BLOOD MONEY

BLOOD MONEY

STORIES OF AN EX-RECCE'S MISSIONS IN IRAQ

JOHAN RAATH

CASEMATE
Oxford & Philadelphia

First published in South Africa in 2018 by DELTA BOOKS, an imprint of Jonathan Ball
Publishers

Published in Great Britain and the United States of America in 2018 by
CASEMATE PUBLISHERS
The Old Music Hall, 106–108 Cowley Road, Oxford OX4 1JE, UK
and
1950 Lawrence Road, Havertown, PA 19083, USA

Hardcover edition: ISBN 978-1-61200-661-1
Digital edition: ISBN 978-1-61200-662-8 (epub)

Printed and bound in the United Kingdom by TJ International

For a complete list of Casemate titles, please contact:

CASEMATE PUBLISHERS (UK)
Telephone (01865) 241249
Email: casemate-uk@casematepublishers.co.uk
www.casematepublishers.co.uk

CASEMATE PUBLISHERS (US)
Telephone (610) 853-9131
Fax (610) 853-9146
Email: casemate@casematepublishers.com
www.casematepublishers.com

I thank my Creator for keeping me safe during stormy times, when I could easily have succumbed. I am also thankful to my wife for her love, support and understanding, and to my mother for her prayers, patience and support. Our work in international conflict zones took me and other private military contractors away from our loved ones for many years, and many men never made it back. I honour these men and their families.

I am indebted to my Special Forces brothers, in particular Chris Delport, Johan (Jakes) Jacobs and Johan (Grobbies) Grobbelaar, and others who worked in Iraq, for providing information to verify facts and details to flesh out the story. I am part of a brotherhood that is second to none, and for this I am grateful. 'There exists a bond between men that spilled blood and suffered hardship together that outsiders cannot understand' (Anon).

I dedicate this book to my father, who passed away on 29 October 2016 when I was halfway through the manuscript. I am saddened that you never got to read my story, but I also find peace in the knowledge that you understood what your son did for a living and what I stand for. Rest in peace, Dad.

Give me 20 divisions of American soldiers and I will breach Europe. Give me 15 consisting of Englishmen, and I will advance to the borders of Berlin. Give me two divisions of those marvellous fighting Boers [in reference to the Anglo-Boer War] and I will remove Germany from the face of the earth.

– *Field Marshal Bernard L Montgomery*

The Americans fight for a free world, the English mostly for honor and glory and medals, the French and Canadians decide too late that they have to participate. The Italians are too scared to fight; the Russians have no choice. The Germans for the Fatherland. The Boers? Those sons of bitches fight for the hell of it!

– *General George (Old Blood and Guts) Patton*

Contents

Preface

Iraq has a history that goes back thousands of years. In 3100 BC the land between the Tigris and the Euphrates rivers was called Mesopotamia, later Babylonia. Major developments in human history, including the invention of the wheel, the planting of the first cereal crops, the development of cursive script and mathematics have their root here.[1]

However, from the start of record keeping, this ancient civilisation has been engulfed in war. For thousands of years, the area of modern-day Iraq has been a battleground for different civilisations, kingdoms and tribes who have fought for the title of ruler and later caliph, including the Byzantines, Abassids, Persians and Arabs.

In modern times, warfare has consumed the country since World War I, when British and French diplomats laid down the boundaries of Iraq, Syria, Jordan, Kurdistan and southern Turkey. During World War II the British led a campaign in Iraq to restore their imperial ally, the Regent of Iraq. Saddam Hussein came to power in 1979. In the preceding years he had been instrumental in the creation of the Iraqi military forces and the nationalisation of the oil industry as a member of the government and leader of the ruling Baath Party. By the 1980s the Baath Party was dominated by Sunni Muslims.

A year after Saddam came to power, Iraq invaded Iran, a Shia Muslim country. The war lasted nine years and led to the death of over a million people on both sides. In 1990 Saddam invaded Kuwait, which led to the first Gulf War. He also brutally suppressed the Shia-majority Arabs and Kurds in the country throughout his rule.

In my career as a private military contractor (PMC), and even more so since I started working in Iraq in 2004, I have often been asked by family members, friends and people in general, 'What kind of work do you guys do over there?' So I decided to tell the story of my journey to Iraq, where I worked as a PMC until late 2017, in an effort to answer this question and to create greater public awareness of the nature of our work there. This is the first eyewitness account written by a South African of what it was like to work as a military contractor in Iraq. In this book I hope to give the South African public a better understanding of the events that took place in Iraq after the regime of Saddam Hussein was overthrown in 2003 with the help of the US.

An important misperception I want to counter is that we did not go to Iraq to wage war. I and other PMCs went there to protect people and assets. The role of PMCs was mostly to escort convoys supplying construction materials for essential infrastructure – anything from power plants, roads and military bases to hospitals, schools and oilfields. These convoys also transported critical supplies to the personnel who worked at these sites. Our job was also to guard the personnel and the installations.

That being said, in a war zone one inevitably gets drawn into the conflict, and that made our work dangerous. Many PMCs had to use firearms against attackers in Iraq, but this was to defend the lives of those under their protection and their own lives. As my story will reveal, we acted defensively, not offensively. Although PMCs often have to defend their lives and the lives of their clients through armed reaction, they are not permitted to engage in offensive combat roles, as this could be classed as unlawful by the UN in terms of international humanitarian law. They can be deployed as bodyguards, training officers, consultants and guards at static locations, such as embassies, oilfields and other key installations, such as power plants, communication networks and airports. Where PMCs are deployed to augment military personnel in protection duties and at installations, it critically frees army soldiers for combat.

When I started thinking of writing a book on the stories of private security contractors in Iraq, my thoughts were to write it solely from a South African perspective and to record the experiences of the South Africans who worked in Iraq after the 2003 war with the US. However, when I began consulting my old diaries, notes, photos and hard drives containing operational information, it became clear to me that PMCs from across the globe contributed greatly to the security goals set by the US government, coalition partners, semi-government groups, non-governmental organisations (NGOs) and private companies.

For nearly 15 years, I have worked, lived, laughed, bled and shed tears with PMC colleagues from the US, UK, South Africa, Uganda and other African countries, and Australia, New Zealand, Fiji, Nepal, Georgia, South America, Europe and Eastern Europe. An estimated 35 000 to 50 000 security contractors worked in Iraq from 2003 to 2008 alone. Although this is mainly my story, I have included the experiences of other PMCs whom I worked with and knew well. The book reflects the dangerous nature of the PMC's work and includes stories of bravery, humanity, humour and survival.

Many books have been written on private military security companies and contractors in Iraq, many by journalists who harbour a negative view of these companies. This book is not intended as an analysis of private military security companies, but was conceptualised rather as a personal journey to illustrate the daily lives of PMCs working in Iraq.

I am a bit like a crow – I like gathering things and managed to find notes in old diaries and electronic reports on external hard drives covering my early years in Iraq. But much of this book is written from memory, and the memories of colleagues and other PMCs. Memory might have failed me in a few minor details, but I have tried to describe events as accurately as possible. I also drew from media reports and Wikipedia as my main research sources to double-check information on organisations and events.

In PMC circles, Iraq and Afghanistan are referred to as either the 'Sandpit' or the 'Sandbox'. From time to time, I will call Iraq the Sandbox because, for me, this name seems more appropriate than Sandpit, which reminds one of a place where children play. A sandbox refers to a litter container used by pets to urinate and defecate in, and, in my mind, the term not only encapsulates the desert that dominates the geography of Iraq, but also speaks of the shit that went down in that troubled country.

And since my story takes place against this conflictual background, I have included a chapter in which Iraq's history, culture and some of the political and belief systems are briefly discussed. For further context, I describe the terrorist organisations and militias that flourished in the country after the 2003 war.

I have also included photos that offer some visuals of our lives as PMCs and depict the Iraqi landscape and city scenes. A note to sensitive readers: some of these photos are fairly graphic. This isn't intended to shock but to give the reader a true sense of the levels of violence and bloodshed we were exposed to.

I need to point out that the title of this book is meant ironically and shouldn't be misconstrued as meaning that PMCs earn their money by being hired killers. The term 'blood money' refers not only to the dangers we were exposed to, but also to the price we had to pay for doing the job. Close to 40 South Africans lost their lives in Iraq over six years, and more than double that number were seriously wounded or maimed as a result of their protective work.

Around 500 PMCs lost their lives in Iraq and another 1 000 private contractors, such as drivers, aviation personnel and logistical, construction and maintenance workers, were killed – often in grue-some ways. PMCs shed blood for the same reasons that the US and Coalition Force (CF)[2] soldiers did. Many human-rights groups and investigative journalists have written about these private contractors who made the ultimate sacrifices in Iraq.

I would like to quote an extract from Sir Arthur Conan Doyle's *The Great Boer War*, which has stayed with me ever since I first read it:

> Take a community of Dutchmen of the type … who defended themselves for fifty years against all the power of Spain at a time when Spain was the greatest power in the world. Intermix with them a strain of those inflexible French Huguenots, who gave up their name and left their country forever at the time of the revocation of the Edict of Nantes. The product must obviously be one of the most rugged, virile, unconquerable races ever seen upon the face of the earth. Take these formidable people and train them for

seven generations in constant warfare against savage men and ferocious beasts, in circumstances in which no weakling could survive; place them so that they acquire skill with weapons and in horsemanship, give them a country which is eminently suited to the tactics of the huntsman, the marksman and the rider. Then, finally, put a fine temper upon their military qualities by a dour fatalistic Old Testament religion and an ardent and consuming patriotism. Combine all these qualities and all these impulses in one individual and you have the modern Boer.

With the word 'Boer', Conan Doyle is referring specifically to the white settlers who trekked to the Free State and the Transvaal from the Cape Colony and started the two Boer republics. However, I believe these qualities reflect the abilities of *all* ex-South African military and policemen, regardless of the language they spoke or the colour of their skin. South African PMCs are not only white, or only Afrikaans-speaking. There were also black security personnel and English-speaking colleagues within our ranks.

Conan Doyle's quotation, however, is a good reminder of the basis on which our soldiering skills have been built and tuned over the centuries. We all worked together, bled together and shared the many different aspects of life in Iraq together.

I never expected to make much money by publishing this book. Rather, my goal was to tell my story, so that the families and friends of PMCs and the general public can understand the kind of work we did in Iraq. I decided that I would donate a portion of my royalties to down-and-out South African PMCs who got injured or maimed, or to charities dealing with child victims of the war in Iraq. The Sandbox provided for me all those years, and I would like to try to make a small difference in aiding the victims of the endless cycles of violence this part of the world has seen.

Johan Raath, sandbox.stories@johanraath.com

Historical background to the war in Iraq

If you know the enemy and you know yourself, you do not need to fear the result of one hundred battles; if you know yourself but not the enemy, for every victory gained you will also suffer a defeat; if you know neither the enemy nor yourself, you will succumb in every battle.
– Sun Tzu, The Art of War

Ever since my days in the South African Special Forces (SF), or the Recces, I have taken a keen interest in international politics and terrorism. I have also lectured and held seminars on these subjects. As part of our SF training, we underwent courses in enemy tactics and procedures, as well as guerrilla warfare training aimed at combating an unconventional threat.

Before I deployed to Iraq, I researched the threat and terrorist patterns there. I was intrigued by the complexity and intensity of the terrorist and insurgency attacks when I started working there. After the ground war concluded in March 2003, various groups came to the fore to launch attacks against US forces, their Coalition Force (CF) partners and PMCs. The threat and number of mainly Sunni-aligned mujahideen fighters[1] grew steadily, with opposing Shia militia forces also coming into play.

International terrorism is nothing new. Terror tactics can be traced back to biblical times when Jewish and Palestinian groups opposed Roman rule in AD 66–73, using unconventional warfare tactics. However, I believe the Iraq War shifted the intensity and regularity of terrorist attacks in the Middle East and globally.

The US military defines terrorism as the calculated use of violence, or threat of violence, to inculcate fear, intended to coerce or to intimidate governments or societies in pursuit of goals that are generally political, religious or ideological.[2] According to *Encarta Dictionary*, terrorism is political violence – in other words, violence or the threat of violence, especially bombing, kidnapping and assassination, carried out for political purposes.

There was a huge rise in terrorist incidents in the latter part of the 20th century, with an explosion of radical militant terrorist attacks in the mid- to late 1990s. In the new millennium, international terrorism shifted into overdrive, especially after the 9/11 attacks on the US in 2001. The Bush administration decisively chose to go after terrorists following the attacks in New York and Washington. Afghanistan was first in its sights. Shortly thereafter Iraq was invaded. There is divided opinion on whether this was the right strategy, but the aim of this chapter is not to speculate on the ethics of the decision, but rather to report the hard, cold facts that presented a threat to the CF and private contractors in Iraq.

Up until the Iraq War, the terror groups in Iraq consisted mainly of Kurdish and some Sunni jihadi elements, such as the Kurdistan Workers' Party, the Kurdish Democratic Party, the Patriotic Union of Kurdistan, the Islamic Movement of Kurdistan, the Kurdistan Islamist Group, Kurdish Hamas, the Tawid Islamic Front and Jund-al-Islam. Other smaller militant Kurdish groups, such as the Second Soran Unit and the Reformist Group, also joined Ansar-al-Islam (AI) in the early 2000s. Of these organisations, AI was the most active Kurdish terror group, perpetrating attacks against locals and foreigners.

Saddam Hussein ruled Iraq fearsomely for 24 years. His power base, the Sunni-dominated Baath Party, used force through his very efficient intelligence cells, backed up by an experienced military and his Revolutionary Guard Council. In 1995 Iraq established a paramilitary group known as the Fedayeen Saddam, which was loyal to Hussein and the Baathist government. Shortly after the 2003 ground war was concluded, and Saddam's fall in April that year, many of these previous Baathist elements and former military and intelligence officers went underground and started attacking the US and the CF.

Some of the first suicide bombings were committed by AI in northern

Iraq in 2003, and by former soldiers from the Saddam era in Najaf and Baghdad. That year another organisation, Jamaat al-Tawhid wal-Jihad (later al-Qaeda in Iraq, or AQI, and today Islamic State in Iraq and Syria, or ISIS), attacked US and CF private contractors and Iraqi civilians.

Abu Musab al-Zarqawi, the leader of this group, was a Jordanian-born Islamist militant who had received training in Afghanistan in the late 1980s and early 1990s. It is said that he first met Osama bin Laden in the late 1980s in Afghanistan. In the run-up to the 2003 war, he organised so-called resistance cells in Baghdad and northern (Kurdish) Iraq to resist the expected US invasion. Zarqawi was implicated in the Canal Hotel bombing, the United Nations headquarters in Baghdad, in August 2003. In mid-2004 al-Zarqawi rebranded his organisation al-Qaeda in Iraq.

Abu Musab al-Zarqawi, founder of al-Qaeda in Iraq.

On 10 May 2004, Zarqawi struck fear into the heart of the world by beheading Nick Berg, an American who had gone to Iraq in search of opportunities. The murder was videotaped and circulated the world in a flash, leading to his followers giving Zarqawi the nickname 'sheik of the slaughterers'.

In July, Washington increased the reward for information leading to Zarqawi's capture from $5 million to $25 million – the same bounty offered for Osama bin Laden, who was behind the 9/11 attacks. Zarqawi celebrated his rise up through the West's most-wanted rankings by recording another video, in which he talked about famous Muslim warriors, implying his own place in the chain of great men, before making an impassioned plea for Muslims from around the world to join him.

Furthermore, bin Laden gave him his blessing, announcing in a broadcast on an Arab news channel that 'our mujahed brother Abu Musab al-Zarqawi is the emir of the al-Qaeda for Jihad Organisation in the Land of the Two Rivers'.[3] By cooperating with Zarqawi, al-Qaeda could share the credit for his successes.

Soon Zarqawi started making references to a caliphate (an Islamic state) where he would be the leader. However, late in 2005 he declared war on the majority Shia population in Iraq and ordered attacks on Shia mosques and high-profile individuals. By then Iraq was ruled by a Shia-dominated government. Zarqawi believed Shia Muslims, Christians, Jews and any other religious groupings were infidels. This took the country into a civil war phase.

Around July 2005, al-Qaeda's second in command, Ayman al-Zawahiri, said in a statement that while it was acceptable to kill Americans and Iraqi soldiers, the bombings and attacks on Shia mosques and AQI's execution videos were sending out the wrong message. To ordinary Muslims, images of dead Shia children and beheaded Bulgarian truck drivers were not inspiring, but rather repulsive.[4]

Zarqawi is seen by many as the 'grandfather' of ISIS.[5] His cruelty and gruesome methods eventually disgusted bin Laden.

From 2004 to 2006, AQI was the main terror group in Iraq. In July 2006 Zarqawi was killed by a US air strike outside of Baghdad. After his death, some of Zarqawi's followers maintained attacks against the US forces, their coalition partners and private contractors. Another group of his followers retreated into northwestern Syria where they would go underground, regroup themselves and emerge as an organised terrorist military force in 2013. They announced themselves to the world as ISIS when they invaded Mosul, northern Iraq, on 10 June 2014.

AQI, AI and the ex-Baath Party militant groups were all Sunni organisations. Various jihadists (an Islamic militant who fights against the enemies of Islam) joined their ranks from countries such as Saudi Arabia, Jordan, Egypt, Libya, Tunisia, Morocco and Chechnya, and a number of other countries. Initially these fighters were responsible for most of the attacks against the CF and private contractors.

With Zarqawi's rise, the majority Shia population started organising their own militias to fight the Sunni insurgent groups. In this, they were supported by neighbouring Iran.

The Iraqi Shia cleric Muqtada al-Sadr is the leader of the Sadrist Movement and of Saraya al-Salam, a Shiite militia. Despite not holding office in the Iraqi government, he is one of the most influential religious leaders in the country.[6] After the 2003 war, al-Sadr called Saddam Hussein the 'little serpent' and America the 'big serpent'. It is important to note that since the Shah of Iran was overthrown by Islamic fundamentalists, there has been animosity between Iran and the US, with the Iranian government referring to America as the 'big Satan' and Israel the 'small Satan'.

Initially I found it counter-intuitive that the Shia militias had such hatred for America, especially since the US forces had toppled their arch-enemy and handed over the power to the Shia majority after decades of brutal suppression under Hussein. However, it soon became clear that Iran played a big role in the new Iraq and fuelled the anti-American sentiment and propaganda.

In May 2003, al-Sadr issued a fatwa – a ruling on a point of Islamic law – that allowed theft, looting and racketeering against the CF as long as 20 per cent of the looted earnings went back to his Sadrist party, which controlled the Mahdi Militia.[7] The fatwa was well received, especially by the poor, of whom there were millions in Sadr City, a large slum in eastern Baghdad.

In April 2004, simultaneous attacks by Shia militias against the US military and CF took place in Sadr City and the southern provinces, notably Basra and Najaf, where these militias enjoyed overwhelming support. The next day al-Sadr declared jihad (religious war) against the CF. The following month, the CF closed down a propagandist newspaper in Sadr City, which led to a revolt by the Sadrist Movement's armed wing.

In those days, there were serious casualties on both sides of the war against the US forces, their CF partners and private contractors – a trend that would continue for years to come. Later in 2004 and early in 2006, more Shia militias joined the jihad against foreign forces and contractors, the most prominent being the Mahdi Army, the Badr Brigade, Kata'ib Hezbollah and Asaib Ahl al-Haq. All the Shia militias had strong backing from Iran and many militia members received paramilitary training there. Many of the special, highly destructive roadside bombs that killed hundreds of CF members and civilian contractors emanated from Iran.

As PMCs, we had to contend with several new threats after 2003 when ex-Baathist Shia militants, Zarqawi's insurgents and the Kurdish AI started attacking the CF. These jihadist attacks on foreigners went into overdrive from March 2004.

It was incredibly challenging to plan your protection details, as there were so many threat factors to consider and outsmart. We soon realised that these terror groups and militias had not only the US, the CF and the new Iraqi security forces in their sights, but all of us PMCs as well. They saw the private contractors as foreigners who sided with the CF, as most of the PMCs in those years worked on US government projects.

Although South Africa was never part of the CF, South Africans were designated, like personnel from the CF, as expats. After the war, many countries joined the efforts to rebuild and stabilise Iraq by sending small contingents of military personnel to the Sandbox. By April 2004, just over 10 000 South Africans were registered in Iraq on the American Department of Defense badging system.[8] Around 200 of these were genuine qualified Special Forces operators, or Recces, and several hundred more laid claim to this status. Since the inception of the South African SF units in 1972 until the day I finished this book, there were fewer than 1 100 SF operators who had qualified in the organisation's entire 45-year history.

We found that, in general, the Iraqis had more time for us South Africans and the other non-CF third-country nationals (TCNs), such as Fijians, Nepalese, Ugandans, Zimbabweans, etc, as we never formed part of the official CF, which had fought them in 2003, but also because we could more easily gel with the locals.

But, in general, the enemy viewed us as infidels and could not easily distinguish between different expat contractors. So, regardless of race, colour or creed, we got tarred with the same brush as the CF and got attacked from all sides by terrorists, militias and jihadist fighters.

Towards the end of 2005, relations between Zarqawi's followers – disenfranchised Sunnis – and al-Sadr's followers – the Shia militias – were at boiling point. During 2006 the civil war between these religious groups was at its peak. While their differences go back centuries, the militants within both these groups had one thing in common: their hatred of all foreigners. To make matters worse, criminal gangs with little other loyalty than to their greed for money started to commit crimes, such as kidnapping and blackmail, under the cover of all the chaos taking place in Iraq at the time.

A new group of terrorist organisations and militias emerged after the invasion of Mosul in June 2014, but this will be discussed in later chapters.

Acronyms and abbreviations

AI Ansar-al-Islam

AQI al-Qaeda in Iraq

ARCO Archirodon Overseas Construction

BaOC Basra Operations Command

CF Coalition Forces (Multi-National Force – Iraq)

Comms communication(s)

CPP China Petroleum Pipeline

DoD card US Department of Defense card (also known as Common Access Card)

E & E escape and evasion

EFP explosively formed projectile (or penetrator)

EWAC Ellis World Alliance Corporation

FBI US Federal Bureau of Investigation

IED improvised explosive device

Intel military or political intelligence

ISI Islamic State in Iraq

ISIS Islamic State in Iraq and Syria

Medevac medical evacuation

NCO non-commissioned officer

NGO non-governmental organisation

PMC private military contractor

PMF Popular Mobilisation Force

SAS Special Air Service

SF South African Special Forces

STTEP Specialised Tasks, Training, Equipment and Protection International

SUV special utility vehicle

TC Triple Canopy

TCNs third-country nationals

UAE United Arab Emirates

VeeBid vehicle-borne improvised explosive device

List of maps

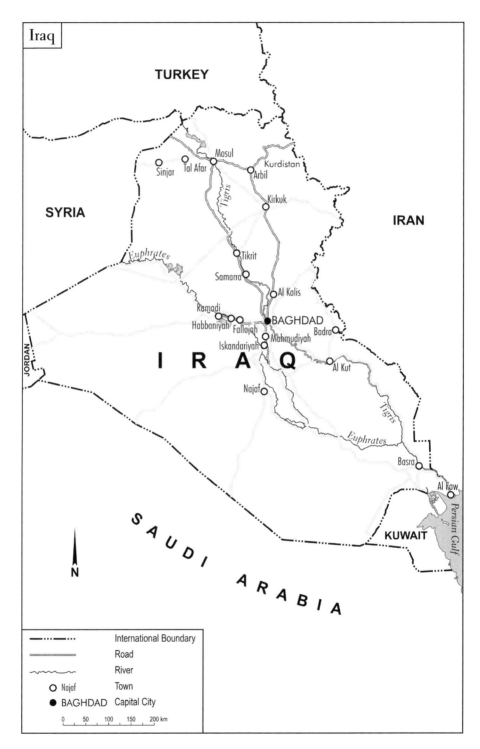

Map 1

1

Good morning, Baghdad!

The smell of Baghdad was the first thing that hit me. Because of the bombings, the city's sewerage system had disintegrated, leaving the city smelling like one massive turd. It was not uncommon to see open sewage seeping out of damaged pipes and floating into the Tigris and Euphrates – along with the bodies that could be occasionally spotted in the rivers.

It was April 2004, just over a year after America had invaded Iraq to topple the regime of Saddam Hussein. In those days, no commercial airlines flew into Baghdad – all flights were chartered or people flew there in private planes. I arrived at Baghdad International Airport in an old private chartered jet. As we approached the airport, the pilots put the plane into a downward spiralling dive, much to the horror of the passengers, who thought we were going down.

During the flight, I had found out that the pilots were South African, so I understood immediately that the alarming approach trajectory was nothing more than a safety manoeuvre. South African Air Force pilots adopted the same procedure in the 1980s when they flew personnel into the operational area for deployments during the Border War in Namibia and Angola. The idea was to avoid approaching the runway in a straight line for too long, as this would allow attackers to take aim more accurately with surface-to-air missiles, rocket launchers and small-arms fire. Instead, they would take the plane down in a corkscrew motion, then level out shortly before touching down. It was a very scary manoeuvre when you experienced it for the first time, although I understood the value of it. Still, I was surprised that a non-military aircraft, a Boeing 727, was performing this hair-raising descent tactic.

At the airport I was met by the team from the Steele Foundation, the American private military security company I worked for at the time, who had just won a contract in Iraq. I had been deployed by the Steele Foundation to Iraq as a team leader and personal protection officer, a bodyguard basically, for American engineers working on expanding and upgrading the Musayyib Power Plant, a key but ageing electrical power station southwest of Baghdad. My other duties included securing the site with static guards and providing armed-escort transport from Baghdad to the site and back for clients and our own team members.

The team from the Steele Foundation escorted us to the parking area, where they handed us flak jackets (bullet-resistant vests) and informed us about the notoriously dangerous stretch of road between the airport and the city, called Route Irish, for some reason (roads were given code names by the CF). This was one of the main roads into Baghdad used by foreigners and security forces, and the insurgents knew this. The road also had several US military and Iraqi checkpoints. It was a magnet for the terrorists. I was therefore taken through the emergency drills should we get hit.[1] These were pretty standard in our line of work.

Between the end of 2003 and well into 2005, Route Irish was considered one of the most dangerous stretches of road in the world. Many soldiers, PMCs and citizens were attacked on this 12-kilometre strip of perilous highway, and a number paid the ultimate price. Drive-by shootings, roadside ambushes and suicide bombers targeting the checkpoints were commonplace. In one incident, video footage showed how insurgents killed three PMCs in April 2005 in cold blood following an ambush.[2]

In the later years of the conflict, private military security companies charged upwards of what may seem like an exorbitant $3 000 to ferry people from the airport to Baghdad. But the costs were justifed: armoured sport utility vehicles (SUVs) with armed PMC escorts do not come cheaply, especially as the client expects these escorts to protect his or her life with theirs.

Once on the road, the drivers hit the throttle and went hell for leather. This, it turned out, was to try to outrun possible improvised explosive device (IED) blasts and sniper fire. They drove at an average

of 120 km/h. Despite the speeding – or perhaps because of it – I made it safely to the hotel.

My first accommodation, and temporary operations base for a couple of weeks, was the Babylon Hotel in the Red Zone on the west bank of the Tigris. The Red Zone is the term used to refer to parts of the city immediately outside the perimeter of the safe area, known as the Green Zone. This was the 10-km² high-security international enclave established in central Baghdad following the Allied invasion. The Green Zone was on the other side of the river from our hotel. This was the governmental centre of the US Coalition Provisional Authority, the transitional government that ruled the country between April 2003 and June 2004. To this day, the Green Zone is still the hub of the international presence in the capital.[3]

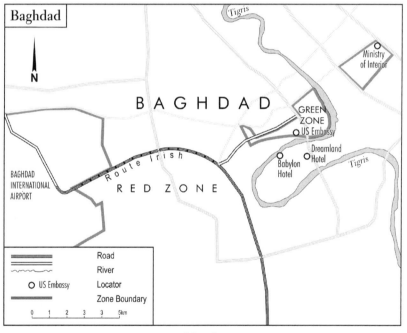

Map 2

Once I got to my room, I unpacked my gear and started putting together one of the most essential items when working in a war zone – my escape and evasion, or E & E, bag. This is a backpack that contains all your essential survival gear in case you have to leave an

3

operational area in a hurry. Americans call it a go bag or a grab bag; others refer to it simply as a runaway bag.

I had somehow managed to get all my security equipment – known in contractor circles as one's 'contraband' – into Iraq. As well as my E & E bag, this kit included a GPS device, knives, a tactical vest, first-aid kit, heavy-duty clothing, boots, a multi-tool knife, parachute cord, compass, signals mirror, strobe light, torches and other tactical gadgetry.

After I had sorted my E & E bag out, my next job was to clean and conduct a functionality test on the AK-47 issued to me.[4] I was satisfied that the AK-47 would more than likely fire. Although it is advisable to get to a shooting range as soon as possible with a new weapon to test-fire it and zero the sights, in the military contracting world such a luxury is not always possible. But I reckoned I was good to go.

A few days after my arrival at the Babylon Hotel, we were having breakfast in the restaurant area when we heard a loud bang and, a split second later, the large glass windows shook violently. The shockwaves, it turned out, were from a car comb that had gone off a few hundred metres from the hotel in the vicinity of the checkpoint that led over the Tigris to the Green Zone.

A couple of seconds after the blast, some joker in the restaurant shouted out, 'Good morning, Baghdad!' We all laughed at the comic reference to the Robin Williams movie *Good Morning, Vietnam*. I had just witnessed what the situation was like in Baghdad, and if I hadn't known it before, I realised then that my time in Iraq promised to be an interesting adventure.

The Triangle of Death

Two weeks after I arrived in Iraq, I was due to lead a team on a reconnaissance mission to the Musayyib Power Plant. Our mission was to set up a base to receive and secure the first engineers and other workers from Southeast Texas Industries Inc., the engineering firm building the plant on a contract from the Iraqi Ministry of Electricity. We were a six-man configuration – three local nationals and three expatriate security contractors.

The facility was about 120 kilometres southwest of Baghdad. The route there and the area that we were to reconnoitre were in the so-called Triangle of Death (not to be confused with the Sunni Death Triangle, which is northwest of the city). The Triangle of Death got its name from the heavy combat activity and sectarian violence in the area between 2003 and 2007.

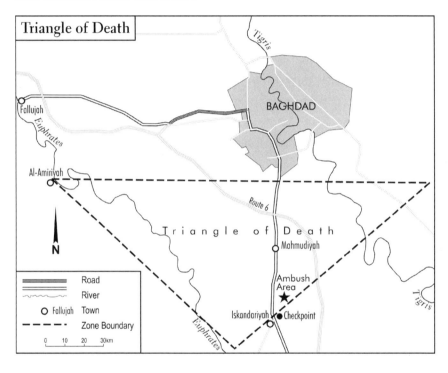

Map 3

Our team members were all armed with assault rifles – we had five AK-47s and one M4 between us. We all also carried 9 mm pistols. When we set off that day, we initially weren't wearing our body armour, as the idea was to blend in, low-profile, with the locals. But, after a while, I got a bad feeling about the area and asked the team to put on their vests. (Later, wearing body armour would become standard operating procedure and it was mandatory for all team members to wear body armour vests with ballistic plates in the front and back carrier pouches.[5])

We were travelling in two unarmoured (known as soft-skin) vehicles. Two of the Iraqis were in the front in a Pajero SUV and the rest of us followed in a BMW 740. The customary procedure was that the local guys would drive in front, so they could speak in Arabic to the Iraqi security forces, who manned most of the checkpoints. At many of the major checkpoints, the US forces had a greater presence, in which case the vehicle with the expat contractors would approach the checkpoint first to liaise in English and to present our US Department of Defense cards (commonly called DoD cards), or Common Access Cards. The DoD or CaC card proved that you were security-vetted and cleared to work on US government contracts. As a private military contractor, you couldn't move anywhere in Iraq without one.

We headed south on National Route 6 (known in CF jargon as 'Route Bismarck'). At around 10:30, shortly after we had turned onto a secondary road, we approached a checkpoint where the men in our lead vehicle showed their paperwork to the security forces and we followed with our DoD cards.

Not long afterwards, I spotted an old black Opel that was occupied by a group of young men. The strange thing was that they were trying to overtake us on the right – Iraqis drive on the right-hand side of the road. They then pulled off the shoulder of the tarmac road and onto the dirt.

I thought it odd but just wrote it off to bad driving, which I'd heard was typical of young Iraqi men. By then we were driving at about 140 km/h, a standard practice for private security teams in those days – the idea being to drive faster than the normal traffic to prevent too many vehicles from passing your convoy and to thwart rolling ambushes from the rear. But despite our speed, the Opel eventually managed to pass us on the outside, kicking up a massive ball of dust in the desert. Seconds later, the vehicle started swerving left aggressively and was back onto the asphalt road, pushing in front of us. They were clearly trying to split up our convoy.

As they overtook, the Opel driver glanced at me fleetingly and I can still vividly recall the look in his eyes. He was just a few metres away when they passed us. His pupils were dilated and he had an intense look of hatred and anger in his eyes. For a moment, I thought he might be under the influence of narcotics, but later I realised I was staring into the eyes of a mujahideen fighter who was drunk not on any substances, just emotions of hate welling up from his religious and sociopolitical convictions.

The next moment, I saw two men lean out of the front right and rear left windows armed with AK-47s. They opened fire on our lead vehicle. Bullets smashed the rear windscreen of the Pajero.

'Contact front!' I yelled immediately.

One of our team members in the back of the BMW, Ali Tehrani, wasted no time. Positioning himself at the back window, he opened fire on the Opel with his M4. The attacking vehicle was in the line of his two o'clock. The attackers immediately turned their attention to us and fired back at our vehicle before they slowed down and veered off the road.

I remember the cracking sound of the AK-47 bullets as they tore through our windscreen. A friend's Garmin GPS and my digital camera were on the dashboard – the bullets pierced both. A piece of a bullet struck my bulletproof vest in the chest area, and another piece broke off and lodged in my left forearm (and is still there to this day). That's how close it was.

In the midst of all this, our Kurdish driver drew his pistol and started firing back at the attackers through the windscreen, now destroyed by bullets, while at the same time trying to control the speeding vehicle with his left hand. We were doing 160 km/h, taking incoming fire and some of us were trying to return fire – it felt like I was in a Hollywood action movie, but one with a potentially lethal real-life outcome.

Our driver got so carried away with firing his pistol that at one point I had to block his right arm when he pushed the gun in front of my face in an attempt to fire at the attackers sideways. I leaned over and grabbed the steering wheel of the BMW, which had swerved dangerously across the road and in the process I dislocated my left shoulder. At the time the adrenaline numbed the pain. (I had to get reconstructive surgery for this a couple of years later.)

I remember very clearly seeing how the attacker shooting at us from the rear window slung his AK-47 over his shoulder, pulled a pistol from his belt and started spraying lead our way again. In hindsight, this showed a level of training and proficiency, because it is a tactical drill to sling your assault rifle when you are out of ammunition or have a jam, and to continue shooting with your handgun.

By this time the Opel had disappeared from sight – presumably Ali's return fire had hit their vehicle – but then we heard shots being fired from our rear as another car with shooters pulled in behind. Our rear window shattered. Brian Smith, one of the expat team members and our project medic, was bleeding from his forehead but, thankfully, he was not seriously injured. He and Ali even managed to fire a couple of rounds at the second vehicle.

By now, our speeding convoy was fast approaching another check-point and the attackers disappeared into the desert on secondary roads. When we arrived at the checkpoint, we reported the ambush

Happy to be alive ... from left, Iraqi driver Arish Farouk, me and Iraqi driver Ali Tehrani after the ambush in May 2004.

and realised that the driver of the front vehicle had been shot through both arms, close to the elbows. Brian stopped the bleeding. Fortunately, the bullets had not hit any bones or arteries, which meant the driver had managed to keep control of the Pajero.

After swapping drivers and trying to make comms with our people back at the hotel, we drove like hell for the rest of the way. We were soon at our destination at the Musayyib Power Plant. The US forces there had a forward operating base with a small medical bay, where we got help for the injured driver. Brian and I were weren't seriously injured, it turned out; the bleeding was caused by some grazes from flying glass and debris. Brian organised a medevac helicopter and our driver was airlifted to Baghdad for medical treatment.

We also made contact with the rest of the team at the Babylon Hotel. By then a convoy from another private military security company had arrived at the base, a team from the ArmorGroup on assignment in the area. Their British team leader agreed to assist us with a lift back to Baghdad.[6] For now, the shot-up Pajero and BMW were left there to be recovered later.

I still do not know how we managed to escape serious harm – or even death – that day. After less than two weeks in Iraq I had had my first eyewitness experience of what it was going to be like. It was an eye-opener, a real baptism of 'fire'. Welcome to the Sandbox, I thought to myself.

2

From Special Forces operator to private military contractor

Ever since I was a boy, I had always wanted to be a soldier. I had first heard of South Africa's Special Forces, also known as the Recces, and these men's stories of bravery, in my teens in the early 1980s. When I was called up for my two-year national service, I attempted the SF selection course and one-year basic training cycle. I was part of only two groups who were allowed to do their basic training in the SF. I have therefore known only the SF environment.

I passed the gruelling courses and became a Recce operator in 1986. It was no easy feat. Today I believe the hardships of the training I was put through, along with the skillset I eventually acquired in my seven years in the SF, perfectly prepared me for the PMC circuit.[1] During my last three years in the unit, I served in the SF training school, where I fared quite well as an instructor, perhaps because I come from a long line of teachers.

When the Gulf War broke out, I was a sergeant at 1 Reconnaissance Regiment, working at the SF training school's 1.2 Commando in Durban. In the Gulf War, a coalition of forces from 35 countries, led by the United States, acted against Iraq's invasion and annexation of Kuwait in January 1991. In many ways, this conflict changed the face and understanding of warfare. It was also the first time that live war broadcasts could be viewed on television around the world (with CNN taking the lead in this regard). I remember how we would scram to the non-commissioned officers' mess hall at teatime, or rush through meals to get to the solitary television to watch real-time war during news flashes and live crossings.

The cameras had night-vision capabilities, and I vividly remember those green images of tracer rounds during the war against Saddam's forces in Kuwait and, later, the invasion of Iraq. I also remember the coverage of Scud missiles that Saddam aimed at Israel being shot down by US and Dutch Patriot missile defence systems.

As SF combatants, our work was always conducted in utter secrecy – hence we were dubbed the 'silent soldiers' – so it amazed us that such revealing real-time information about combat missions was transmitted to the whole world. But this was the start of reality-TV-style news coverage of war and it set the stage for modern news broadcasting in war and conflict zones.

After I left the military in November 1992, I opened a security training school in Durban for tactical and VIP protection, complete with an indoor shooting range and vehicle skid pad. I ran VIP/ executive protection courses. It was work that I enjoyed. However, a year or two later the South African government started regulating security training in an effort to set a minimum standard for the industry. This might have been a noble idea but the problem was that these standards were based on the lowest criteria required per subject and I did not agree with this approach, as I believe that one should aim for the highest standards. When it comes to protecting people's lives, training must be comprehensive and at the highest level, which inevitably makes it difficult to pass such training courses.

My thinking in this regard, coupled with the fact that there were just too many ex-servicemen, ex-police officers and so-called private security specialists in the market working as bodyguards, caused me to reconsider the direction I wanted to move in. It was time for a change. In the mid-1990s, I got involved in international high-threat security, working on VIP protection tasks in Mozambique and specialised training in North Africa. Here the standards were set by the professionals I worked with – and by me. This was the start of a long journey for me in the global high-threat private-security sector.

This is probably a good time to bust a popular myth about body-guards. The general perception is that bodyguards need to be large, over-muscled Rambos who wear sunglasses and have a bad attitude. I blame this perception on Hollywood and the movie industry. Although gorilla-sized protectors might be useful to guard actors and pop stars, and to keep crowds at bay, the reality is that the modern-day, high-threat close-protection officer needs to be a highly skilled, intelligent, well-trained operator with a specific skillset and experience. He also uses prevention rather than cure to keep clients alive.

Although I happen to be tall and weigh around 105 kg, I find that smaller, athletically built operators can move more nimbly in and out of armoured cars, are generally quicker in contacts and less prone to injuries because the more muscle bulk you have, the easier it is to get injured. However, it does help to have a bit of weight when you work in crowds, as I discovered first-hand when I worked on the protection details of a couple of presidents.

After I closed my training centre, I started working as a PMC on a training task in North Africa where we trained SF soldiers. I then worked on the presidential election campaign in Madagascar in 2001, followed by specialised tasks in southern Sudan and Sierra Leone, including medical search and rescue missions, combat medical training and infantry training. In 2003 I was recruited to serve on the presidential protection unit in Haiti. When President Jean-Bertrand Aristide was removed from power in a rebel uprising in 2004, the Steele Foundation had won the contract in Iraq to secure the power plant. They deployed me to the Sandbox shortly afterwards.

The rise of private military security companies

The phenomenon of mercenary armies is as old as war itself. Mercenaries were deployed in the wars of the Roman Empire, by Alexander the Great, the Persian Empire and during the Anglo-Saxon wars. The period after World War II saw a decline in the use of mercenary armies because the superpowers believed it was important to maintain and deploy their own permanent armies during the Cold War. This would change after the fall of communism in 1989, however.

In the African theatre of conflict, mercenaries such as 'Mad' Mike Hoare, Bob Denard and David Stirling achieved global fame, and often notoriety. These, and other private soldiers fought campaigns in Africa during the Cold War with government and rebel forces alike. Stirling, a World War II veteran and the founder of the SAS, was probably the first to privatise mercenary services by founding a formal structured security company in the 1960s to run military operations. But such private security operations were still generally regarded with a degree of distaste and viewed as mercenary activities, organised by small specialised groups of ex-soldiers who networked in secrecy to recruit and execute paramilitary tasks in global conflict zones.

After the end of the Cold War, when millions of military personnel worldwide were laid off or resigned, the services of private military security companies really began to come to the fore. The birth in the early 1990s of the truly modern-day private military security company in many ways changed the nature of warfare. I believe the time is near when the international community will accept that the use of private soldiers and private armies to combat international terrorism, and to act as auxiliary peacekeeping forces, is a viable and sustainable option.

Although private military security companies[2] can, and have been, commissioned to operate as private armies, the role of the PMC is principally to train, mentor, advise and protect clients. In other words, PMCs are mainly involved in defensive operations and do not have the mandate of a military force to go on the offensive to hunt down and destroy enemy forces.

A UN convention that was passed in 1989, and which became effective in 2001, classes PMCs as mercenaries and prohibits the use of such security specialists. However, the US, UK, China and Russia are not signatories to this convention and the US does not accept the classification of PMCs as mercenaries. Since the Gulf War and during the conflict in Bosnia and Kosovo in the late 1990s, the US has used private military security companies who employ PMCs on mainly US government-funded missions. The term 'private military contractor' started doing the rounds during the 1990s, but it was really with the advent of the Afghanistan and Iraq wars that the term received credence.

A number of South Africans played a prominent role in the development of private military security companies. In 1989 the protracted Border War between South Africa and its allied forces, and the South West African People's Organisation and the Angolan Armed Forces, with the backing of Cuba, the Soviet Union and East Germany, came to an end. After the 23-year-long conflict finally ground to an indecisive halt, democratic processes replaced military actions. This caused many soldiers and SF operators to leave the South African Army and consider other options in the form of private military security.

In the early 1990s Executive Outcomes, a South African company, was formed as a private paramilitary force. The company, founded by Eeben Barlow, a former intelligence officer, was run by commanders who were former SF officers. The company consisted mainly of ex-soldiers from the ranks of the SF, 32 Battalion, the Parachute Battalion, Koevoet (the police's counter-insurgency unit) and other combat units, such as 101 Battalion, and infantry and mechanised units.

After the war, Executive Outcomes was contracted by the government of Angola to assist with specialised training and operational oversight in the government's fight against the Unita rebels (who had, ironically, been South Africa's Angolan allies in the Border War). Their success in Angola led to Executive Outcomes becoming involved in other African conflicts, such as in Sierra Leone, where they assisted the government with similar training, operational planning and oversight in their fight against rebel forces.

Executive Outcomes mounted successful and sophisticated missions, even if they were involved in various hair-raising operations where the odds were often stacked against them. Their operations took their toll in terms of losses and casualties. Still, these were relatively low considering the kinds of missions Executive Outcomes was involved in, and they accomplished a great deal in terms of controlling the civil wars in Angola and Sierra Leone, and also in South America and Indonesia.

Many in the industry view Executive Outcomes as the first truly modern private military security company. Many of those who were employed by the company went on to initiate operations for other private military security outfits internationally, including missions in Iraq after 2003.

Although the US government used private military security companies in a limited capacity after World War II and the Korean War, it was really only after the Gulf War in 1991 that the US started relying more heavily on them, so that it could free up soldiers in the US Army. In the mid- to late 1990s, private military security companies were used more regularly by the Clinton administration in conflict zones such as Kosovo and Bosnia and Herzegovina. Two prominent American private military security companies at the time were DynCorp, and Kellogg Brown & Root.

One of the economic rationales for private military security companies is that it is very expensive to supply and maintain a fully integrated permanent army, complete with life support, air and land travel, as well as personnel benefits, such as medical cover and pensions. Private military security companies pay PMCs a much larger salary, but keep the support costs down, as they do not require an air force, hospitals, mess halls, etc, as a permanent army does. Not having to contribute to servicemen's pensions also drastically reduces costs.

The services of private military contractors can be terminated at a moment's notice. All of us in the business know that you might have a job today but tomorrow you could be on the street. Private military security companies do not keep employees on their books once contracts have been ended; you are contracted only for a specific mission or job.

The real boom in the private military industry was seen after the 9/11 attacks, following which the US launched a global war against terrorism. Afghanistan was the first in America's crosshairs, as Osama bin Laden, who was responsible for the 9/11 attacks, operated from that country.

It was also decided to invade Iraq to topple the regime of Saddam Hussein because it was believed that Iraq had weapons of mass destruction. The American government wanted such weapons to be dismantled before they could be used in a terrorist attack.

In March 2003 US forces invaded Iraq. Hussein's regime was overthrown within a month but he was on the run for several months before he was caught in December that year. However, this did not bring an end to the hostilities. Firstly, as mentioned in more detail in the chapter on the history and background to the Iraq conflict, in the resultant power vacuum widespread sectarian violence flared up between the two main Muslim groups, the Shias and the Sunnis. Secondly, it brought on a long guerrilla insurgency against the American and other CF members by jihadist militants and other militias. These groups saw the CF as infidels and believed it was their religious duty to expel them from Iraq. What was initially expected to be a quick and resounding victory soon turned into a bloody and drawn-out conflict that lasted longer than the Vietnam War.

It was during this post-invasion period that the use of private military security companies and private security contractors escalated, setting a trend in military practice for the years to come.

Last days in Haiti

When America invaded Iraq, I had just arrived in Haiti to work in the presidential protection unit for the Steele Foundation. All presidents require some level of protection, but in Haiti there was a rebellion brewing against President Aristide, and hence the requirements for added security. I was the senior agent on the presidential protection team, assisting with operational command of his and his family's daily protection. The rest of the team consisted of former American and British soldiers and law enforcement officers. From Haiti, we would follow the war in Iraq with keen interest, watching the live broadcasts on TV.

I was part of the protection team for President Jean-Bertrand Aristide of Haiti during a visit by President Thabo Mbeki in January 2004.

From April 2003, rumours were circulating that security contracts for Iraq were being offered. The conflict clearly wasn't drawing to the expected rapid end after the invasion. Everybody's ears pricked up, as PMCs are always on the lookout for the next good meal ticket. Towards the end of July that year, the first stories broke about attacks on contractors, convoys and foreigners. We were going to be in demand, it seemed.

I was right: terrorist attacks started escalating the moment the Iraq coalition invasion was over. One of the most significant bombings during this time took place on 19 August 2003 when a massive truck bomb exploded at the UN headquarters at the Canal Hotel in Baghdad. More than 450 kg of high explosives were detonated and 22 people were killed in the blast, including the UN special envoy to Iraq, Sérgio Vieira de Mello. Over 100 others were wounded. The attack had been masterminded by Abu Musab al-Zarqawi, whose jihadist organisation later morphed into ISIS (see the earlier chapter on the background to the Iraqi conflict).

About a month later, a suicide bomber blew himself up at the same hotel. The UN withdrew its mission a few weeks later. Its withdrawal was a sign of the instability of the country and the inherent danger of working there. It also highlighted the fact that the real war against the insurgents was not over, even if the ground war had been won.

In November the Haitian presidential protection unit had a high turnover of personnel because a number of the American and British guys left to take up new contracts in Iraq. We followed their experiences in Iraq with great interest. Then, towards the end of 2003, I was asked by senior managers at the Steele Foundation to help them recruit three former South African SF members to deploy in Iraq on a pilot project for the company. I got hold of Renier (PP) Hugo, Johan (Jakes) Jacobs and Anton Beukman, all ex-colleagues of mine (some of whose exploits the reader will learn more about later in the book). The three men were deployed to Iraq in January 2004.

At the time, I considered putting my hand in the air to go there myself, but I had just been promoted to senior agent on the protection detail, and decided to stay in Haiti longer, as the management had shown faith in my abilities on this protection task.

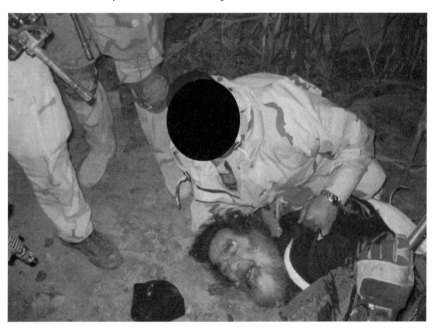

Saddam Hussein was captured by American forces on 13 December 2003
(US Army photo).

On 14 December 2003, President George W Bush announced that Saddam Hussein had finally been captured. The wily old fox had managed to evade the CF for nine months, hiding out in an underground bunker near his home town of Tikrit. When he was found, he was in possession of two AK-47s and $750 000, but offered no resistance.

At the time, many extremists voiced their disappointment that Saddam did not put up a fight to the end. Be that as it may, the infamous Saddam Hussein was captured. He was tried by an Iraqi court for crimes against humanity and sentenced to death by hanging three years later.

There was elation in Iraq that the man who was seen as the arch-enemy by the Shiite majority had been captured. However, the terrorist organisations let it be known that his overthrow would not slow down or bring an end to their resistance to the US and the CF, and the government they had put in place after the invasion.

Our contract in Haiti came to a sudden end when President Aristide was ousted in a civil uprising in February 2004. Our security team had to remove him and his family from Haiti on the advice of the US government after a violent rebel movement against his rule gained momentum. The team contacted various African governments to request safe haven for the exiled president and his family. He eventually ended up in South Africa after President Thabo Mbeki granted him asylum. He and his family lived in the country for a number of years before returning home.

And so by March we were out of work, but we soon heard that the Steele Foundation had been awarded the Musayyib Power Plant security contract. A number of the Haiti team, including me, were offered contracts on this protection task.

The prospect of working in Iraq was exciting, although we knew it was going to be very dangerous – a number of contractors had already been killed by the time we deployed in April 2004. I wrote to my family explaining my decision, trying to allay their fears, as the news was riddled with gruesome stories from that part of the world.

But I saw it as a serious challenge, and one that could bring high rewards, financially, physically and mentally. I felt that it was a mission that was more in line with the kind of work SF soldiers like me did. Unfortunately, the lure of high salaries in return for working in high-risk areas also drew many second-string security operatives to Iraq.

I was flown to Amman, Jordan, where I was briefed about my new mission in Iraq. Then I was off to the Sandbox, ready to deploy and to face whatever this country could throw at me.

After that ambush on the road to Musayyib, I decided to study closely the terrorist groups that operated in the region, as well as the tactics, techniques and procedures they deployed. Although I had analysed various case studies on insurgent and terrorist attacks before my deployment to Iraq, I now realised that the ideology, motivations and modus operandi of our many different enemies were not as straightforward as I'd initially thought. I was also surprised by the sheer number of militia groups that were active in the country. During the Iraq conflict, there was a particular use of terminology regarding the various groups. In the Iraq context, militias were militant Shiite Muslim groups with strong support from Iran. Many Iraqi government security forces belonged to militia groups. The insurgents were Sunni mujahideen and fedayeen soldiers. Their ranks were made up of local terrorists, usually former Saddam-era soldiers and Baath Party members, and foreign jihadist fighters from countries such as Saudi Arabia, Kuwait, Morocco, Algeria, Libya, Egypt, Tunisia, Chechnya and Afghanistan. Fighters from outside Iraq were referred to during this conflict as insurgents. However, in the end, we described all militants as terrorists because all of them tried to kill locals and foreigners in Iraq.

One major challenge of being a PMC is that you are confined to being on the defensive all the time. The enemy has the advantage of surprise, knowledge of the location, method of attack and timing, so we had to be extra vigilant and deploy our best skills to plan and execute our moves to outfox the enemy. Unfortunately, this was not always possible, as there were only so many roads you could use and areas in which you could move around.

That is why things like the attack on our convoy shortly after my arrival in Iraq happened. Many teams that went out on missions on the highways and byways of Iraq knew it was just a matter of time before they would be hit by IEDs or get ambushed. Unfortunately, it seemed that for quite some time the bad guys had most of the routes and areas of operations covered. But the show had to carry on and the teams had to absorb these blows.

South Africans in the Sandbox

By the time I arrived in Baghdad, a number of private military security companies had set up shop in Iraq and quite a few South Africans I knew had been working in the country for some time. Meteoric Tactical Solutions was a South African close-protection security company founded by former members of the Police Task Force, or Taakies, and the SF. Meteoric won some of the first contracts available to private military security companies in Iraq. They performed well and paved the way for other South Africans to achieve success in the Sandbox.

In mid-2003 another South African security company, Safenet Security Services, sent a representative to Baghdad to initiate operations there. Neil Reynolds, a Border War veteran and friend of mine, was tasked to go to Baghdad to initiate operations for Safenet. The company landed contracts and went on to employ many ex-SF members and other South Africans on various missions across the country.

A group of former Recces who were contracted by British security company Olive Group to protect employees of General Electric also helped to put South Africans on the map in Iraqi contracting circles. The work done by this group in August and September 2003 to protect General Electric employees contributed greatly to the supply of power-generation materials, and therefore to the overall reconstruction effort in Iraq.[3]

A former Recce, Chris Delport, was one of the first Olive Group employees in Baghdad to do threat assessments and reconnaissance missions for General Electric. The tall, athletically built Chris had qualified as a Recce in 1992, the year I left the SF. We only really got to know each other when we both worked for different outfits in the Sandbox. Chris qualified as an SF sniper and excelled in this field.

Back then, Chris stayed in the Palestine Hotel in the Red Zone, an area notorious for car bombs and rocket and mortar attacks. He once explained to me that they would never stay higher than the tenth floor, since upper floors fell in the arc of fire and there could be flying shrapnel during attacks and explosions. The lower floors at the Palestine Hotel were better shielded thanks to the 12-foot reinforced-concrete T-walls that lined the outer perimeter. It was the sort of reality of everyday life in Baghdad that we would soon all become attuned to.

From September to November 2003, when they were setting up Olive security operations in Iraq they had four teams, running missions out of the hotel, and Chris was the only South African among them. They would pick up General Electric engineers and escort them under security to power stations all over Baghdad for assessment.

It wasn't long before Chris got the opportunity to select his own team, and he asked a number of fellow South Africans, then all based in the south close to Basra, to join him in Baghdad. Chris selected Mathys (Diff) de Villiers and Brandt Brecher, along with Paul Heany (ex-Royal Marine) as his driver. The rest of his team were a mix of young and old South African PMCs, including Recce legends such as Menno Uys and the late MP Viljoen. Soon all the team leaders were ex-SF guys.

General Electric was awarded a contract by the US Army Corps of Engineers, which included refurbishing and replacing switchgear for substations all over Iraq. Many reconnaissance missions and assessments had to be conducted before General Electric could even consider deploying any of their engineers to anywhere in Iraq, and rightfully so.

Chris told me the South Africans were favoured for these missions owing to their ability to navigate, adapt to the hostile environment, endure time at the target location and return with facts. He and his team did more than 12 reconnaissance missions and covered thousands of kilometres within four months in soft-skin vehicles.

Early in 2004, Olive obtained a villa to base themselves from in the Green Zone and everyone relocated to this heavily fortified area. Some GE projects got under way and people were sent to various locations all over Iraq. By mid-2004, all four Olive teams operating from the Green Zone consisted entirely of South Africans.

The US military and other CF started taking note of the South Africans in the Green Zone. One day Chris was invited to attend a US Army Corps of Engineers meeting. He asked Diff to drive him to the appointment, the idea being that Diff would remain inside the vehicle while Chris met with the engineers. When he came out of the meeting, Diff was nowhere to be seen. Chris remembered the huge relief he had felt when he suddenly spotted two bare feet sticking out from under the hood of a Humvee parked next to his SUV. While Chris was away, Diff had decided to 'explore' the military vehicle's chassis – apparently overtaken by curiosity, as these vehicles weren't available in South Africa at the time.

The US soldiers were speechless – they had never seen anyone crawl that deep under a Humvee. This, together with the fact he was not wearing any shoes, meant Diff quickly became a legend around the Green Zone. He also used to go for runs barefoot in the afternoon. Soon everybody in the Green Zone was talking about South African Diff and his barefoot ways.

On one occasion, Chris and Diff had to travel to Kuwait to pick up a General Electric convoy. When they arrived at the Navistar control station at the Kuwait border crossing, the temperature was in excess of 55 °C. When Chris approached the Navistar officer to receive the paperwork for the convoy, the officer and his team were moving from one spot to the other because the tar was so hot that the rubber of the soles would melt after a few seconds. That kind of heat put the temperature of the asphalt close to 80 °C. When Chris returned to their vehicle, Diff asked why everyone seemed so restless. When Chris explained about the temperature of the road surface, the barefooted Diff had to bend down and put his hand on the tar to be able to understand what Chris was referring to. Diff stood on the same spot for 15 minutes in his bare feet without feeling the heat.

When one US soldier noticed Diff was not wearing shoes, he literally dropped everything he had in his hands. 'Look, this motherfucker ain't got no shoes!' he cried out.

Chris, Diff and a few other South Africans decided it would be sociable to open a bar in the Olive compound for colleagues and other contractors. They had one built and decorated it with flags representing all the countries that formed part of the CF. In no time the Olive Bar became a renowned Thursday-evening gathering spot for PMCs of all nationalities from the various security companies, such as Blackwater, Reed, Aegis, Kroll and ArmorGroup. People would drive across Baghdad to share war stories and listen to the South Africans talking about bygone days working for Executive Outcomes or fighting in the Bush War.

The Olive teams traded their beers and Jack Daniel's for meals-ready-to-eat (MREs) with US soldiers who manned a telecommunications point adjacent to the Olive compound.[4]

The US military's meal, ready-to-eat (MRE) is quite an upgrade from the ratpack.

Also on the recreational front, Chris and his team established the Baghdad Rugby Club in the Green Zone. Nine countries participated in a weekly touch rugby event, in which Brits, Aussies, Americans,

Fijians, Romanians, Italians, French and even Japanese participated (they could not play full contact rugby because of the risk of injury).

In January 2004, the first South African contractor in Iraq, Francois Strydom, was killed in an ambush in Baghdad. By the end of that month over 50 contractors had been killed in Iraq, the majority of them truck drivers for the American logistical firm Kellogg Brown & Root.

Although a number of contractors had been killed in the latter part of 2003 and the beginning of 2004, the first major incident involving PMCs was the gruesome killing of four security personnel from Blackwater in the streets of Fallujah in March 2004. Their bodies were mutilated, burnt, dragged through the streets and hanged from a bridge outside the town, which became known as Blackwater Bridge.

This incident was widely reported in the media and first brought to the world's attention how private military security companies were active in large numbers in Iraq. It also brought to light how some of these contractors were undertaking paramilitary-style protection tasks that required soldiering skills. The enemy deployed guerrilla warfare-style attacks, not only against the CF, but also against the private contractors guarding and protecting CF officials, NGOs and civilians, such as the engineers who worked for companies that were contracted to help in the reconstruction efforts in Iraq.

There was no shortage of coverage of the deaths of contractors who worked in Iraq; the PMCs knew that their work was extremely perilous. Yet the promise of big-buck salaries still lured individuals from all walks of life to work in the Sandbox.

This kind of life might sound exciting and smack of Hollywood glamorisation of the lives of military and security contractors. But the reality is that working in the Sandbox in those early years was dangerous, tiresome and painful. Most guys' partners and families could not get used to the men being away from home for years on end. A lot of PMCs who worked in Iraq had cosy assignments where they were stationary in a CF base or safer location, but most of us were exposed to the dangers that the country dished up, and all had to get used to being separated from their loved ones for many months on end.

The following chapters illustrate what this reality was like, and take the reader on a journey that describes the kind of existence that we as PMCs led in the Sandbox.

3

A taste of everyday life in Iraq

In April 2004, I moved into our camp near the Musayyib Power Plant along with the rest of the team who had been deployed to work on this project. Our daily routine was to run motorcade convoys to the airport to collect engineers from Southeast Texas Industries, who were arriving in Iraq, and bring them to the camp. The journey took around two hours and, as mentioned, passed through some very rough territory – the Triangle of Death, a hotbed of insurgency, including a run on the notorious Route Irish.

The camp was in a flat, sandy area adjacent to the old power plant. At that point only the camp's border wall and entrance gate had been erected. Accommodation units, offices and other infrastructure, such as sewerage and water services, still had to be constructed. Supplies for these were trucked to the site, mainly from Turkey. The first units that arrived were set up for the security team. Our living quarters were a large containerised room with eight single beds and steel cupboards. We had a communal toilet.

Most accommodation units in remote camps in Iraq consisted of containerised housing units, also called 'hooches', Portakabins or caravans. This is a modified shipping container with insulated walls, air conditioning and a couple of power sockets. Such a unit normally measures around 3 x 4 metres, but they vary in size. A unit is usually furnished with a single or double bunk bed, a small cupboard and a small table and chair.

(On my next assignment, in northwestern Iraq about two months later, the units we were allocated were very small – just 3 x 3 metres, which is acceptable for one person, but we struggled when we had to share a hooch. On a later tour[1] I once had to share a cabin with a burly ex-US Marine, the late Brian Dolan. It took a very coordinated effort for the two of us, both tall and weighing in excess of 100 kg, to move around in such a small space. Just getting out of our beds and getting dressed had to be executed with military precision, something akin to synchronised swimming.)

What we called home in Iraq: containerised housing units, or 'hooches'.

The hooch of an American private military contractor at Al Kasik.

In addition to the motorcades, we also escorted the engineers to areas of the plant where they were working on the power facility. Initially, the foundations had to be prepared to support the heavy General Electric power modules, such as transformers and other power-generating equipment. For the construction, large trucks hauled in a special track-driven crane from Turkey. This was so large it had to be brought to the site in sections, and a team of engineers assembled the monstrosity in stages. When the crane was built, it almost toppled over while manoeuvring a heavy object. People scampered in all directions, but fortunately it stayed upright.

The power plant was next to the US military's forward operating base, Iskandariyah, which was both a good and a bad thing. It meant that we had access to medevacs and Intel, and the US military could deploy a quick-reaction force to our location if the camp was attacked. But it also meant our camp was often the target of mortar attacks. During one particular incident, there were eight detonations inside and at the perimeter wall of the compound. We suspected that the mortars that hit us were often aimed at the military base (a mortar is considered as an area weapon and it takes some skill to fire it with pinpoint accuracy at a target). Because of the risk, the engineers decided to construct an underground bunker where we could take shelter during incoming rocket or mortar fire. During these attacks, the sentry in the towers, or the first person who heard the detonations, would shout 'incoming' over the radio, and everybody would run for the bunkers or into hard cover, which is any solid building where you could lie flat on the ground, away from windows and doors.

If you were out in the open, it was best to just hit the deck with your arms and hands covering your head. Running around like a headless chicken could easily get you killed if a mortar or rocket landed close to you. On one occasion, the mortars and explosions were so close to our small camp that our hooch's windows and bathroom mirrors shattered.

Getting mortared and rocketed so regularly was mentally exhausting. We constantly had to be vigilant and we were anxious because bombs could rain down on us at any time. We also had to ensure the sentries, radio comms and emergency drills were all working properly should we need to raise the alarm for everybody to scramble to the bunker or hit the deck.

Towards the end of April 2004, shortly after we had moved to the camp, stories of prisoner abuse at the notorious Abu Ghraib prison west of Baghdad started surfacing. The media were onto it in a flash. A number of US soldiers and a handful of private contractors were implicated in the scandal. It is generally the feeling among contractors that from the end of that month the floodgates opened in terms of attacks on private military security companies and security contractors. There is no doubt that the Blackwater deaths in Fallujah and the Abu Ghraib incidents exacerbated the situation.

In the weeks after our ambush on the road, I noticed that my left shoulder was continuing to hurt badly. It was only when I had it checked out months later that I was told that my shoulder was dislocated and that a small piece of shoulder bone had broken off and some tendons that anchored the shoulder joint were torn. It required reconstructive surgery but I decided against it, because I did not want to interrupt my career and leave the Sandbox. For many months I could not lift my arm above my shoulder, but at least I could hold onto the stock on an AK-47. So I stuck it out, even though it was very painful.

This, combined with an injury I'd sustained to both my heels during my military days and an old back injury that flared up, meant I experienced chronic pain. In the mid-1990s doctors and neurologists prescribed chronic pain medication for the condition in my heels, and since then I had been taking these meds to get some relief. Since I had access to painkillers, I kept increasing the dosages so that my body could keep up with the demands of my work.

Heat and flies

Aside from the human dangers we were exposed to, daily life in Iraq brought a number of other challenges, many from the natural environment. For starters, we had to get used to the incredible heat. In southern Iraq the air temperature can often reach 50 °C and beyond. In the direct sun it gets even hotter. We often measured temperatures of well over 60, sometimes over 70 degrees, while working in the sun.

(Fact checkers will now probably go onto Google to check the hottest temperatures ever recorded. They will see that it was 57 °C in the western hemisphere – in Death Valley in the United States – and 54 °C in the eastern hemisphere, in Kuwait City, but these temperatures are the average air temperature in the shade. Put a thermometer in the direct sun for an hour and see what happens ...)

South African colleagues who took care of engineers in southern Iraq measured temperatures in the direct sun with industrial thermometers to determine the expansion and contraction of power lines. They recorded temperatures of up to 83 °C. This is hot enough to bake eggs on a vehicle's hood after 30 minutes! The South Africans managed with the heat, but the British guys battled. One of my colleagues from my Haiti days, a Brit, always had to go out dressed like he was going to the North Pole. He had to cover every inch of his skin and even had to work with gloves on as the sun caught his hands one day and the skin blistered.

My British colleague Kevin Williams covered up completely to protect his skin.

Given the heat, the engineers decided to work from 06:00 to 12:00 and take a siesta until around 15:00, and then they would work until around 18:30. During these breaks, I would get into my running gear, put a 'camelback' hydration pack on my back and grab my

AK-47 with double mags, and run a couple of kilometres around the inside perimeter of the base. This flabbergasted some of the British and American guys, but I believe it helped me to get conditioned to working in the heat, and it kept me fit.

We quickly discovered some of the golden rules of working in extreme heat – find shade when you can or generate it with hats, cover up with clothing and stay hydrated. It was common to drink up to 12 litres of water a day while we were working in the sun in bulletproof vests, tactical jackets, cargo pants and boots, which caused excessive perspiration.

But finding the right kind of water was crucial. In Iraq the manufacture and supply of bottled water is a huge business because the regular mains water supplied by the water authorities is unsafe to drink. Between 2004 and 2007 the US and CF consumed roughly 1.5 million bottles of water – a day. Most Iraqi civilians who can afford it also drink bottled water. Unfortunately, the poor rely on the government supply of water from the two main rivers and dams. As a former combat medic, I had prepared a medical lecture for new team members arriving in the country to warn them about the unsanitary conditions they would face. In this brief I warned personnel on the dangers inherent in the water supply. I explained that water contamination created the greatest short-term health risks from the consumption of water contaminated with raw sewage, runoff water contaminated with faecal material and fish contaminated with toxins. Human waste would flow into open gutters and storm drains, mixing with the overflow of garbage. At times bodies were observed in the rivers but these were normally cleared quickly when reported. Leakages in the water supply lines were also a problem. These were caused by locals illegally tapping into the water pipes, and by insurgents sabotaging the water supply network. Another risk to short-term health was the supply of ice, as most ice is made from local tap water, and not from sanitised spring or treated water. Food was also kept chilled on ice made from ordinary tap water, and transported in wheelbarrows and open trucks. Supplying sufficient amounts of potable water was one of the biggest challenges for the new Iraqi government.

So we had to take great care not to ingest any infected water. We made our own ice by packing the freezers with bottled water and then breaking it into smaller pieces. You also had to keep bottles of water in the bathroom to brush your teeth with. When there were problems with the water pipes or pumps, you had to take a 'bottle bath' by using a face cloth and bottled water to clean with. When you took a shower, you had to take care not to swallow even a drop, as a very small amount could make you sick.

My second and third months in Iraq introduced me to some more of the country's natural 'wonders'. Like all desert environments, Iraq is by nature a very dusty place. During May, and particularly June, we got acquainted with the desert wind known as the *shamal*, a strong northwesterly that emanates from the Mediterranean and blows across Syria and Jordan, south towards Kuwait and Saudi Arabia, where it funnels into a narrow and intense band onto the Persian Gulf. The shamal causes dust storms, particularly in the dry summer months.

A sandstorm engulfs a US military base in Iraq in 2004.

We had a taste of such a sandstorm on site during June. I'd experienced severe sandstorms in the Sahara many years earlier when I worked in North Africa, but for many of the guys in our team this was a first.

During a shamal storm, you had to get indoors – and stay there. The dust cloud can be several thousand feet high and can stay in the air for up to five days. In August 2005, a shamal storm that blanketed Baghdad caused all air travel to be cancelled, and nearly all shops closed and public activity came to a halt. One hospital alone in the city treated over 1 000 people for respiratory difficulties, and more than 100 died.

The dust gets in everywhere, even into the pores of your skin. For this reason, nomads and traditional desert dwellers cover their bodies with cloths from head to toe, including the traditional *shemagh*, or head scarf. Because of the shamal threat, I always carried a shemagh scarf and dust goggles in my E & E bag.

In Iraq, the dust is a force to be reckoned with, and therefore
you have to cover up.

Then there are the flies. I have been to a number of African countries, but never before had I encountered as many flies in one spot as I did in certain areas of Iraq. There must have been at least a million flies per cubic metre. I have seen white cars turn to black under swarms of flies.

It is a special kind of lazy fly that hangs out in the Sandbox. They move in slow motion, and seem to crawl slowly over your skin, making them more irritating than a regular fly that will quickly buzz away when disturbed. They stick to you, and to any surface, and only move when you swat them.

They are a tough breed too. I have seen 'dead' flies miraculously reviving themselves a minute or so after being swatted. I guess the unsanitary conditions in the country play a large role in this phenomenon. At least when the shamal blows hard, the swarms of flies seem to diminish for a while.

Many scary, yet unfounded rumours about camel spiders did the rounds.

We also had to get used to the camel spiders. These sand-coloured spiders look menacing, move fast and have large pincers to catch their prey. During our first few months in Iraq, some emails did the rounds in the contractors' world claiming that these fearsome-looking creatures were very dangerous and many a contractor was very scared of them. But none of this is true. Although they become aggressive when challenged, these spiders are not venomous and are perfectly harmless to humans.

Culture shocks

As well as having to get used to the challenges nature brought, we also had an interesting time getting to know our Iraqi employees and their culture. Needless to say, there were a few things that surprised us, while other cultural practices, especially around religious values and traditions, were important to take note of and respect.

For instance, one morning after night shift, one of the expat shift leaders told us an interesting story. Since the night-shift guards were often caught napping, he had decided to address the problem with the Iraqi guards. He was surprised by their response. They tried to convince him that their 'Iraqi DNA' was different from ours and that, genetically, it is impossible for them to stay awake for a 12-hour shift without catching a nap.

They acknowledged their shortcoming and asked us to let them work for only four to six hours, maximum, before rotating them. We decided to give it a try, but alas, we still found the guards napping during their short shifts. In the years that followed we realised that it was near impossible to keep the Iraqi guards awake for an entire shift. This problem also presented itself during the day shift.

Since there was a shooting range next to the US military base, two of my South African colleagues and I decided to take the Iraqi guards, among whom were some Kurds, to the range to check and zero our weapons, and to do some shooting practice.

Everybody was kitted out with AK-47s, and after we had explained the safety procedures we did some dry drills and weapons orientation. Once the live firing started, we realised that very few of the Iraqis could hit the targets consistently. They blamed problems with the sights, so we took the rifles and fired them to check. The sights were working fine, and my observation over the next decade was that this problem might well be genetic too.

We gave some basic instruction and things got a bit better, but I soon came to the conclusion, and this was confirmed many times during the next couple of years, that the Iraqis cannot shoot particularly well (there are a few exceptions, of course).

But, for us, a serious problem was the Iraqi of shooting wildly in the air when they celebrate something or get excited. The Iraqi national soccer team had been banned from international participation in the 1990s. So, when the team qualified for the Asian Cup Finals sometime in 2004, Iraqi fans in Baghdad let rip with celebratory fire. Most of us foreigners, who still had to get used to this method of celebrating, thought a large-scale attack was breaking out. Many ran for cover and went into combat mode until the locals pointed out that it was merely celebratory fire.

Something these happy shooters do not take into account is the laws of gravity and physics: whatever goes up will eventually come down. All those bullets that were fired into the air come back to earth and often retain enough energy to wound and even kill people. I know of at least two Iraqi security force members who were wounded in such incidents. It makes one wonder how many civilians have been wounded or even killed when thousands of rounds are fired into the air. Either way, we learnt quickly to move indoors and away from windows and doors when the Iraqis were celebrating.[2]

Also on a cultural note, a common mistake foreigners make is to sit with the soles of their shoes pointing towards an Iraqi. The sole of the shoe is considered dirty, and for this reason shoes are placed outside mosques, most restaurants and certain official buildings. I saw videos of Iraqis placing their shoes in the mouth of Saddam's statue in Baghdad after it was torn down – the ultimate insult. And George W Bush had a shoe hurled at him by a reporter during a press conference when he visited Baghdad in 2008.

Another big no-no is not showing respect for religious rituals, such as daily prayers (which are followed three to five times a day), and holy seasons, such as Ramadan, Eid and Ashura.

Muslims are not allowed to eat pork. It was possible to bring some pork or bacon into the country, but you had to be very careful not to let any Iraqis touch or cook it. Moreover, if you made a dish containing pork or bacon, you had to mark it clearly and tell the Iraqis in the team or in the compound about it, so that they would not eat it accidentally, as this would lead to a riot.

Another tradition is that most Muslims use their right hand to eat with, to pass gifts and to greet people because this hand is seen as the 'clean' hand, or the one to do noble things with. You are supposed to use your left hand to clean yourself after using the toilet, so the left hand is considered 'unclean'. Still, this rule isn't set in stone. One will often see younger Iraqis wave at you with their left hands or hand you goods with their left hands.

'Funny English'

It became apparent immediately after my arrival in Iraq that there was an insurmountable language barrier between the Iraqis and the foreigners, with much communication lost in translation. In those days, very few locals could speak English, although the city dwellers in Baghdad managed better than the people in rural areas. Most Iraqis who could speak decent English had studied overseas or had studied English at a local university.

It was not easy to find Iraqis with English language skills and many also bullshitted their way into a job by having a few well-rehearsed pat phrases ready and by nodding their heads when you asked them questions. Those who were proficient in English were paid more and found work with the US military and the CF as interpreters. The private military security companies were far behind in the queue when it came to finding decent translators, however.

One day at the power station, a group of Iraqis came to see me. They told me they had a big problem – they could not understand some of the American and British guys in the team because, as they said, they spoke 'funny English'. I had to laugh. As someone who had learnt to speak a bit of English only at the age of 18, and given that English is my third language – after Afrikaans and 7.62 mm – I completely empathised with them. They said it was easier to understand the South Africans – I guess because our English is often just as broken as theirs – it's a bit like drunks who manage to communicate with one another, I suppose.

While on the theme of communication, another big mistake Westerners made in Iraq was to shout and swear at the Iraqis, often using the F-word. This has no effect, as it's perceived as incredibly insulting behaviour. It was also not a good idea to discipline an Iraqi employee in front of other Iraqis because it is seen as very demeaning and as something that will make them lose face. Once they get the idea that you have insulted them, it becomes very difficult to remedy a bad situation.

Fortunately, I didn't succumb to these behaviours. I'd learnt a long time ago not to raise my voice when I get angry or excited. Naseer, an Iraqi colleague, who would later become a friend of mine, once told me that they would get very concerned when I started speaking quietly as my eyes grew darker. They could obviously read the danger signs.

During my first months in Iraq, I learnt another valuable lesson. A guard had brought me a radio I had requested, and I said *dankie*, thanking him in Afrikaans out of habit. I was just trying to be courteous. A short while later, the Iraqi supervisor came to see me with the guard in tow. Why had I insulted his guard? he wanted to know. It turned out that he thought I had called him a donkey, which is seen as an impure animal. I had to apologise there and then. Later on, some of the Iraqis learnt a few basic Afrikaans words and phrases. A few of them could even hold short conversations in Afrikaans.

And, in turn, we learnt some basic Arabic; it was important to be able to speak at least a few words. If you knew how to greet people in Arabic, count to ten, say 'turn left/right/keep straight' as driving instructions, problem or no problem, power or no power, you could often count on a good response. It was also very important to understand and correctly use religious phrases and greetings, such as:

Salaam Alaikum – Greeting (literally 'may peace be upon you'), to which you reply: *Alaikum Salaam*.

Insha'Allah – God willing. A phrase often used if the outcome of a desired result is unknown.

Allahu Akbar – God is greatest.

Allah Balkher – God bless us all (used by traditional Iraqi males before a meeting).

Hum-dAllah – God bless you or bless your heart, also the expression used when someone sneezes.

Alhumd Allah – Thanks to God, praise be to Allah.

Shukran – Thank you.[3]

The Iraqis not only understood our broken English better than the

English spoken by the Americans and British, but in general they also got on better with the South Africans. One reason is that we were never part of the CF; another is that we had our own identity and culture, which they did not associate with citizens of other English-speaking nations. Many of them were also fascinated by Afrikaans and the fact that it stems from Dutch, Flemish and German – this definitely helped to distinguish us from English-speaking nations during the war. In many an Iraqi's mind, speaking English was synonymous with being an infidel. In our line of work, I've often found it tactically useful to speak a language that less than 0.05 per cent of the world's population can understand. In the early 2000s, when I worked in southern Sudan with a number of American PMCs, they handed the radios to me and my fellow South Africans for us to coordinate our movements in Afrikaans because we knew the government of Sudan was listening in.

In Iraq we did the same thing when we didn't want the Iraqis to know what we were planning. I have been called a 'windtalker' on a few occasions in my career (a 2002 movie by the same name tells the story of two US Marines who, during World War II, were assigned to protect Navajo Indian Marines who used their native language as an unbreakable radio cipher to coordinate movements).

VeeBids and air strikes

In May I encountered my first suicide car bomb, or, in military terms, a vehicle-borne improvised explosive device (VBIED), commonly called a VeeBid. I was doing guard duty on the tower closest to the camp's vehicle access gate one morning, when I saw an old box-type car slowly moving towards a small checkpoint on the road outside the camp that led to the power plant complex. What I saw and experienced then would become a regular occurrence in the coming years.

Suddenly, there was a fireball. The sound reaches you a split second later, and the blast waves hit you like a sledgehammer. This particular explosion's blast wave was enough to push me backwards against the walls of the guard tower. I cannot recall the amount of casualties, but US explosive ordnance device technicians later informed us that they had found pieces of metal, which suggested 82 mm high-explosive mortars had been used, and that the power of the explosion indicated that more than a single mortar shell had been deployed in this attack. We realised then that we were indeed inside the Triangle of Death. And the mortar and rocket attacks, and ambushes, in the area did not relent.

Having been trained in demolitions and the use of explosives, I was well aware of the effects of a high-explosive blast. That car bomb and the destructive speed of the air displacement created by the high explosives led me to reflect on how Hollywood has created a myth. Heroes in action movies are seen outrunning an explosion, the huge fireballs behind them as they run out of a building or dive out of harm's way. This is totally false, as high explosives detonate at between 3 000 and 8 000 metres per second: no living creature can outpace that destructive force, which creates a blast wave that destroys anything in its path. It is true that blast waves follow the path of least resistance and exponentially lose their force if distance and matter (cover) can be gained before the blast. But outpacing an explosion – never.

One afternoon while I was on tower watch duty, I heard the sound of a fighter jet overhead. I eventually spotted it just as it went into a nosedive from high altitude. At one point, it levelled out, and then the pilot pulled the nose of the plane into an almost vertical climb again. I saw a massive explosion around 4 kilometres away and then realised that the plane had dropped a bomb. The whole camp shook after the explosion.

Later we learnt from the guys at the forward operating base that they had called in an air strike on a team of insurgents who had been spotted lobbing mortars at their location. The plane had dropped a 500-pound bomb. I had never before witnessed such a powerful explosion and I had to wonder how much of the insurgent group was left to be buried. During this period, I read Intel reports that the US were peppering the Taliban and al-Qaeda terrorists in the mountains of Afghanistan with bombs that weighed over 10 000 pounds. I reckon anybody witnessing such an explosion, if they were lucky enough to survive it, must have thought Armageddon was upon them.

4

Badlands: Northwestern Iraq

I survived my first three-month stint, known in PMC circles as a rotation, in the Sandbox and flew back to South Africa at the end of June 2004 for some rest and recreation. While I was on leave, a manager from the Shaw Group, an American construction and environmental company, contacted me and offered me a contract for the position of team medic[1] on a Shaw project they were working on to revamp the Al Kasik military base in northern Iraq.[2] Al Kasik is around 60 kilometres west of Mosul.

I agreed to deploy on this mission at the end of July after my leave, as the salary was better and our project at Musayyib had suffered many setbacks and security incidents. It was time for a change of scene. This time, I had to enter Iraq via Kuwait, since no commercial airlines were flying into northern Iraq at the time, and I then took a US Air Force plane from Kuwait City to Mosul. The Shaw Group had been contracted to upgrade existing buildings at the military base – which had been built as a tank brigade base during the Saddam era – and build a water-treatment plant.

The Shaw Group had teamed up with one of the largest construction companies in Iraq, which was owned by a prominent local family. The company's CEO was a sheik, whom I will call FK. I met FK for the first time when he came to visit Al Kasik in August to check on the progress of the project. I introduced myself over some strong Turkish coffee. FK spoke English well and he was clearly a well-educated and intelligent man. After the pleasantries, he asked about my professional background and for my view on Iraq. He seemed interested in my VIP protection and high-threat management skills.

He then asked me to draft a proposal to provide protection teams in Baghdad for his company's offices, a bank in which they held shares

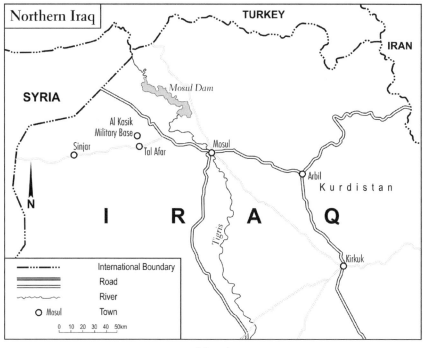

Map 4

and the Dreamland Hotel,[3] which I later discovered he owned. I agreed to help him and we exchanged email addresses. This was the start of a long business relationship and a good friendship.

The Shaw Group had its own internal security division. The site security manager was an ex-US Marine and the security team a motley crew of South Africans and a couple of Americans from diverse military backgrounds, some ex-law-enforcement officers and other auxiliary security personnel. The base was close to the troublesome village of Tal Afar and the area was a hotbed for Sunni insurgents, who infiltrated the country from Syria, and there was a large Sunni support base for the guerrillas in the vicinity of Mosul. These were truly the country's 'badlands', and a decade later became the hub from where ISIS terrorists and insurgents would operate, as well as forming part of their self-declared caliphate.

So, it was perhaps not surprising that, less than two weeks after arriving for my second rotation, the base was struck with a coordinated complex attack.[4] I was out protecting a group of engineers who were working in one of the buildings overseeing the construction work of the Iraqi subcontractors. We heard a massive explosion nearby, and moments later a second enormous explosion went off in another part of the base.

The security team at Al Kasik military base in August 2004.
I am in the back row, second from right.

As the team medic, I was called on the radio to tend to casualties. First I had to secure the clients under the staircase of one of the buildings, away from windows and doors, and then sped off in a bakkie to our camp. On my way there, we were rocked by more blasts and I then realised that we were under mortar or rocket attack, or both. There were explosions all around the base and smoke was rising.

When I got to our camp, I saw some bodies and a lot of blood in the foyer of the building where our Iraqi engineers worked from. I marshalled members of our security team to ascertain which casualties were still alive and to assist in triage, the medical process of prioritising which casualties need medical attention first. After emplacing field dressings, or bomb bandages, and tourniquets on the injured, I tended to an Iraqi whose right arm was severed at the elbow; he was fast bleeding to death.

After fastening a tourniquet on his upper arm, I placed an artificial airway in his throat and proceeded to run two intravenous drip lines on his left arm and ankle. It was difficult to find a vein on his arm, as he had lost a massive amount of blood and was in shock, but I managed to find a vein in his lower leg. The patient was fading away fast and I had to perform cardiopulmonary resuscitation twice. I managed to keep him breathing, and his heart was beating, but after around 20 minutes he died.

I was tending to other casualties and delegated tasks to team members who were able to help with measures to stop the wounded bleeding. The US military personnel in the base arranged medical-evacuation helicopters from Mosul and the most serious casualties were flown to more sophisticated medical facilities.

A room at Al Kasik after the attack in August 2004.
The blast was about 25 m away.

Eight people died that day, mostly Iraqis, and many more were wounded, including expatriates. But it was a miracle that so few perished during what turned out to be a major coordinated attack. Looking back, there were some factors that contributed to the minimum loss of life that day. Two suicide VeeBids (water tankers) had been detonated – one at the dining facility and another at the headquarters building. But the terrorists got their timing wrong, as it was not mealtime when the tanker detonated outside the dining building.

Several chefs and cleaners were killed or wounded, but there would have been many more casualties had the hall been full.

An engineer stands in the crater left by one of the bombs, while I look on.

The second vehicle exploded outside the base HQ, but caused only one fatality – an Iraqi soldier on guard duty, who was the closest to the explosion. A few of the Shaw Group engineers, and our night-shift-duty security personnel, including fellow South Africans Awie Wessels and Nico Lee, were in the building and close to the exploding water tanker. In the explosion, bunk beds and steel furniture were tossed around by the force of the blast along with two security personnel who were close to the explosion. Awie later told me they were flung around the room with the furniture like clothes in a tumble dryer. But the reinforced-concrete buildings of the old tank base were very strong and had been designed to withstand attacks. One of the 107 mm rockets also hit the HQ building from the east. It was fortunate that it did not detonate, as it struck the building close to a window next to where some of our people were staying.

Awie came to see me a few days after the attack complaining about headaches, and I noticed a yellowish discharge from his nose. This pointed to possible serious concussion that might have caused brain fluid to escape from the skull via the facial orifices. I wanted to arrange to medevac him but he insisted on staying, as he was concerned that he might be sent home and lose his job. I kept monitoring him and the condition eventually cleared up.

It was only many years later that Awie and I – with my broken shoulder – both discovered that we could have applied for Defense Base Act (DBA) insurance, which was a type of cover that companies took out for people working on military contracts funded by the US government. If a contractor got injured to the extent that he could not perform his security functions any longer, then the insurer would pay the individual's medical costs and a salary for as long as he could not perform the same kind of work. Anyhow, Awie survived and managed to work, but he suffered from headaches for many years.

After this attack, security measures were stepped up. There were dedicated search lanes for trucks entering the base, and another separate pedestrian entrance for day workers who walked to the site from the nearby village.

During the next year and a half, I worked at the Al Kasik base and it got peppered with rockets and mortars on a regular basis, mainly 107 mm Chinese rockets and 82 mm Eastern bloc mortars. Such was the regularity of these attacks that we soon learnt how to distinguish between the different sounds made by the mortars and rockets. A mortar comes down with a whistling sound, whereas a rocket emits a 'ssshhh' sound as the rocket propellant burns and propels the projectile forward. One of the South Africans at the base recalled how a rocket had once sailed over the guard tower, barely missing the tower while he was on night shift. On a number of occasions, the 107 mm rockets failed to detonate, and then we had to clearly mark the location of the warheads, so that the explosive ordnance disposal teams could destroy them.

Members of the Iraqi security forces and an American PMC, Sean Hill, with an unexploded 122 mm Katyusha rocket, September 2004.

I also decided to institute training sessions on protective and combat arms on the range to ensure that there was cohesion among the team. They came from different security backgrounds and needed to be able to function as a well-oiled unit in the event of an armed attack.

The site tended to be quiet on Fridays because the Iraqi contractors and workers went to their mosques to pray, so on Fridays I used to take the team to the shooting range, where we would go through tactical and combat training exercises with handguns, assault rifles, machine guns and sniper rifles (Russian Dragunov SVDs). One thing I'd learnt about Americans a few years before, during a visit to the US, and from the ones I worked with in Iraq, is that they love their guns. I'm a gun nut myself, so this suited me fine. I pushed the team hard, and it yielded good results. The training was also a great team-building exercise.

The American engineers from Shaw asked us if we could teach them how to use the AK-47s and PKM machine guns. I thought this was a good idea; they would understand how to use the arms that the security team used in case a security officer went down next to them and they might have to pick up a weapon and defend themselves. It was also a good time to show them what kind of drills to expect from the security team in case of an attack. After some contact drills and exercises at the firing range, our clients were much better prepared and worked more in harmony with the security team.

Team members practise long-distance shooting during range training day at Al Kasik.

Meanwhile, the security team gelled and their reaction times got faster, especially after we showed them that, for close-quarter combat in urban and semi-rural areas, they did not need all the accessories often used with their weapons, such as telescopes, holographic sights, bipods and torches, as these slowed them down. We practised contact drills with clients in foot formations and safety sweeps, shooting back at 'attackers' while providing body cover for the clients. We shot from vehicles and simulated exercises that mirrored the real conditions on site.

In one exercise, we would line up with a couple of engineers in front of us and then simulate a contact. The engineers would hit the deck while the private security officer fired shots over them towards the imaginary targets, and then move next to them in a kneeling position while engaging the target; then a tactical withdrawal to the vehicles would be carried out. We also practised fire and movement, and breakout-of-encirclement combat exercises.

During contact drill training, our clients had to get used to someone shooting over them.

I organised other training classes that I deemed useful for the team. We had a former police bomb-disposal expert on the team, who arranged some good training sessions involving IEDs and mine warfare, and how to perform a counter-explosive vehicle search. We got the engineers involved as well, so that they knew how to search their vehicles themselves while waiting for a private security officer to become available before going out on site.

I also conducted first-aid training, and held classes on how to use an automatic electronic defibrillator, a useful tool to revive a patient who has suffered a heart attack or has other conditions that cause the heart to stop beating. We did GPS navigation classes, camp defence drills, and I organised a class on how to survive a chemical-warfare attack. We involved the clients in some of this training, such as how to recognise IEDs and survival skills during chemical attacks.

Improvised protective gear worn during chemical warfare training.

For security purposes, it was standard operating procedure to search all vehicles and Iraqi workers entering and exiting the base. The main reason for searching incoming vehicles and personnel was to detect explosives and weapons that might be smuggled in and used in an attack.

The exit search procedures were mainly to control theft and pilfering, but also to prevent bomb-making materials from being smuggled out. We found that light switches, electric cables, power sockets, and particularly air-conditioner main switches were disappearing from the base. I later learnt from Intel sources that such electronic components were being sold to insurgents, who were always looking for components they could use. Any kind of circuit breaker was useful to a bomb maker, as it could be connected to electrical wiring and coupled to a detonator and energy source. They also used washing-machine timers, keyless vehicle remotes and automatic garage-door switches. By activating the switch on timers, and by initiating a circuit breaker, the terrorist could trigger and explode his IED. The air-con circuit breakers were especially handy, as most have a time delay, which could be used to great effect by insurgents to commit acts of terror, allowing them to get out of the area after they had activated a bomb.

Our searches had to be thorough, as some electronic parts could be hidden in clothing and compartments of bags. Some perpetrators cottoned on to our security procedures and, to get round them, would throw the stolen componentry concealed in plastic bags over the fence and retrieve them later once they had exited the base, so we placed guards around the perimeter to look out for this. The guards were also trained to scan the desert plains to detect suspicious movements as precursors to possible attacks.

Another challenge for the expat security officers was to ensure that the local guards did not steal rounds out of the AK-47 magazines. An AK bullet could fetch a couple of dollars on the black market, so we had to inspect all weapons and magazines at the guard posts daily and ensure that the magazines were filled up and weren't missing a round or two. Luckily, this was easy, as AK-47 magazines are designed to help the user quickly establish if they are filled to capacity, which is normally 30 rounds.

The guard usually had a number of excuses if you found a magazine was missing rounds, and they mostly blamed the shift before them. It was a continual game of cat and mouse, and we had to stay sharp to not let this kind of pilfering take place on our beat.

Our over-watch position on the roof of the office building was manned 24/7. While I was on guard duty at night, I could engage in one of my favourite hobbies – stargazing. I was fascinated by how the constellations in the northern hemisphere were all 'upside down' compared to the southern hemisphere. With the help of star charts, I was able to identify quite a number of constellations that I was unfamiliar with during these long night shifts.

Comms gremlins

The 2003 war had destroyed many telecom systems from the Saddam era. Hence, international calls were near impossible without satellite or expensive specialised communications equipment. When the first PMCs arrived in the Sandbox in mid- to late 2003, there were no working cellphone networks, and it was a challenge communicating with one's family. I had acquired a hand-held satellite phone for my travels in remote parts of Africa and could use this for making calls in Iraq; the problem was that calls were well over a dollar per minute, and charge cards for this system were not readily available outside of Baghdad.

Consequently, schedules were arranged to allow people to communicate briefly with family members. However, most types of satellite phones only work when you are outside, and they don't function well in low-lying areas, so it was best to get to higher ground for a good signal. Twice while I was on calls, we took incoming mortars and I had to scram for cover.

Companies usually installed satellite-dish systems for internet connectivity, but in the early days they were slow and to transfer even a 1MB data file could take frustratingly long. There was no Facebook, Twitter, WhatsApp, Instagram or other social-media platforms then, and we used either Hotmail or Yahoo's video-call facilities, where you had to plug a webcam into the PC and battle forever to get a grainy picture going.

Some private military security companies made a satellite phone available for their security teams to use, maybe once a week, to make short personal calls. However, many abused the system, leading to costly bills. This invariably meant the privilege was taken away. In 2004 cellular licences were awarded to cellphone companies but it took years to build the cellphone towers and infrastructure to service the population outside of Baghdad, so at remote sites connectivity continued to be a challenge.

The Battle of Fallujah

From April 2004, the security situation in the country deteriorated, and attacks against the CF, Iraqi security forces, PMCs and other civilian contractors escalated. That month, the US Marines also launched an operation that became known as the First Battle of Fallujah, or Operation Vigilant Resolve, following the gruesome execution of the four Blackwater military contractors.

Their stated goal was to root out the hard-core extremists who operated out of the town. However, the operation was stopped a week into the campaign because the Iraqi government accused the US Marines of killing ordinary civilians.

In November the US forces, aided by the CF and Iraqi security forces, decided to attack Fallujah again to break the insurgents' stronghold on the town. It was thought that al-Zarqawi and a number of Baathist insurgent commanders were using Fallujah as a springboard to launch attacks on Baghdad and other areas in the greater Anbar Province. This became known as the Second Battle of Fallujah.

By then I had become accustomed to watching coverage of conflicts on TV, but I was once again dumbstruck by how international news crews were now shadowing the attacking force during the operation. I remember how, weeks before the Fallujah attack, the news crews would report on the training and preparation of the US Marines outside Fallujah. In hindsight, I guess the insurgents knew in any event that they were going to be attacked, but it still seemed odd that a force would publicise their preparation and timing to the enemy on the news.

The battle raged on from the first week of November until the third week of December 2004. The CF managed to break the stranglehold that the insurgents had on the town, but it was a bloody battle, fought in the streets and buildings of Fallujah, with serious casualties on all sides. Around that time, by studying Intel reports and speaking to the US personnel at our base, I started seeing a pattern: the number and intensity of attacks against foreigners increased exponentially after the Battle of Fallujah.

While patrolling the guard posts on the perimeter, I learnt from the local guards about the mood and general feeling of the Iraqi people. About a month after the Battle of Fallujah, some of the guards told me that they had heard rumours that Zarqawi had been wounded during the battle and was hiding in a mosque near Mosul. I passed this information on to a CF liaison officer but, evidently, Zarqawi was either not there or had fled the area, as he would eventually be cornered only in 2006.

In October and November 2004, the Al Kasik base started filling up with more US troops. During this time, one of our military points of contact told me that, stored in a room in the base, there were some parcels that had been sent by the US public to the troops in Iraq for Christmas. The American people would regularly send presents to their troops stationed in combat zones around the world as a token of their appreciation. There were also letters from kids thanking the soldiers for what they were doing.

Our contact said we could help ourselves to some of these gifts. We decided to wait until all the soldiers in the base had had a chance to help themselves first. When I finally went in, I scored a pair of military sleeping pants, some shaving cream and a very large tub of sweets called Twizzlers, which I had never seen before. To this day, they are one of my favourite treats, although they are not sold in South Africa. We were very touched by our Christmas gifts from the kind-hearted folks in America. I ate so many sweets that I got stomach ache.

5

A Black Hawk encounter

The Sandbox offered no respite. Although we had some degree of control over the security at the Al Kasik base, we faced grave danger every time we went outside it. The road between the base and Mosul (where we went for official liaison with the US military) became increasingly risky and many private security teams were ambushed along it. It was therefore decided that Shaw Group personnel would travel by helicopter – partly because we had no armoured cars available to transport people in safety. Fortunately, as we were working on an official US government contract, we got permission from the US military to use their helicopters to transport personnel. From that point on, any of us who were due for rest and recreation leave would fly out by helicopter to the Mosul airfield, where we would catch a military plane to the US military camp in Kuwait City. On one of these trips to Mosul, we noticed that the pilots were pushing the chopper hard. We enjoyed the thrill of flying at low level, as one could get a sense of the speed.

In November 2004, I was asked to go to Mosul to investigate whether the security personnel could obtain US DoD cards from the US military offices there, instead of having to travel to Baghdad for this purpose. I was quite excited when I first got into a Sikorsky UH-60 helicopter, better known as a Black Hawk. Another US military passenger jumped in and we took off.

On the way, there was a scheduled stop at Tal Afar, only 15 kilometres away. When we landed there, the pilots switched off the engines and told us we had to wait, as fighting had broken out between the US forces and insurgents close to the helipad. Some of the door gunners and flight crew were tired and lay down on the concrete landing pad to rest. But my fellow passenger and I hung onto our rifles; I wanted to keep an eye on the dirt walls around the helipad in case an insurgent tried to break through.

As we were waiting, one of the pilots approached me and we started chatting. I asked him to take a photo of me by the Black Hawk (this is the cover image for this book).

'So, what kind of music do you like?' he asked.

'Heavy metal,' I said.

'You a fan of AC/DC, then?'

'Fucking yeah! It's one of my all-time favourite bands.'

The next thing, the pilot produced a small boombox, placed it in the gunner's opening on the helicopter and started playing AC/DC's 'Thunderstruck'. Man alive! I couldn't believe it – here I was in a war zone, the good guys fighting the bad ones around me; I was making friends with the Black Hawk pilots and, to top it all, listening to AC/DC! Life was good.

'Thunderstruck'! Note the boombox in the door gunner's position of the Black Hawk helicopter, October 2004.

After we had landed, we heard that insurgents had fired shots at the helicopter in the vicinity of Tal Afar – a hotbed of extremist activity. Thankfully, the belly of a Black Hawk is reinforced and can withstand a certain degree of small-arms fire. Because of the noise of the rotor blades, we didn't hear a thing and were completely oblivious to what was happening.

But, as we approached Mosul, my fellow passenger and I noticed smoke billowing from the top of the cabin. Now, this is quite a worrying thing to see. We pointed it out to the door gunners and they must have reported it to the pilots on their headsets. When we landed in Mosul, a fire engine pulled up next to the landing zone, and the crew indicated that we had to move away from the chopper – fast. We grabbed our gear and gorilla boxes,[1] and ran as quickly as our tired bodies would allow. Fortunately, it turned out that it was just some wires in the console that had short-circuited.

After a leave rotation, Awie and I had to travel from Dubai to Baghdad and then on to Mosul. On this trip, we caught a Black Hawk ride from Baghdad to Mosul airfield with some American soldiers. It is incredibly noisy inside a helicopter, especially when you're flying with the doors open. Awie slept for most of this long flight. He and I had shared a hooch in Al Kasik, so I had become (slightly) accustomed to his very loud snoring, akin to a lion growling in the distant bush. For some reason, he took his snoring to new heights on this flight. At one point, one of the American soldiers shouted in my ear, 'Is this guy all right?' We could hear his snoring above the noise of the rotors and the roar of the air rushing into the chopper. I gave them a thumbs-up and jabbed Awie in the ribs. For about a minute he snored less loudly. Everyone merely shook their heads.

I managed to set up a system by which our personnel could obtain their DoD cards from Mosul. In the process, I had to stay over in the military-style barracks at the Mosul airfield on a few occasions. I looked forward to the splendid food served in the dining facility there, but a really great treat was being able to visit the US military store (known as a post exchange), and buy things from the local vendors next to the store where anything and everything could be found. There was an Iraqi shop that sold Persian carpets and I took some back home for at least half the price I would have paid in South Africa.

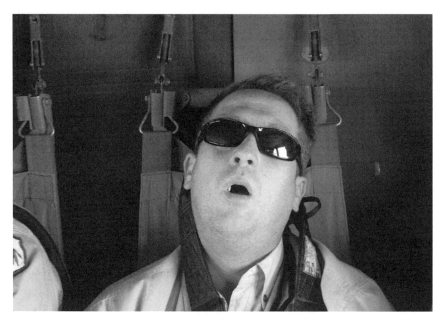

The greatest snorer in the Sandbox – South African Awie Wessels during a flight on a Black Hawk.

During the latter half of 2004, two local men who worked with the Iraqi building subcontractor at Al Kasik were shot and killed in Mosul while on company assignments to purchase supplies. It was the start of a trend that escalated because the insurgents viewed Iraqis who worked for the US military – mainly as interpreters – or for private foreign companies as colluding with the infidels. Like us, they were considered by the extremists as traitors for helping the foreign intruders in their holy land. It therefore became increasingly risky for Iraqis to work for the CF and private contractors. A decade later, Mosul would become the heartland of the ISIS insurgency and a main pillar in the formation of the Islamic State's caliphate (more on this later). Without the help of the Iraqis, the reconstruction efforts in the country could never have taken place. The participation of these nationals was key for various reasons, including their language skills, ability to liaise with local-government entities and assistance with key purchases.

By December I had survived my second four-month rotation in Iraq and made plans to travel to South Africa for the Christmas holidays. I organised a Black Hawk ride to Mosul, where I bumped into an old SF buddy of mine, Johan Grobbelaar. The energetic and outgoing Grobbies had qualified as an SF operator a number of years after me, and we had both served at 1 Recce Regiment at the Bluff in Durban. Grobbies is known for his quick, sharp responses, both mental and physical.

Former Special Forces operator Johan (Grobbies) Grobbelaar in 2004.

I noticed that Grobbies had a bloody field dressing around his lower leg and was limping. I enquired about his injury and he proceeded to tell me the most incredible story of what had happened to him just a day or two before.

Grobbies was working as a private security detail team leader. His team had been ambushed outside Mosul on their way to us at the Al Kasik military base. He had been tasked to escort two clients, expat senior management members of a catering company, to various American military bases in the north of Iraq where they were to do inspections of the US military's dining facilities and have meetings. On the first day, they were due to cover a large distance, including a visit to a forward operating base before ending up at our base.

The night before, Grobbies had put together the details of the mission using intelligence from the US military. This was possible thanks to the well-established ties between PMCs and the US military at the time. The intelligence covered aspects like route status, insurgents' modus operandi, danger areas, safe havens and other useful mission information. Team leaders were required to draw up a detailed and thorough mission execution document, which included maps, comms charts and emergency plans.

Grobbies' team consisted of three other expatriate security contractors – an Italian, an American and a Romanian. In addition, he had 11 Iraqi security guards who acted as shooters and drivers. Grobbies' own convoy consisted of four GMC Suburbans, two of which were armoured to level B6;[2] the other two were non-armoured. These two soft-skin vehicles acted as 'gunships', fulfilling the role of a counter-assault vehicle, with one driving ahead of the convoy and the other soft-skin covering the rear of the convoy. The two clients travelled in the first armoured vehicle, while the second armoured vehicle acted as a backup, in case the first got disabled.

On 14 December at about 15:00, the convoy of four vehicles left Mosul and took an offramp leading to a road that exited the city. From there it was about 60 kilometres as the crow flies to their final destination for the day, the Al Kasik military base. They immediately noticed that the road was particularly quiet. Grobbies, who was in the leading soft-skin vehicle, instructed the rest of the team by radio to keep their eyes open and to be alert.

Seconds later the team drove into an ambush. The attack started with AK-47 fire followed by an explosion from an IED. The team immediately returned fire and drove through the ambush, as per the standard drill. This ambush was a few hundred metres long, but the convoy made it through without any casualties or breakdowns.

But it wasn't over. Shortly after, the team was shot at again with AK-47s and PKM machine guns, and they took RPG fire. There were also more IED explosions. The terrorists had set up a series of successive ambushes.

During the fourth of these, Grobbies' vehicle was hit by machine-gun fire and by an IED blast. The vehicle was immobilised and three of the team members, including Grobbies, were wounded. As rounds penetrated the vehicle, Grobbies and the driver received shrapnel wounds to the head, which bled profusely. The driver slumped back in his seat with his hands in the air, which made Grobbies think that he was seriously wounded.

Grobbies then pushed his left leg over in an attempt to get control of the accelerator and drive the vehicle out of the ambush,[3] when he realised the engine was dead. The vehicle still had some forward motion and he grabbed the steering wheel to steer the vehicle to the side of the road, where it came to a standstill. At his command, they got out of the vehicle quickly because they were basically sitting ducks. As they got out, they spotted a number of corpses lying by the road, some shot in the head and one with a knife embedded in his throat. This gruesome scene made all the Iraqis hide behind the vehicle. (The other vehicles had by now moved out of the initial ambush site to take the clients to safety and left the one vehicle stranded in the kill zone. They had left on Grobbies' instructions and tried to return several times but the enemy fire was too heavy. It was only later that they could return to assist the remaining pinned-down team members.)

At this point, they took PKM fire from a vehicle to their front left, sniper fire from their rear and more small-arms and RPG fire from a position to the left rear of the vehicle.

Grobbies first focused on the threat from the vehicle. After eliminating that, he moved to the right-hand side of their vehicle. There he found the Iraqis, who were so overwhelmed they were just lying on the ground shooting aimlessly into the sky. After ordering them to conserve ammunition and to shoot only at the insurgents, he repositioned two of them and indicated their arcs of fire to them.

While shooting at visible insurgent positions, Grobbies worked his way from the front of the vehicle to the rear. He had to change his magazine but the only decent cover he had was the front of the vehicle. Even though the insurgents would be able to see his silhouette, he went ahead, as he had no other choice. The second time he knelt down for a magazine change, the attackers noticed his silhouette and he got shot in his leg, just under the knee.

He tested his leg to determine if it was still functioning – no bones or arteries had been struck. He moved back to where the Iraqis were lying and spotted a two-metre-high sand wall on the right-hand side of the road. He worried that the insurgents might use this as cover and close in on them.

They had to get away from there. When there was a lull in the fire, Grobbies jumped into the vehicle to retrieve his E & E bag, and while maintaining fire on the insurgents, he and the five Iraqis now left with him made a tactical withdrawal from the kill zone.

After about 200 metres, Grobbies spotted some houses, and there were some trucks parked on a side road. At one of the houses he found two women and a child, and asked them for the keys to the vehicles, so that he could escape the carnage less than a kilometre away. One of the women explained to one of the Iraqis, who was translating, that the vehicles did not have fuel and that they did not have the keys anyway. Grobbies then realised that the situation was dire, as his Iraqi team members were hapless and in a state of zombiness, and some of the terrorists had started moving towards them, while another group was approaching them from a different direction. Things were going south at a rapid rate.

Grobbies spotted a wadi (dry river bed) to their northwest, and to the northeast there was a downward slope from the little hill they found themselves on, which ran towards open fields where there was no cover. There was also no cover to the south or west of their position, and the attackers were now approaching fast. He then saw a mud hut with a straw roof that was used as a sheep pen and checked it out to see if they could use it as a defensive position from where they could ambush the insurgents. Inside, he considered this grim situation, taking a couple of deep breaths to compose himself.

With renewed determination, he exited the sheep pen and led his men to the wadi where they would at least have some cover against sight and fire. But, on their way, they were spotted by their attackers, who started shooting at them from the road and from their rear. As Grobbies returned fired, he saw two of his Iraqis deserting their positions and running away from the incoming fire. About ten insurgents attacked them and Grobbies managed to kill three during this contact.

This created a lull in fire on the attackers' side, which afforded him a chance to get up while shouting at the three remaining Iraqis to follow him. As they were ascending a hill, they took concentrated incoming fire from all the insurgents, and from various directions. During this madness Grobbies detected a different pitch from the attacking rifles and realised they must have been using the Heckler & Koch MP5 submachine gun the team had abandoned during the initial ambush. At this point, one of his Iraqis was killed.

Although they were completely exposed, the three of them had to continue running up the hill, as there was no other cover or escape route. It was steep and they had to slow down at times to catch their breath but they kept moving. When they reached the top of the hill, they were relieved to finally be outside of the attackers' direct sight and line of fire. At this point Grobbies thought they might actually have a chance of escaping death or worse …

When they descended the other side, he spotted the two deserters running towards the Tigris through fields. Grobbies decided to follow them, as he knew there was a US forward operating base some 10 or 20 kilometres further on near the river. But they had hardly gone a few metres than Grobbies spotted another group of terrorists moving into an ambush position for them. They stopped dead in their tracks and ducked out of sight again.

A sense of desperation overcame Grobbies. He said a quick prayer asking God to help him in this doomed country so far away from his own. The only thought now going through his mind was that he wanted see his wife one more time. He explained to the remaining two Iraqis that it would be suicidal to continue north, but they would not listen to reason. They left him, thinking that they could somehow make it out alive.

By now more insurgents were approaching the hill from the other side, and another group was behind him. This is when his SF training kicked in, and he realised that the only way to survive was to move forward, towards the enemy in the direction of the front side of the hill and then to conceal himself as best as he could before ambushing the insurgents as they came into view on their final ascent of the hill. He would lay maximum fire on the enemy, identify a weak point and use this to break out of his encirclement. His E & E bag was too heavy to sprint with if he managed to break out, so he decided to take only his spare magazines and a pullover (it was winter) out of the bag, and jettison the rest.

Once in position on the edge of the hill, Grobbies had a good view of the ploughed field and could see some of his Iraqis who had abandoned him down below. He decided to leave one round chambered in his 9 mm pistol: as a last resort, he decided he would shoot himself rather than let the insurgents capture him and cut his head off for the whole world – and his wife and family – to see.[4] As he waited for the enemy to come pouring over the edge of the hill, he spotted the insurgents going after the two Iraqi team members who had left him behind. When some time had elapsed, he realised that his assailants must have thought that the entire group was with

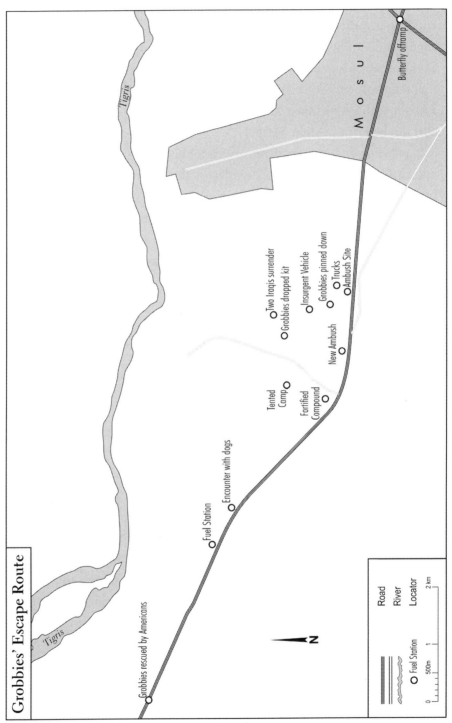

Map 5

the two Iraqis and therefore, presumably, they had not bothered to continue up the hill towards his position.

Gunfire erupted down below in the valley, where the four remaining Iraqis now found themselves. As Grobbies watched, the insurgent fire forced one team member to head towards the river, one guy turned east and two hid down in a dry river bed. After a few minutes, the Iraqis hiding in the river bed raised a white cloth signalling their surrender. A vehicle approached them. There were two insurgents in the rear, one with a PKM and the other with an AK-47. The occupants got out, tied the two Iraqis up and bundled them into the vehicle before driving off.

Another vehicle moved in the direction of the Iraqi who had headed east. The vehicle disappeared behind a hill and some shots followed. Grobbies assumed the insurgents had killed him. The vehicle then reappeared and the insurgents chased after the remaining Iraqi, who was now close to the river. At 18:05 Grobbies saw and heard more shots – this man didn't make it either.

Grobbies remained where he was, as there were no trees or shrubs to provide cover, and waited there for the sun to set. As the light faded, he went back to retrieve his runaway bag when a slight movement caught his eye. It was a vehicle slowly heading towards him. They were back. He immediately went to ground, using his bag as cover and got the driver in his sights. He was about to shoot at the occupants when the vehicle stopped for a few moments before it turned around and moved away again. Not taking any chances, he remained in position and decided to only start moving after last light.

As team leader, Grobbies was responsible for navigational duties and communication with his HQ. However, during the ambush, the satellite phone and GPS had been left behind in the vehicle. He told me he'd felt like an idiot for not attaching his equipment to his battle jacket, as he had been taught during his SF training. He knew every step of the journey they had been scheduled to make – the result of his detailed mission planning – and he knew exactly where he was and which way he had to go to escape. But he had no way of contacting his

HQ or the American military to ask for help (as mentioned, this was before extensive cellphone coverage was available in Iraq).

After assessing the situation in the dark, Grobbies decided it was best to head northwest towards Al Kasik, which was about 50 kilometres from his position, using the main highway as a navigational aid. As he had been taught in his SF days, he would stay parallel to the road but at a tactical and safe distance from it. The priority was to determine how far he had moved away from the road. There was a power line that crossed the road, which he followed as a navigational aid as he started heading towards the road.

As he walked through a field with a slight upward slope, he spotted seven insurgents, all lying evenly spaced, but facing away from him towards the road in an ambush formation. They were blocking his escape route. After keeping them under observation for a while, he leopard-crawled north for about a hundred metres until he reached an irrigation ditch; he got into it and started heading west. Grobbies said to me that at that point he felt like a robot just going through the motions.

He reached another road, heading east–west, where he waited, observing the road and the surroundings. The occasional vehicle passed and although it was pitch black he could make out a fortified compound about 150 metres away on the other side of the road. The building had guard towers at every corner, but there were no lights or any other signs that it might be occupied. Periodically, vehicles swept past his position, most probably insurgents looking for him. Somewhere to his left was the main highway, and without many options left, he chose to follow the road northwest as far as he could. He waited until a bakkie had gone past, after which he got up, crossed the road, making use of anti-tracking methods as best he could, and then followed the road, a short distance in from it, so that he wouldn't be spotted in the headlights of vehicles.

Just as he was about to continue, another vehicle approached. He ran for about 40 metres before going down. He was boxed in – there was a road behind him, the main road to his left, the fortified compound ahead and what seemed to be a wadi (which turned out to be an earth-removal construction site) to his right. He waited until the vehicle had passed. There was still no sign of life in the compound, upon which he decided to approach the compound through what he thought was the wadi. He climbed down a steep embankment and, at the bottom, unexpectedly found himself inside a tented camp.

In the dark he could make out figures sleeping there and had a close call when somebody passed just a few metres from him. Grobbies decided it was too risky to remain there and he left. With only one option remaining, he hunched over and, stealthily, over open ground, approached the walls of the fortified compound and, using the walls as cover, skirted around and then away from the compound until he encountered a ditch about 200 metres away. Feeling relatively safe, he approached the road to plot his position.

In the dark, he now realised that he was on the outskirts of Mosul, and he could identify another building about 150 metres away and, next to it, what seemed to be a communication mast. Sensing an opportunity that he might be able to communicate from there, he moved closer. As he approached, the building came into view more clearly. It turned out to be a double-storey house. Outside, a dog was barking continually and every now and again a man would appear through a door on the upper floor and smoke a cigarette. Grobbies decided to go in.

Making sure his M4 assault rifle was cocked and ready, he burst into the house, going in low and quick, ready to apply his urban-warfare, room-clearing and house-fighting techniques – only to find, inside, a man, his wife and a child, all wide-eyed and staring at him, shaking with fear. In his broken Arabic, he enquired about communications, vehicles and water. The first two were not available, but the woman did bring him some water and a packet of biscuits.

This put him a little more at ease, but he was still very nervous – and rightly so, as Mosul was swarming with insurgents and any Iraqi found helping a foreigner would be executed, mainly by public decapitation. The man then took him to a building at the rear of the house, hiding him there in case other Iraqis might show up. The

Iraqi asked him to stay there and told that he would return later. He wanted to lock the gate but Grobbies refused to let him. Inside he found some more water. Grobbies knew that he should leave, but he was so exhausted by the day's events that he waited for about an hour.

He left, taking up a position nearby where he could monitor the house, to see if the owner left, or if anybody else approached. He then dug a hole to the one side of the enclosure surrounding the communication mast, and proceeded to sanitise his aching leg wound with Johnnie Walker Red Label whisky, which was in his E & E bag and which had been intended as a gift for one of the clients. The wound was deep enough for him to be able to insert the length of his finger into his leg. The whisky worked its magic and the pain subsided. He inserted a piece of a field dressing (bomb bandage) into the wound, and used another bandage to wrap it tightly around the wound. Once finished, he buried the wrappers and material in the hole and covered it.

Realising that this was not a safe position to be in, he moved on, executing a dog-leg manoeuvre – often used to ambush the enemy if you are being tracked – to observe if he was being followed (there was the possibility that the owner of the house would by now have alerted insurgents). After about an hour, he was satisfied that everything seemed all right, upon which he stood up and headed towards the road.

When he reached the road, his original intention had been to hijack a vehicle, and soon he saw headlights approaching. He realised, however, that he would expose himself in the headlights and that the vehicle might well be full of insurgents, so he decided to abandon this plan. As he waited for the vehicle pass, it dawned on him that he would now probably have to walk 50 to 60 kilometres – the distance to the nearest US forward operating base – and this with a bullet hole through his leg. He set off, and after a while he reached a ridge from where he spotted a fuel station. Stopping to observe it for a while, he noticed an Iraqi guard and another local, who seemed to be the supervisor, entering a building. Neither were carrying weapons. Some large trucks were parked there, but he could not tell whether the drivers were sleeping inside them, or whether there were any other people in the trucks. There were also two bakkies parked nearby.

He stealthily approached the building that the supervisor had disappeared into, taking care not to be seen by the guard. After executing a quick house-clearing-style entry, à la Special Forces, he found that the room was empty. But there were internal doors, so he prepared himself for the next room and went in.

Inside were nine Iraqi men and the supervisor he had spotted earlier sitting behind a desk. He ordered them to move to one side of the room so that he could observe them, while simultaneously keeping an eye on the window and door. He asked for the keys to the bakkies, but they were having none of it. It became clear that they were afraid to help a foreigner. The situation was getting hopeless.

At that moment Grobbies heard vehicles outside and one of the Iraqis managed to explain to him that it was the US military. He went outside. There was a convoy of Humvees parked about 100 metres away. As he started walking towards them, the convoy drove away, but then, after a short while, it came to a halt again. Grobbies once again walked towards them but the convoy started moving again and this time they kept on driving away from him. He then decided to turn around and kept on walking north.

Shortly afterwards he saw some bright lights in the distance. After about three and a half kilometres, he saw that it was a prison set back about 150 metres from the road. He thought that it would be guarded by Iraqi officials and that there would possibly be an American contingent present. Grobbies decided to pull his day-glow signal panel (VS-17 panel) from his runaway bag and approached the nearest watch tower. A guard shouted at him to halt when he was about 50 metres away from the tower. He explained that he needed help and medical assistance, upon which the guard told him to sit down while he notified his superiors.

Nothing happened and after a while Grobbies asked the guard if they were coming to help him. The guard answered that they were struggling to open the gates. While he was waiting, he heard the guard shouting at him; he was pointing to the horizon. It was a US military convoy approaching. It was late, 23:55, and the US forces might well have mistaken him for a terrorist in an area rife with insurgent activity. Grobbies was concerned that the US contingent might open fire on him, so he decided to place his weapon and E & E bag down and approach the convoy unarmed and without carrying anything that might have been construed as weaponry or explosives.

When he was about 100 metres away, he held up the day-glow panel and shouted as loudly as he could to the convoy. Grobbies banked on the US military forces making use of their night-vision equipment to spot him but, to his amazement, the convoy just sped past him. When the convoy was about two kilometres away, he saw it stop, turn around and head back towards him. Grobbies was now unsure whether the convoy had seen him the first time they had passed him and if the convoy commander had been aware of him, so he started moving closer to the convoy with his VS-17 panel held up high. When he was about 50 metres from the road, he shouted for help again, but once again the convoy sped past and stopped – this time around 500 metres further down the road and then turned around again.

Grobbies then realised that they must have seen him, and were probably going through this routine to exercise due caution. They approached him slowly and he held up his DoD card. All he could make out were the bright lights of what looked like a Bradley Fighting Vehicle – a tracked armoured personnel carrier – approaching him. The lights blinded him, and he felt the earth vibrate. To his right was another Bradley. Grobbies slowly turned towards the second Bradley and heard a voice saying 'he's good' echoing through all their radios.

Even though he hadn't seen them dismounting, soldiers were already on the ground, approaching him. In an instant, he found himself flanked by soldiers pointing their weapons at him. After they had checked out his DoD badge, he explained to them what had happened. After hearing his story, they told him to get inside one of the Bradleys where they treated his wounds. He was then taken to a military hospital by the Mosul airfield.

During the trip to the hospital, the officer commanding the Bradley praised Grobbies for his bravery and for keeping his cool. He then handed him a Bronze Star Medal,[5] saying, 'You deserve this more than me.'

Over a period of about ten hours, Grobbies had covered a distance of about 13 kilometres on foot through very hostile territory while wounded. The ambush and Grobbies' successful escape from almost certain death at the hands of extremists was subsequently used as a case study by various PMC teams to study the lessons learnt and to be better prepared should they ever find themselves in a similar scenario.

When I bumped into Grobbies at the Mosul airfield, it was the day after his horrific ordeal. He greeted me with a smile. I was terribly glad that he was alive.

On my way back to South Africa, I passed through the US military camp in Kuwait City again. After we had landed at the military airfield, as I was waiting for a bus to take me to the main base complex, I witnessed a touching moment. Soldiers were loading four coffins draped with the American flag into a military cargo aircraft. There were about half a dozen soldiers moving the caskets and another was in charge of loading them into the plane. They were acting very respectfully and saluted each coffin as it disappeared into the belly of the aircraft. That moment was a stark reminder of what war was all about, and the sacrifices soldiers must make to serve their country.

6

Tremulous times

By mid-January 2005, when I got back to Iraq after my leave, there had been some changes in our security team and I was promoted to site security manager for the Shaw Group's project at the Al Kasik base. At this time the base security was outsourced to another American private military security company called EODT Security Services. Between the US forces, the Iraqi Army, EODT and our security team, we beefed up security measures, particularly access control, which now included dog searches and physical inspections. There was an entrance lane for vehicles and a separate entrance for pedestrians, mainly casual workers who entered the base in the morning and left in the late afternoon. All vehicles were thoroughly searched, and water tankers were checked over properly. All workers and visitors entering the base were inspected with a hand-held metal detector and patted down, and all bags or parcels were opened and inspected. With these new measures, it was now much harder for any would-be suicide bomber or insurgent to get into the base.

By March my tactical training sessions with the team were going really well. Everybody shot straighter and reacted much faster during their contact drills than they had six months ago when I had started the training programme. It was now time to step up the training exercises a notch. I introduced several moving and tactical exercises – shooting from vehicles and while dismounting from vehicles and scrambling to cover (we created wooden barricades for this), and shooting while on the move.

One of my favourite exercises was called 'the running man'. Here, the shooter would start at the 200-metre mark, kitted out in flak jacket and with full tactical combat gear, and in the ready position. Upon blowing a whistle, the shooter takes cover in the prone position and fires ten shots at his target. Before getting up, he has to do a speed magazine change and then sprint to the 100-metre mark, where he hits the deck again and fires another ten rounds from the prone position. The mag change drill is repeated before he sprints to the 50-metre mark and fires another ten shots from a kneeling position. He has to do another speed mag change and then sprint to the 25-metre mark where he fires ten shots at his target from the standing position, puts the rifle on safe, slings it behind his back, draws his pistol and moves as quickly as possible to the 10-metre mark to fire ten shots at the target.

This is all done against the clock. To determine the trainee's combat-factor score, I take the score of his 50 shots and divide it by the number of seconds it took to complete the exercise. Each shot is worth five points, so a full score would be 250 points. If, for example, the shooter scored 200 points (an average) and it took him 100 seconds to complete the course, his score will be a factor of +2.0. The shooter with the best factor was given a 95 per cent mark, and the rest of the team would be benchmarked against this. I never gave anybody 100 per cent, as there is no such thing in tactical combat shooting – you can always do it a bit quicker, and hence score better.

This is a good exercise for testing various strengths, and it points out many weaknesses to the shooter. Firstly, your gear needs to be packed tightly in holsters and pouches, and securely attached to your body to ensure you do not lose anything, as happened in ambushes with guys I knew in Iraq. Secondly, you need to be fit, as sprinting, hitting the deck and getting up quickly again with full combat gear and flak jacket is exhausting. Even the shortest of firefights will tire you out good and proper. Thirdly, the exercise forces the shooter's heart rate to increase and causes trembling while aiming. This mimics the adrenaline release stimulated by the distress of real-life attacks, so this exercise also demonstrates your marksmanship skills in difficult, fast and furious combat conditions. Lastly, the guys with injured knees and backs, and other medical conditions, could not keep up, so this exercise was a useful indicator to me of who I could use on the protection team, quick-reaction force or for private security officer duties. The medically unfit guys could be used in operations rooms, as static guards or in other less physically demanding positions. I had been hurt badly myself but I stuck it out, as, in my mind, I had to be combat fit if I was going to lead this outfit.

Of course, the scoring system meant that a trainee might have a negative score. If you shot badly and only landed 100 points on target, and your time was 110 seconds, then your combat average would be 0.90. Awie, for example, battled to break into a positive factor and it floored him every time. He could not live with the idea of a score below zero when I announced the results. Eventually he pleaded with me to simply give him a zero score because the negative factor really played on his mind. He was somewhat appeased after I explained to him that the point about the factor scoring was that it was designed to track your improvement each week, even if it jumped to a less negative result.

One Friday, before starting the running man exercise, Awie came up to me and said I should push him really hard to help him break his dreaded below-zero results. He asked me to whip him with an AK-47 cleaning rod on his backside while running between stations, so he would move faster. We set up for the exercise with me standing like a bully ready with the metal ramrod in my hand.

Here I am on the range at Al Kasik demonstrating the 'running man' exercise.

I blew the whistle and off we went. The whole team was watching this spectacle. As I pummelled him on his backside, puffs of dust flew from his pants, as we had been training hard on the dusty range. As if this was not funny enough, Awie – who is a bit of a clown – jumped in the air like a goat being bitten by a snake, grabbing his bum with one hand and shouting 'hee-haa'. Of course, this made the team crack up, but, lo and behold, by the end of the day Awie's time was better, and he finally moved up into positive-factor territory. However, to this day Awie can still not understand how someone can shoot a sub-zero score on a range.

Awie wasn't the only character around. We were responsible for the protection of a number of engineers, some of whom were great, and rather unique, individuals. At this point we were looking after three older engineers – Ken McCool, Joe Smith and the late George Droby, who all kept us smiling. George used to call me 'Doc' because I was also the team medic.

Like many older people, they would be up at the crack of dawn. Most Iraqis, on the other hand, do not wake up early, and it was difficult to get them to report to work on time. One Iraqi, who used to be a teacher, had especially limited English-language skills. But he had one favourite line whenever he had to speak: 'Congratulations, mister, you have done a very good job.' I suspect he thought these words would smooth over most situations (and it generally worked). One morning, however, Ken got very worked up after this Iraqi had pitched up late. He gave him a really good drubbing in his Southern accent. After Ken had finished hauling him over the coals, the Iraqi, who had probably not understood a word of what had been said to him, simply smiled and said, 'Congratulations, mister, you have done a very good job.'

I could see Ken turning red – he was very close to exploding. I took the Iraqi to one side and called a guard who could speak a bit of English to try to explain that he had to arrive at work earlier. After a while, when I thought I'd got the message through, he simply did it again – 'Congratulations, mister, you have done a very good job.'

From left, engineers George Droby (RIP), Joe Smith and Ken McCool,
with an American PMC in 2005.

By this time even I was running out of patience, so I thought it best
for Ken and I to leave. Inside our car all we could do was look at each
other and shake our heads.

Then there was fellow South African PMC Dana Jacobs, my
assistant site security manager and a veteran of Koevoet, who once
caught a snake on site. It turned out to be a poisonous snake – from
the viper family – and capable of delivering a deadly bite. Dana kept
the snake in a large glass jar in our little security management office
where he and I were stationed. Needless to say, most of the personnel
were horrified by the creature and refused to come near our office.

A couple of days after he had caught the snake, I noticed the glass
jar was empty. There was some commotion in the engineers' office,
which was across the hall from ours. Everybody in the building had
heard about the viper's escape and there was a frantic search going
on for it. Some guys scrambled to get a decent set of boots on, while
others even had their AK-47s out to hunt the snake down. We had to
calm everyone's nerves to prevent a possible shooting in the building.

Eventually Dana found the snake, which was subsequently released

The pet snake of fellow South African PMC Dana Jacobs.

into the desert. To this day, I do not understand how this snake managed to open the jar by itself. When I asked its 'owner' what had transpired, he just gave me a wry smile …

Carnage

During 2005 I was still working as the team medic, as well as site security manager. When I was in the SF I had trained as a combat medic at 7 Medical Battalion, the specialised combat medical unit of the South African Defence Force, which deployed with the SF and other special-operations groups. I qualified as a combat field medic, and later as a combat paramedic. I have always had in interest in medical matters and have been able to help people who were seriously ill or wounded on several occasions.

One such an instance was when one of the Shaw engineers, Paul Ingersol, felt ill, presenting symptoms similar to those of malaria patients. Now, I almost kicked the bucket when I contracted cerebral malaria in 2002 while working in southern Sudan and Kenya. But, in Iraq there is only around a 3 to 5 per cent chance of contracting this dreaded disease, so I was hesitant to put it down to that. Also, the symptoms are similar to those of dengue fever, hepatitis and other viral diseases. So I decided to treat Paul symptomatically, giving him low doses of pain medications, keeping him hydrated and placing him on an old, trusted broad-spectrum antibiotic, doxycycline (doxy), to treat the fever. We then arranged to get him out of the country as soon as possible. When Paul made it to the US, doctors established that he had indeed contracted malaria. They said the dose of doxy had probably saved his life.

On his return, Paul gave me as a gift a Swiss Army knife, which, he explained, had been handed down to him from his father. He had planned to give it to his son. I refused to take it. I told him I was merely doing my duty, but he insisted. So I took the knife to South Africa, where it has been on display in my man cave until today. I still feel bad about keeping it and have since decided to try to track Paul down and return it to him.

On another occasion an engineer fell ill with an intestinal infection and was in bad shape. I placed him on Ciprofloxacin (Cipro) and metronidazole (Flagyl), and ensured he stayed hydrated and rested. He got better and was back at work after some time. He was very grateful and gave me his brown leather computer bag with various handy compartments. Since then, the bag has travelled with me all over Iraq and to many African countries.

Combat medics do their work as a matter of duty, and sometimes in very severe conditions, without an expectation of seeing their patients again, and with no desire to be praised. Sometimes patients survive, sometimes they don't. These gifts were reminders, however, of medical cases that had a happy ending and of good times in my career.

My skills as a paramedic stood me in good stead at Al Kasik too. Despite our increased security measures, a big explosion hit the base early one June morning. When the blast went off, I was in a bakkie at the pedestrian gate trying to determine how many of our Iraqi employees were pitching for work. I was around 80 metres from the explosion and the blast rocked my bakkie pretty hard. I instantly knew it was a suicide bomber. A large plume of dust and smoke was rising and there were blood-curdling screams from the area where the workers were waiting outside the gate to enter the base through the search lanes.

The area was quickly sealed off and, the next moment, the base ambulance approached at high speed. By now, I had announced the explosion on our internal radio system and instructed my security team to secure the engineers in what we referred to as 'hard buildings' and to stay away from the gate. I asked Dana to bring my medical bag to the gate and to help me assess the situation.

There was utter pandemonium. Bodies and body parts were strewn all over the desert. I joined the US corpsmen[1] in assessing and treating the wounded. By this time locals from the nearby village, where most of the day workers came from, had started gathering about a hundred metres away. They were extremely restless and wanted to get to the dead and wounded to see if their relatives were safe.

I was tending to a young Iraqi male who showed no vital signs (i.e. no breathing or pulse), when I heard gunshots ring out from where

Sixteen Iraqi workers died after a suicide bomb attack
at Al Kasik's pedestrian entrance in June 2005.

the villagers were congregating. Everybody scampered for cover, but if I left the patient, he would not survive. Fortunately, it turned out the villagers were not shooting at us, but in the air out of frustration.

During this ordeal, Dana stood his ground next to me and gave me cover while I worked on the seemingly dead Iraqi. This showed his commitment to his team members without regard for his own safety. Soon all the emergency personnel and base security personnel were tending to the wounded and performing triage.

I managed to get the Iraqi breathing with an artificial airway, and got his pulse going with cardiopulmonary resuscitation. I found a vein in his arm and ran up an intravenous bag drip. I kept him breathing and he was taken away by the corpsmen medics in the ambulance to be medevaced to a higher-care facility in Mosul. I later learnt that he survived. It felt good that I, as a combat medic, had succeeded in reviving him from a comatose non-breathing state.

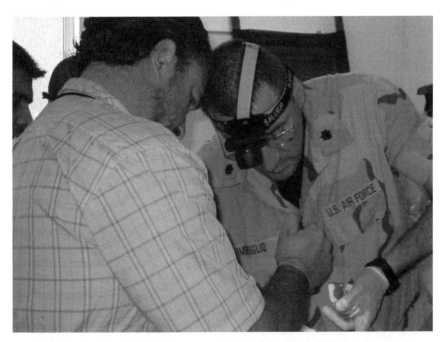

I assist a US military medic in treating one of the wounded after the attack.

By now we had figured out that the explosion was a person-carried IED attack, which is technical military jargon for a suicide bomber.

We found small metal ball bearings scattered around the explosion site and embedded in the flesh of the victims. It became common practice in Iraq for suicide bombers to pack their explosives with pieces of metal to make their bombs more lethal.

Witnesses later reported that the suicide bomber had made his way into the crowd gathering outside the base before he caused an argument and started shouting at people. This drew attention and a crowd had gathered around him. That was precisely his plan – it was then that he blew himself up. That day, 16 Iraqi workers were killed and over 22 wounded. Back at the medical bay inside the base, I assisted some corpsmen medics and tended to more wounded.

As the base CF personnel and medics started collecting the bodies and limbs, they found the suicide bomber's head entangled in the razor wire on the perimeter. It had been blown clean off his body. The Intel guys told us later that he was apparently a Saudi Arabian citizen.

The CF personnel and medics took care to collect and match as many body parts as possible, so that the families could bury most of the remains of their lost ones. I remember a large pile of limbs and flesh that were collected and placed outside the medical bay inside the base. We lost many workers, one of whom was a 14-year-old boy who worked in the base as a cleaner and general worker. Seeing his lifeless body enraged me, as it always would in the years to come, whenever I saw reports and photos of children who had been blown up by fanatical suicide bombers.

This incident was a good reminder that we were dealing with cold-blooded killers, drunk on the warped interpretation of their religion, and in many cases high on drugs given to them by the terrorist ringleaders to enhance their 'courage'. The families of the suicide bombers, and the bombers themselves, are brainwashed by jihadist militants into believing that becoming a martyr in this way will reserve a special place in heaven for them.

After this incident, the security measures were stepped up even more. Observation posts were created so we could scour the desert with binoculars in an effort to detect all movement outside the base.

Our engineers were spending a lot of time working on the waste-water treatment plant, which was outside the base, so we established an observation post there, as the area was exposed and it would not have been difficult for insurgents to sneak up close to the plant and shoot at the engineers.

Manning the observation post at the waste-water treatment plant at Al Kasik in May 2004.

As mentioned, the base often got attacked from further afield with rockets and mortars, so the security team decided to extend their patrols further out from our perimeter. During one such patrol, the team found steel pipes buried at an angle in the ground, facing our base. These firing positions were camouflaged with hessian bags and sand, ready to be used as mortar launch pads at any moment.

A US Strike Force unit was based at Al Kasik at the time and they also patrolled the outer perimeter and desert surrounding the base.[2] Around September or October, two of their members were killed in action in the area. I felt incredibly honoured when the base commander invited me to a memorial service for the fallen soldiers. When the US military has such services, especially for elite units, they are normally exclusively for Americans. It was also very moving when they played Barry Sadler's 'Ballad of the Green Berets' at the end of the service.

Clampdown on the security industry

From April 2003, when the first PMCs arrived in Iraq, until mid-2005, there was very little in the form of local legislation regulating the security industry. Most security firms were foreign-based and worked under the laws of the Coalition Provisional Authority[3] and those that applied in the CF countries. With the increased demand for PMCs from the end of 2004, and the large influx of contractors at the beginning of 2005, however, things started to get out of control. There were too many cowboys in the Sandbox, and not every security operator had the right soldiering and combat skills, or prior experience of working in conflict zones.

Increasingly, reports of 'wildcat' shootings of Iraqi citizens started circulating. The media enjoyed fuelling this craze, and in certain cases where contractors had to legitimately shoot at locals to defend their own lives, or the lives of their clients, the media were quick to pounce on the PMCs and make a meal of it.

Consequently, the Iraqi government decided to reel in the security companies and around July 2005 the Ministry of Interior passed a raft of new laws to regulate the industry. All security company employees, both foreign and local, had to undergo a vetting process, had to be registered with the Ministry of Interior, apply for weapons licences and register all armoured vehicles and other 'controlled' equipment. They also put a moratorium on the use of any squad-type weapons, such as mortars, rocket launchers and hand grenades, as well as items like flares.

They were adamant and aggressive in the application of these rules and regulations. All security companies had to quickly fall in line with the new legal framework. There was a lot of resistance, but, in the end, it was the right decision to regulate the security industry in the Sandbox.

In September 2005 I had to travel to Baghdad to meet with the Shaw head-shed (a military term for commander or senior leaders). During the briefing, I was told that the Shaw Group wanted to send me to Saudi Arabia to get a project started there. I was called to Dubai by the Shaw Group regional security manager, who offered me a job as the security project manager on an oilfield development in eastern Saudi Arabia.

A couple of days later, I flew to Saudi with the Shaw security manager in Baghdad to conduct a site visit and recon of the area with a view to drawing up a security plan for the project. I did not particularly enjoy the assignment, as it was not in my normal line of work, namely, high-threat environments. After the trip I worked out of Dubai for a short while, where I drafted the security plan.

Then, in October 2005, I was approached by the vice president of Iraq operations for US construction and engineering firm Ellis World Alliance Corporation (EWAC). They wanted me to be their country security manager for upcoming reconstruction projects awarded to the group by the US Air Force Center for Environmental Excellence, as well for some contracts for the US Army Corps of Engineers. It looked set to be a challenging position but I wanted to get back to the Sandbox, so I accepted the offer and resigned from the Shaw Group.

The Hamra hammering

I arrived back in Baghdad in November. This time round, my accommodation – and place of work – was a hotel in the Red Zone – the Dreamland. At the hotel I met some EWAC engineers and personnel. I was tasked to set up a security team for EWAC, so they could start working on contracts that had been awarded to the company.

Shortly after my arrival in the Red Zone, the Al Hamra Hotel, which was about a hundred metres from the Dreamland, got hit by two suicide bombs. On 18 November, at 08:15, there was a large explosion to the south of our location. Within a minute, a second, larger blast went off in the same area. The first blast blew out several of the windows, glass panes and doors at the Dreamland. When the second blast went off, everybody at the hotel had already taken cover and the security team had taken up their fighting positions. I went up to the roof for observation purposes and to report developments over the radio.

The Al Hamra was a large hotel on the border between the upmarket Jadriya and Karada districts, about half a kilometre south of the Green Zone. It was frequented by foreign news and TV agencies; *The Washington Post* team were stationed in a building between us and the Al Hamra.

An apartment block next to the Al Hamra Hotel after the blast
in November 2005.

The initial explosion was caused by a suicide bomber who drove a white van into the 12-foot-high concrete T-wall barriers designed to protect the hotel against VeeBids. This was supposed to create a gap for the second suicide bomber, who drove a water tanker, to get through. The plan was for the tanker to get as close as possible to the hotel foyer before detonating and causing maximum casualties but, fortunately, it got stuck in the rubble created by the first blast. The bomb went off by the side of the hotel and 15 people were killed, with around 40 wounded – mostly Iraqi families who were in an apartment building next to the hotel.

In the aftermath of the blast, we went over to take photos and check out the scene. Some of the reinforced-concrete wall sections, which weigh around three tonnes, had been picked up and thrown over a hundred metres through the air, causing them to smash into the apartment block, destroying it. It was a mess. Once again I witnessed the apocalyptic destructive power of high explosives.

We had to replace glass panes, windows and door frames, and remove various pieces of broken furniture from our building after the blast. The experience sharpened our senses and provided a stark reminder of where we were and what the enemy's goals were.

This attack against the Al Hamra happened at a time when the terrorists were focusing their attacks on areas where foreigners and news agencies and reporters congregated. A month before, a triple suicide vehicle attack had been carried out in a similar fashion at the Palestine Hotel in central Baghdad, where employees of Associated Press, Fox News and other organisations lived and worked. In that attack, which killed 17 Iraqis, one vehicle blew a hole in a concrete blast wall, opening the way for a cement truck packed with explosives to penetrate the compound. The truck detonated a few feet inside the compound after US troops had raked the vehicle with gunfire. The driver, like the Al Hamra assailant, got stuck in the debris. A third vehicle bomb went off a short distance away. These were dangerous times for foreign civilians who lived in hotels in and around the Red Zone.

First EWAC assignment

Towards the end of November, my first mission with EWAC was to travel to Mahmudiyah, a town in the Triangle of Death, to conduct a security threat assessment and write a risk-analysis report with a view to developing a full security plan. The area I visited was earmarked for new buildings and infrastructure for an Iraqi Army base, a project of the Iraqi Ministry of Defence.[4] It was close to where we had been ambushed in May 2004 on the way to Musayyib.

EWAC decided to subcontract a new up-and-coming British security company, Blue Hackle,[5] to conduct our private security detail moves and to assist us with the overall security efforts. By then, 'hard-cars', or armoured vehicles, had become more popular and Blue Hackle acquired a couple of low-profile (sedan) armoured vehicles. These early specimens of armoured vehicles were not as well armoured as the later norm of level B6 vehicles, but it was a good start, and at least the windows and doors could withstand small-arms fire, although not armour-piercing rounds.

Blue Hackle supplied us with some expat PMCs and the protection team's move to the Mahmudiyah base was arranged. The area earmarked for the base was next to a small police station. It was not a large area, about a hectare, and not far from the main road (ASR Jackson) and next to a railway line. The site was surrounded by triangular sand defence walls, or berms, with razor wire on top. There were a few derelict buildings inside the camp, which was at that point manned by the Iraqi Army. However, the biggest part of the area was clear and open, which is where the construction was going to take place.

We came across a pile of unexploded ordnance, leftover bombs and munitions that did not detonate, in the middle of the base. This was problematic. I took photos to determine what force protection measures had to be erected to secure the base. Force protection measures include T-walls, Jersey barriers (smaller concrete walls designed to redirect traffic at checkpoints) and Hesco barriers (metal-framed baskets with liners that are filled with sand and stacked on top of one

another); erecting guard towers and metal screens; and installing razor
wire, floodlights and security cameras.

Much planning and preparation were done during the next month,
so we could kick off the project early in 2006. The rigour of the
overall security plan for such projects was crucial, so that the US
government would approve them and release funding – and rightly
so. It was not uncommon for the security portion of the overall
budget to be between 3 and 6 per cent of the total project value. In
other words, if it was a $100 million project, the security costs could
run between $3 million and $6 million over the contract period. This
allowed us to plan properly for the protection measures needed to
keep our clients and workers safe and alive.

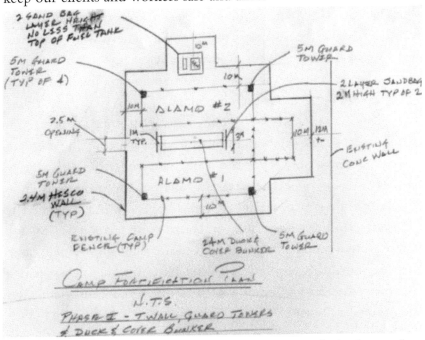

A field sketch by engineer Jack Scott of safety measures to be implemented
at the Alamo camp at Mahmudiyah, in the Triangle of Death.

This budget apportionment would, however, change dramatically
in the new Iraq, post-December 2011, when companies started to
lower the overall budget for security services to around 1 per cent
of the project value – and sometimes even less. This was because,

by then, the CF had suppressed the insurgency to such levels that the terrorists went underground and the militias started leaving the private contractors alone towards the end of 2011 when US forces withdrew from Iraq.

The price of oil was also a major contributing factor to this. When the oil prices started falling below the $100 mark, it squeezed the oil companies' profit margins, and everybody was looking to cut costs. I have figured out over the years that the last budget that companies work out when planning projects is the security budget, and the first budget they cut when they feel the pinch is the security costs.

I developed a comprehensive risk assessment matrix that stood me in good stead for projects to follow. The immediate priority we identified was to get the unexploded ordnance removed and destroyed, and the area had to be swept and cleared for any buried unexploded mines or other devices. Next we had to secure the entrance to the base and to get bunkers in place, as mortars were flying around the area on an almost daily basis.

Iraqi elections

In October a new Iraqi constitution had been accepted and elections planned to choose Iraq's first parliament, a new president and other leaders after the 2003 war and the toppling of Saddam Hussein. The elections were held on 15 December 2005. We expected a lot of security problems but the CF and Iraqi security forces tightened their security measures, and the elections went down with only a few incidents. Nouri al-Maliki's coalition of various Shia groups won the election.

A British survey showed that more than 80 per cent of Iraqis wanted the Americans and the rest of the CF out of the country after the elections. This was not to be, however, as the coalition government was shaky and violence surged soon after the elections as it emerged that minority groups, such as the Sunnis and Kurds, were slowly being excluded from the democratic processes that were supposed to have been ushered in with the new administration.

Maliki, who had been in exile in Iran during the Saddam era, began to isolate non-Shia groups from political representation. He was emboldened by support from Iran. This stance would continue for many years. It only fuelled the Sunnis' and Kurds' anger, and encouraged them to support anti-government fighters and terrorist groups, such as AQI and AI.

A deadly find – a bag containing explosives, a detonator
and two AK-47 magazines.

Under Maliki's watch, the Shia militia groups flourished and grew stronger, infiltrating all domains of government, and using their official status to persecute segments of the population who were not part of their political groupings or culture. Slowly the optimism of the world and of ordinary Iraqis would be suppressed and diminished as the new democratic Iraq showed itself to be nothing other than a reverse dictatorship, discriminating against minority groups and enriching a chosen few.

During the second week of December, one of our security personnel came across a laptop bag in our open store area where machinery and building materials were kept, around the corner from the Dreamland Hotel. Upon careful inspection, we discovered that the bag contained ten sticks of 200-gram high explosives, a single electronic detonator and an AK-47 magazine. The discovery was made less than a month after the Al Hamra suicide blasts. These materials were exactly what suicide bombers utilised to make their explosive vests with. The yard where the bag was found was used by the construction teams and was only 200 metres from our hotel.

I contacted our Intel liaisons in the US military and we increased security, searches and all-round alertness to maximum levels. These were strange days indeed.

7

A country drenched in blood

Many observers in the security industry view 2006 as the pinnacle of the civil war between the Sunnis and Shiites, and of the insurgency against the CF and other foreigners in Iraq. It was certainly an incredibly busy and challenging year, even if it turned out to be the highlight of my career in Iraq as a PMC.

The security plan for the base in Mahmudiyah that I had drafted was accepted by the US Air Force Center for Environmental Excellence, who oversaw construction projects in Iraq, and we were ready to start work. The first order of business was to create an effective entry control point for vehicles and pedestrians. I planned the force protection measures, and the subcontractors started erecting the Hesco barriers, guard towers, Jersey barriers and boom gates. We also installed 'duck and cover' cement bunkers because the camp was frequently mortared.

I recruited an expat security team in late 2004 and early 2005 to assist me with the project management and security services. Blue Hackle would continue to provide mobile security, while EWAC provided the overall security and personnel management. Most of the guys I recruited for the new team were ex-South African SF buddies of mine. Johan (Grobbies) Grobbelaar (he of the ambush ordeal near Mosul) and Johan (Jakes) Jacobs were among the first I hired. They had had a couple of years' experience on the Iraq circuit and I knew them well from our military days. Chris Delport and Greg Garland, two South Africans who'd had experience working for the Olive Group security outfit, also joined us. I was confident we had a capable and experienced security team. Many had been working in Iraq since 2003. I also recruited some of my former team members from the Al Kasik project – Awie Wessels, James Wheeler, Apollo Pallourios and an American, Adam Leckrone.

All these men were well trained as individuals, but I believed it was necessary to train as a unit. I therefore set up training sessions to allow the team to get used to working together and to standardise the protective and emergency drills we were going to deploy to keep our clients safe. At this stage, the insurgency and guerrilla war in the country had been going on for three years, and most of us had been on the receiving end of a number of militant assaults.

As part of our training, I also gave lectures and courses on international terrorism and terrorist organisations in Iraq, as well as the tactics, techniques and procedures militants deployed against the CF and contractors who worked there. I was able to complement these lectures with our own lived experiences, and we discussed case studies to see what we could learn from them. I organised advanced driving and counter-ambush classes, and managed to arrange for us to use the shooting range at Commando Base 11. (EWAC had been awarded the contract to revamp two Iraqi police bases bordering the Green Zone, called Commando Bases 1 and 11).

This time around, the team was sharp from the word go, as the SF guys had all been previously trained in fire and movement, breakout of encirclement, VIP protection drills and combat shooting, and the men who joined us from Al Kasik had all undergone this training with me two years before. We rehearsed our immediate reaction response and emergency drills regularly and everybody knew what to do in case of an attack.

In January I finally managed to obtain an access card for the US embassy in Baghdad. This was no easy feat, as the US embassy was considered one of the most prized targets in the world by al-Qaeda and other terrorist groups in the country. The vetting criteria were therefore unsurprisingly very strict and you had to have a very good reason for claiming to have business to conduct there. The US embassy at the time was housed in Saddam Hussein's former palace in the Green Zone next to the Tigris.

I was impressed when I first saw the inside of the palace. The building had grand, high domes, it was lined with marble, and there

Inside the Republican Palace, which served as the US embassy in Iraq until 2009.

were many colourful murals, courts, decks and a large swimming pool. This is where the Coalition Provisional Authority, CF commanders and NGO leaders were based, and everything seemed to work a bit better and faster around there.

The food served in the dining facility was second to none. It was a treat to go there just to savour the delicious food that they served up. The embassy had a coffee shop and a large reception area where people working on US government contracts congregated. I often bumped into old military and PMC contacts of mine, and it was always good to hear their stories and take on what was happening in the country.

A trip to the embassy usually also ended with a stop at the PX (Post Exchange) shop across the road from the palace where there was a coffee shop and a pizzeria, which also turned out to be a popular meeting point for contractors.

I was often on the road to the Mahmudiyah base and the Commando Base projects. On one of our trips to Mahmudiyah we got mortared as we arrived at the base. At the time, EWAC had just appointed a new country manager, the flamboyant Rich Mendonca. Rich refused to wear a bulletproof vest or protective helmet – even though this

The Post Exchange (PX) shop (in the background) offered some retail therapy.

contravened the security team's recommendations. When the mortars landed, we scrambled to the closest duck-and-cover bunker – where the team leader from Blue Hackle very loudly reminded Rich that this was precisely why protective security gear should be worn. Rich acquiesced for a little while after that but soon lapsed into the bad habit of refusing to wear it.

Private clients, unlike those from governments, the military or large corporations that have their own institutional health-and-safety standards, sometimes don't see the point of wearing protective gear. They pay the security company's fee and cannot be forced to wear a flak jacket and a helmet. I encountered a small number of such clients over the years and always tried to make them see reason. Later, most companies would make it a standard operating procedure for all employees to wear protective gear, but I still came across directors and managers who refused. Anyhow, we all survived this mortar attack, security gear or otherwise, but some rounds landed inside the base, causing material damage. A few days later another barrage of mortars were fired at the base. One landed close to a building that was being constructed and inflicted more damage. Again, fortunately, nobody was killed or injured. I was relieved that my security plan seemed to be working. The positioning of the bunkers and other force protection measures seemed to help, although luck also played a part.

On the morning of 20 March, a large explosion went off near our hotel in Baghdad. The blast was followed by automatic gunfire. We received word from our observation post on the roof that an IED had gone off on a road in front of the hotel, about 100 metres away. I called it in on the radio and the team scrambled to get to their emergency defence posts to protect us in case of an armed attack.

I ran up to the roof and could make out Iraqi police vehicles through the smoke and dust in the street below. Bursts of gunfire were still flying in all directions. It was a roadside IED aimed at a police patrol. It turned out that the terrorist who detonated the bomb had mistimed the police patrol; a civilian bystander was killed and another wounded.

It was a relatively big blast, with the shock waves ramming chunks of metal into the side of the hotel and shattering many windows. Fortunately, none of our personnel were injured by pieces of glass because one of our security measures was to keep the curtains drawn at all times, which also prevented snipers from being able to see into the rooms at night. That explosion, right on our doorstep, was a good reminder why we had to maintain maximum security measures at all time.

Canine explosives detection

EWAC's projects at Mahmudiyah and Commando Bases in Baghdad were both in areas where car bombs and other IEDs were frequently set off. It became imperative therefore to develop the capacity to search and detect explosives before they could be detonated. It is well known in military, police and security circles that the most effective way to detect explosives is to deploy trained sniffer dogs.

The Iraqi construction company that had worked with the Shaw Group at Al Kasik had now partnered with EWAC. Sheik FK, the owner, and I realised that we needed dog teams for explosive detection and it was my responsibility to find trained dogs and experienced handlers. Several companies were providing sniffer dogs that could detect explosives, and I requested quotes. I found a group in Baghdad based at the airport that had a number of dogs available, as they had recently finished working on certain contracts. This was an attractive solution, as it would avoid having to import dogs from overseas, which was a lengthy and expensive process. I had recruited two ex-South African police kennel masters and dog handlers, André Swanepoel and Ferdie Heynemann.

In March we acquired ten sniffer dogs and had a building near our hotel converted into kennels. Good-quality dog food was ordered through the military shop in the Green Zone. When we collected the dogs, everyone was excited, as most guys on the team loved dogs, and we all knew what a valuable contribution they would make to our overall protection effort.

Explosive-detection dogs have to be retrained regularly to ensure they stay operationally efficient and sharp, so our dog handlers, André and Ferdie, put them through refresher training. The challenge now was to find Iraqis to train as handlers, and this was no easy feat given the fact that Iraqis tend not to like dogs. It is not part of the Iraqi culture to take care of dogs in general. When I was at the Al Kasik military base someone came across a female dog and some puppies in our area of operations. We decided to keep two of them. The team took them in, fed them and ensured they had water.

After six months in our care, they were becoming young adult dogs, full of life and energy, and were good guard dogs too, as they barked at strangers who came into our compound, particularly at night. But this started causing problems with some of the Iraqi day workers, as the dogs barked at them when they entered our area. This led to the workers kicking the dogs from time to time. During this period one of the dogs had enough of this treatment and bit a perpetrator after being kicked.

It descended into a mini revolt, and the Iraqis wanted to kill the dogs there and then. After lengthy meetings with the workforce and management, it was decided that the dogs had to be put down. The Iraqi who had been bitten offered to terminate their lives, but the security team refused to hand the dogs over to them. Suddenly this was becoming a serious problem, and the workers halted work around the compound. After more negotiations, it became clear that we were not going to win this round: if a dog bites an Iraqi it has to be put down.

I made a very hard decision that day to do the deed myself, to ensure it was a swift end for the dogs and not run the risk of the animal being stabbed, hacked to pieces or wounded, and dying a slow, painful death. I lured them outside them camp with some food and shot each one in the head at close range to ensure they did not suffer. I have had dogs since I was a young boy and this broke my heart. I promised myself that I would never again show affection towards stray dogs while working in Iraq, but that was easier said than done.

Back to our search for Iraqi dog handlers. We finally found a few candidates and the training began. After a couple of months, the dogs were ready to be deployed to the projects. (These were already fully trained explosive-detection dogs that had had experience in Iraq. It takes almost two years to prepare newly born pups to work as fully trained explosive-detection dogs, and we did not have this kind of time on our hands.)

Training an explosive-detection dog, February 2006.

The first two dogs were sent to the Mahmudiyah Iraqi Army base. Dog teams were also dispatched to the Commando Base projects. These facilities experienced high instances of IED attacks. All vehicles and pedestrians were searched. On a number of occasions, the dogs reacted positively to traces of explosives on the vehicles. Our vehicles were searched in lanes lined with high concrete T-walls or rows of Hesco barriers to minimise the blast damage if a suicide bomber detonated his device while being searched.

When trained sniffer dogs react positively to the scent of explosives, they are trained to immediately sit down at the spot where they detect the smell. The dogs picked up the scent of explosives a few times. When that happened, the area around the vehicle would be cleared immediately. The driver was taken out of the vehicle, isolated and searched. These were hair-raising moments for the handlers and the security team. Once a thorough search was conducted – and if no explosives were found – the driver would be sent back without being permitted to enter the facility and made to clean his vehicle to remove the background trace of explosive vapour.

Sniffer dogs played a major role in helping to detect explosives in vehicles.

These dogs are so well trained that they can even detect the smell of the vapour emitted by explosives. Some of the trucks arriving at our bases had passed through places where roadside bombs had detonated, and the vapour of the explosives used in the attack would cling to the vehicles. The scent of explosives would also somehow cling to mud that would get attached to vehicles in the rainy season.

During this period, one of the dogs cut his paw badly. With the help of my medical kit, and our in-house medic, Manny Louw, we managed to stitch up the dog's paw in the hotel. We administered local anaesthesia and bandaged him up. He was limping but recovered quickly.

How I became a marked man

The Al-Askari mosque in Samarra, north of Baghdad, is a Shiite shrine that was built in AD 944. It houses the tombs of two ninth-century Shiite imams, and is said to stand near a mystical site – a tunnel into which Muhammad al-Mahdi (known as the 12th imam), believed to be the redeemer of Islam, disappeared in AD 878. Most Shiites believe the so-called Hidden Imam, or Mahdi, will one day reappear as a messiah and bring salvation to Shiite believers. The mosque has immense religious significance for Shiites.

On 22 February 2006, AQI, the branch of al-Qaeda led by Zarqawi, infiltrated the mosque, planted explosives and blew it up. They destroyed the golden dome and much of the rest of the shrine, which is one of the holiest sites for Shiite Muslims. It was one of the worst cases of religious vandalism in modern times. Many observers saw this as the final straw that tipped the two main branches of Islam into a full-blown civil war.

After this atrocity, we became aware of a marked increase in the intensity of the conflict, which was already at an alarming level. Some prominent Iraqis called this their Bloody Sunday; for others, it was Iraq's 9/11. It certainly enraged the Shiite Muslim population, and this was exactly what Zarqawi and AQI had intended to achieve. Blood flowed in the streets and deserts of Iraq, and the aggression was not only seen among civilian from the two branches of Islam, but it was also directed against the CF and private contractors present in the country.

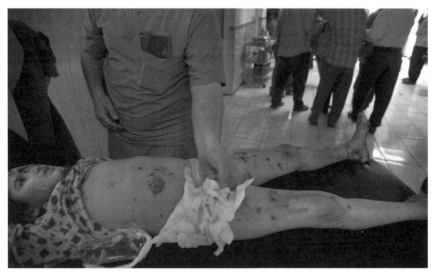

Many civilians, including children, were killed or wounded during the protracted conflict in Iraq, and especially in 2006 and 2007.

After Al-Askari, there were several retaliatory attacks on Sunni mosques and Sunnis visiting them. Zarqawi and his fellow fanatics succeeded in pushing the hatred between Sunnis and Shiites to breaking point. This was a very dark time for Iraq.

As PMCs, we weren't immune to the consequences of this high degree of civil strife and I was personally affected by it. We were drawn into the fray in April 2006 when members of the Iraqi police force happened to raid a house where an EWAC quick-reaction force was staying; the police harassed them.

At the time, I was at one of our project sites, so Grobbies had to take charge of the crisis. His report on the incident tells how the police officers entered the house by force one morning. Two of the police were wounded in the process. They then cuffed 30 of our guards, bundled them into vans, and removed all the weapons and ammunition from the house. Grobbies said that he approached them from our hotel, and the situation soon turned into a Mexican stand-off.

The US military had a contingent who worked with the Iraqi

police. These men were deployed in an observational role only and initially did not want to get involved. But, after shots were fired, Grobbies approached one of the US Humvees, identifying himself with his DoD badge. He explained that the house was used by EWAC's security team to support American engineers working on a US government contract. The Americans then stepped in to help.

The Iraqi police produced court orders for the arrest of six members of our guard force, who, they claimed, were part of some death squad. Although they had no reason or authority to arrest anyone, they insisted on taking the men to their headquarters at the Iraqi Ministry of Interior. The fact that they found RPG-7s and hand grenades in the house was a major problem for us. They also produced two letters, written in Arabic, that they claimed they had found inside the house. These supposedly contained anti-American propaganda, to create the appearance that the guards hated the US and its citizens.

After protracted negotiations, it was agreed that they would take the men to Camp Honor, the notorious detention and torture facility in the Green Zone. There, senior American officers got involved and enquired who the men were working for. Grobbies told them that they worked for EWAC and that responsibility for the security personnel fell under our local partner. They also wanted to know about the owners of the construction partners, the KG Group. Grobbies told them. One of the Iraqi generals accused Sheik FK's family, who are Sunnis, of financing the insurgents. But he assured us that our personnel would be treated properly and looked after.

At this point, the captain in charge of the US contingent at the raid informed Grobbies that they had to approve all operations in our zone and told him that they had not been aware of our presence. Since we had US citizens under our protection, they would block any unauthorised police raids on our location in future.

I discovered later that another Sunni-owned security company in Baghdad had been raided by the police a month before and over 50 of their workers arrested for no apparent reason. It became clear to me that certain Shia militias within the police were operating with impunity and orchestrating killings and abductions of Sunnis all over Baghdad, including those working for private military security companies. One of the main reasons for this was retaliation for the bombing of the Shiite mosque in Samarra, coupled with the marginalisation of Sunnis and Kurds by the Maliki government.

Upon my return, I was briefed about the incident and liaised with our contacts in the Green Zone and at the US Air Force Center for Environmental Excellence about this unfortunate event. Grobbies made contact with the secretary of one of the top US generals in Baghdad. She greatly helped in securing the release of our guards.[1]

I had no doubt that the incident was a set-up, a feud between death squads that operated in the police and certain rich influential families in Baghdad. This happened in the year that saw the largest number of attacks on, and killings of, members of the US military and the CF in Iraq. I strongly protested against this type of action against our employees to as many of my CF contacts as possible. I even went to the 'heart of darkness' – the interior ministry HQ in Baghdad – to object and to warn them to not try such moves again. My outspokenness would eventually make me a target too.

We eventually managed to secure the release of our personnel a month later. After a debriefing, it was clear that they had been beaten and tortured while in custody. We saw the marks on their bodies; some were in a bad state.

These rogue elements among the Iraqi authorities tortured and killed many of their countrymen in the name of so-called justice. They simply created trumped-up charges against certain civilians, some of whom were executed by these militias. I received many intelligence reports in 2006 about the high levels of violence in the country – there was torture, and beheadings and murders, not only by the insurgents and terrorists, but also by the ordinary people of Iraq. I heard reports of family members killing each other for $50, teenage boys tortured to death with electric drills and people beating each other to death with blunt objects.

The violence between Sunnis and Shiites, coupled with the

relentless and gruesome attacks perpetrated by insurgents and terrorist groups, and rogue militias, led to a period of total madness in Iraq. Everybody was affected and all of us had to be exceptionally vigilant, especially those contractors who did not stay in the relative security of the Green Zone, the forward operating bases or the big CF camps and bases

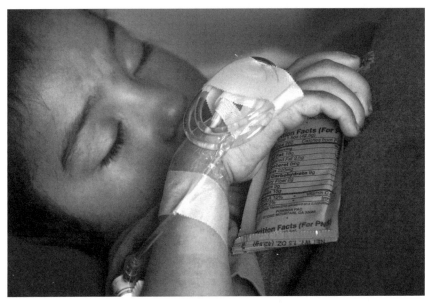

A wounded Iraqi girl clutches an MRE biscuit packet.

After the police raid, our team picked up that we were under surveillance by militia elements within the Ministry of Interior, sometimes by uniformed personnel in official vehicles and sometimes by plain-clothed officials. They were probably angry because, during the raid, two of their men had been wounded, and because we had secured the release of our guards in a short period of time with the help of our friends in the US military.

A few weeks later, some of our senior Iraqi security personnel handed me a piece of paper that had around 25 names written in Arabic. It was a photocopy made by some snitch in the police HQ. They explained that this was a hit list and that a certain militia hit squad was systematically killing off the people on the list. Gravely concerned, they told me that my name and that of Sheik FK, the owner of the Iraqi construction company and partner in EWAC Iraq, were both on the list. I was apparently the only foreigner; the rest were all Iraqis. I knew what was going on: it is a custom in this part of the world to exact revenge for perceived wrongful actions taken against a person or tribe.

These rogue elements wanted to remove me as chief of security for the group either as revenge for preventing them from getting to their initial target(s) or because they thought it might weaken the security team and our defence of the Dreamland, our clients and our local employees. It is possible that the list was leaked to try to scare us away and leave the country, or it could have been a genuine piece of intelligence. Either way, there was concern for my personal safety.

We normally moved around as a team wherever we went, complete with personal protective equipment, sidearms and assault rifles, and drove in B6 armoured SUVs. However, it was decided that I could not go out on my own any more, not even for a walk to the Al Hamra Hotel, the quick-reaction force house or our lay-down yard near our hotel, without a protection team. I found it ironic that the chief protector now needed protection. So I limited my movements around the block, and when I did go for a walk to inspect our posts and see the neighbourhood, I took an expat security team member and a couple of Iraqi guards with me.

We knew these violent elements were unlikely to desist. It was the first time I'd got caught up in the crosshairs of militias and rogue officials in the Sandbox. But it was certainly not the last.

Iraqi employees in the firing line

During the whole of 2006, there were relentless attacks on Iraqi interpreters and other Iraqis who worked for the CF or foreign organisations. Many Iraqis who worked in the International Zone or for foreign companies had to sneak to work in civilian clothes for fear of their lives.

In June I was notified that one of our guards had been murdered after he had left the Mahmudiyah site to buy a packet of cigarettes in the town. He had been shot in the head at close range. His cellphone and company ID card were stolen. The motive for the murder was never established but he was most probably a target because of who he worked for and perhaps because the terrorists might have been after ID cards, so they could gain access to sites where foreign nationals worked and carry out their suicide missions. As a precaution, we shut down the camp while we arranged for a new internal ID system to prevent a possible breach of security.

Earlier in the year, I'd met a young Iraqi woman who worked at a tactical shop[2] near the PX store in the Green Zone. I knew her by her English name, May; she was a pleasant, friendly and vibrant youngster. She spoke good English and had apparently worked as an interpreter for the CF. I used to go to the shop whenever I needed some new gear, but, towards the end of the year, I noticed that May was no longer there. I assumed she had found another job.

Several months later, when I had to go for a meeting with the Multi-National Security Transition Command – Iraq, I noticed a wall of remembrance at the entrance to the building. There was a plaque and a photo of May. I was flabbergasted. She was dead. I asked around but could not get a straight answer about her death. I heard rumours that either terrorists or militia members had killed her because she'd worked for the CF and because of her links to foreigners. By some accounts, it was most likely a gruesome death too, although I could never confirm this. The violence and madness of Iraq had consumed another young, innocent life.

On 29 October 2006, terrorists boarded a bus transporting 17 Iraqis who worked as interpreters for a US private military security company in Basra and executed all of them, dismembering and cutting up their bodies. They strewed the body parts all over the city as a warning.

Various other reports told of Iraqi interpreters and reporters being persecuted and killed. The victims of this lunacy were ordinary civilians, unconnected with the conflict – blue-collar workers, doctors and teachers – as well as Iraqis with links to the CF or foreign entities.

Many reporters lost their lives while covering events, or became targets of the terrorists and militias because of their profession. In 2013, the *Huffington Post* reported that at least 150 journalists and 54 media support workers had died in Iraq between the American invasion in March 2003 and December 2011, when the war was declared over. The number of fatalities was 'higher than any other wartime death toll for the press on record', according to the report.[3]

In 2006 alone, eight reporters were killed – the highest number in a single year during the conflict, followed by another seven in 2007. I saw Intel reports that indicated that reporters were being killed not only while covering events, but were also being hunted down and executed in cold blood in reprisal for their reporting.

Deadly weapon

So-called explosively formed projectiles (or penetrators) (EFPs), which are the deadliest types of IEDs,[4] were introduced into Iraq in 2005 by militia groups from Iran who were opposed to the occupation of Iraq, but 2006 saw a surge in attacks using these types of devices. Between January and December there was a 150 per cent rise in EFP attacks against the CF and private security contractors. Around 30 per cent of US military casualties that year were due to EFP attacks.

It does not matter how well armoured your vehicle is – an EFP will go straight through it, destroying everything in its way. The way these killer bombs were set off was also ingenious. Laser-beam cutters and delayed pressure switches are examples of the level of sophistication built into these devices. Unlike IEDs, which are often home-made, these devices require a far more technical and specialised process. Metal-cutting and pressing machinery is required and the devices have to be assembled by a bomb maker with high levels of technical skill. These skilled technicians of death mostly originated from Iran.

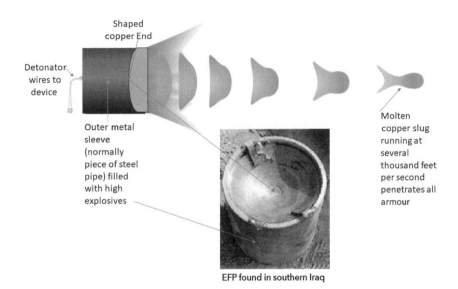

The workings of an explosively formed projectile (EFP).

A REVA armoured vehicle after being hit by an EFP in 2005,
killing a South African PMC.

Although various EFP 'factories' were discovered and destroyed in
southern Iraq by the CF, the militias did not relent; their attacks on
convoys continued. They simply moved on or created new factories

of death. It was the Iranian-backed militias who smuggled, and mainly used, EFPs in Iraq. The insurgents were more inclined to use suicide bombers, car bombs and roadside IEDs.

Because our armoured vehicles could not withstand an EFP blast, we had to select the routes carefully, move at irregular times and switch the vehicles at our disposal around to avoid setting discernible patterns, which attackers could use to 'ping' you.

By mid-2006 Zarqawi and bin Laden had the highest bounty in the world on their heads – set at $25 million. AQI had sown death and destruction, and, over three years, led the country into a civil war. The US military and the CF were desperate to get hold of Zarqawi. In June the US military confirmed that Zarqawi had been killed (on 7 June) in a guided-bomb strike on a house in the village of Hibhib, north of Baghdad. We heard that Delta Force operatives had been poised to hit the AQI safe house to capture or kill Zarqawi, but a sandstorm had prevented them from infiltrating the target by helicopter. It is a pity the sandstorm prevented the Special Operations soldiers from deploying, because if Zarqawi had been captured alive, he might have given them some useful information. In the end, he was killed by the missile strike – probably a fitting send-off for the sheik of slaughterers.

History has taught us that when the head of such a snake is cut off, the creature usually grows back two new heads in no time, and although Zarqawi's death was probably a setback for AQI, it certainly didn't stop them. In fact, it seemed to spur them on, particularly in Anbar, the province that includes the cities of Fallujah and Ramadi.

We heard rumours that the intelligence that led to the attack on Zarqawi's position had been provided by another AQI terrorist. If this is true, I am quite sure the $25 million bounty must have played a part in it. But, in the end, the reward money could apparently not be paid out to a known terrorist. The violence and vicious attacks continued unabated despite the fact the man behind a lot of these acts was now dead.

8

The road to hell

After the Second Battle of Fallujah, which started in November 2004, the CF forced the terrorists out of their stronghold and they set up their HQ in Ramadi, in the Anbar Desert. Thereafter Ramadi became the heart of the Sunni insurgency. The city is close to the Syrian and Jordanian borders, from where many foreign jihadist fighters infiltrated into Iraq to join the struggle.

Between late 2005 and the end of 2006, east Ramadi was probably the most dangerous place in Iraq, if not one of the most dangerous cities in the world. The US military 'froze' the area because it was too dangerous for civilian traffic, commercial convoys and PMCs to move into.

And, as luck would have it, EWAC was awarded a project in east Ramadi in 2006. Before the contract was awarded, I had to travel to the area to conduct the reconnaissance and compile a security plan that could pave the way for the first commercial construction contract in the area since the 2003 war. Getting to east Ramadi was easier said than done. Convoys and PMCs could still travel the perilous route from Abu Ghraib in western Baghdad to Fallujah, and then on to western Ramadi. But the direct route from Habaniyah into east Ramadi – known as ASR (alternative supply route) Michigan – was deemed too dangerous and was out of bounds to PMCs. The route had aptly been given the nickname the Hell Run.

The project EWAC tendered for was to build a new Iraqi Army camp in east Ramadi, next to the US base, Camp Corregidor. This posed quite a problem because it was not possible to travel to the site by road, and during most of 2006 it was too dangerous for regular helicopters – other than gunships and medevacs – to fly into east Ramadi. In June alone there were 293 serious attacks in the area, which led to many casualties on the CF side. We were going to struggle to get our convoys with construction materials and supplies to the site area. I realised the importance of close cooperation with the US forces and the Iraqi Army that operated in the area. We needed their assistance.

From speaking to my CF contacts in the Green Zone, I heard there were US Marine and other military 'midnight convoys' running from the Al Taqaddum Air Base, west of Baghdad, to east Ramadi along Route Michigan. My next step was to get to Al Taqaddum (with a protection team) to go and investigate this option, and to possibly hook up with the US Marines and other military units there.

This was also not straightforward. The short route to the air base was also out of bounds, so we had to take a much longer and more dangerous route through unpopulated desert territory – ideal terrain for roadside ambushes. What should have been an hour's trip from Abu Ghraib turned out to be a four-hour circuitous route through the restive Anbar Province, via west Ramadi and the bottom of Lake Habbaniyah, to the air base.

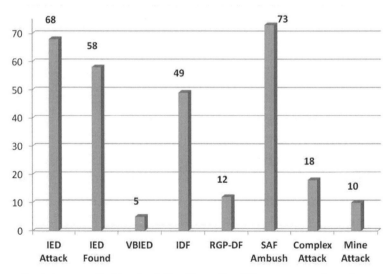

Statistics compiled by the US military for different types of attacks near Camp Tiger in east Ramadi in June 2006.

When we finally got there, I made my way around the massive Al Taqaddum Air Base to find the office in charge of arranging the midnight convoys to east Ramadi. The members of this unit were helpful, and I was scheduled to travel there on the next convoy, which would depart the following night. I arranged overnight accommodation (or 'billeting', to use the military terminology) and got settled into a hooch where a couple of other soldiers in transit were also staying.

Hell Run

Around 20:00 the following evening, I reported to the muster point from where the midnight convoy would depart for Camp Ranger, another US base in east Ramadi. Camps Ranger and Corregidor were only 1.5 kilometres apart. Ranger was smaller and manned by US Army Reserve members. Corregidor was the HQ for other camps in the area and was manned by full-time combat units.

I was placed on a manifest and briefed about the journey. I had my own flak jacket, but had to organise a Kevlar helmet, as this was a standard operating procedure and a requirement when travelling with military convoys. I had my E & E bag, and my leather computer case with me (the one that had been given to me as a gift by the engineer whom I treated). When the convoy lined up in the dark, my laptop bag was too close to the vehicles and a Humvee clipped it. Luckily, my work laptop was a Panasonic Toughbook and survived the accident. My trusted old leather case now had a wheel imprint on it but I restored it later when I got back to Baghdad.

As I explained earlier, the E & E bag contains all your essential survival gear in case of an emergency, should you have to leave an operational area in a hurry. The bag should also contain navigational aids, and I ensured that I always carried a handful of chemical-light sticks (Caylum) to be able to mark a helicopter landing zone at night (a green one and a red one, to indicate the port and starboard sides). Other useful equipment is a multi-tool knife, such as a Leatherman Wave, and a knife with a larger blade than a pocket knife, and, of course, spare ammunition.

I preferred desert 'spec ops' boots to the lightweight sneaker-type shoes that many contractors wore (because they are lighter and cooler) because boots allowed me to carry a boot knife and a small hidden cellphone, and because they better supported my heels, which I'd injured severely in the army. Most guys carried their larger knifes in their E & E bags, along with a small pair of binoculars, a torch with backup batteries, some emergency food (e.g. dates or nuts), leather or neoprene gloves, personal medication, a backup radio and satellite-phone batteries, parachute cord and duct tape.

It also helped to have a day-glow panel (VS-17) to warn CF attack helicopters or fighter planes of your presence and a small US flag to hold up (so the CF didn't mistake you for the enemy) and any other equipment that might help you when you are on the run, or when you have to survive for a short period of time until help arrives.

Some guys didn't like to carry bare essentials, but I always kept a few things on me – just in case. I believe a professional PMC should be prepared 24/7 and that is why I always had my passport, access cards and some cash, usually $500 to $1 000, kept in a watertight wrapping. And I always carried a firelighter, pocketknife, cellphones – and, on missions, a satellite phone – a tourniquet, a wound dressing and a rugged watch with a compass in the leg pockets of my cargo pants, on my waist belt or in my shirt pockets.

I asked the guys in my teams to keep their tourniquets and wound dressings in the left pocket of their cargo pants, so the rest of the team would know where to find these items if you got wounded and your buddy had to use your own medical kit to tend to you. My watch was a Casio G-Shock Protrek with a digital compass, barometer, altimeter and temperature sensor, so I could use it for various applications.

When moving around in high-risk environments, a PMC will wear body armour, also known as personal protective equipment. This typically consists of a bulletproof vest with metal plates in the front and back areas covering the vital organs, as well as a Kevlar helmet. A tactical vest or flak jacket fits over the bulletproof vest, which usually has a pouch for a radio, spare assault-rifle magazines, a pistol with spare mags, a large-bladed knife, a satellite phone, small GPS/compass, field dressings and a small torch (normally one that can fit

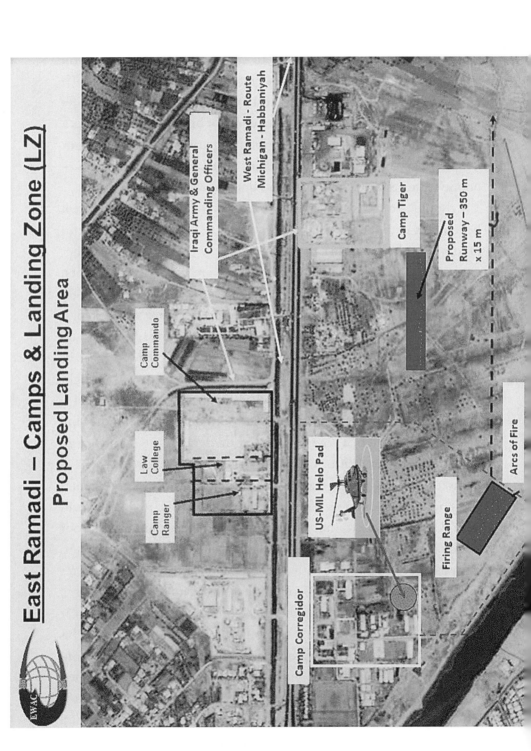

Map showing locations of US bases and Camp Tiger in east Ramadi.

onto your pistol and rifle). Other tactical equipment that a PMC might carry includes a helio mirror (for signalling helicopters and planes), blood-clotting powder (in case you get wounded) and a multi-tool, such as a Leatherman. Many of us rigged our tactical vests with water bladders and hydration pipes to provide ready access to water.

It is essential that the equipment is packed in a way that all these items are held securely to prevent them flying around in situations such as an ambush or shoot-out, where you might have to get out of a vehicle in a hurry and engage in fire and movement.

Our departure was the typical scenario I remembered only too well from my days in the South African Defence Force – hurry up and then wait. I could sense the tension and apprehension mounting in the group. I was wide awake and shifting into high alert. After all, I was about to travel on the most dangerous road in the world, the Hell Run.

Our convoy eventually headed off just after midnight. I guess the timings of the convoys' departures were moved around to break the routine.

The US military deployed explosive ordnance disposal teams to sweep the road in front of convoys. Special armoured mine-sweeping vehicles, which some contractors called daggers, were used to detect and set off landmines and roadside IEDs. The vehicles were designed to withstand quite a blast, and the wheels were set far in front of and behind the main cabin, so that the explosive blast was away from the driver, which is different from a normal vehicle or a Humvee, where the wheels tend to be below the driver. Some of the sweeper vehicles had extension arms, akin to an earth-moving machine's mechanical arm, to deal with bombs and mines.

The convoy moved out of the Al Taqaddum base towards Habaniyah and after a short while we turned left for east Ramadi and our final destination, Camp Ranger. One of my favourite AC/DC songs, 'Highway to Hell', popped into my mind as we pulled onto Route Michigan and headed towards our destination.

It was slow going, as the road was in a terrible state after years of disrepair, and damage caused by landmines and roadside bombs. The vehicles in the convoy used no lights, as this would give the insurgents an aiming point. The military guys were using night-vision goggles, and many of them had a helmet-mounted night-vision device, for which you normally use your non-aiming eye, as they sometimes cause temporary night blindness as a result of the green electronic hue shining on your pupil. So a shooter will try to keep his master eye adapted to the dark, so as to be able to aim a rifle properly.

Fortunately, my eyes are one part of my body that has not been broken, ripped, torn or injured yet, and I have good natural night vision. I could see the outlines of dilapidated buildings, vehicle wrecks and rubble next to the road. We passed US military tanks and Stryker vehicles[1] next to the road at regular intervals, and I realised that soldiers were manning these static patrol posts, whose presence on this insanely dangerous road was to try to safeguard the convoys. It was only about 30 kilometres from Habaniyah to Camp Ranger, but the going was slow and this night the journey took about an hour.

At one stage I heard gunshots and small explosions, and saw tracer rounds pass over the front of the convoy. I was later informed that a roadside IED had gone off but had missed the target, and that the insurgents had fired a salvo of rounds towards the convoy before disappearing into the night. Thank goodness that nobody got injured on this trip – this was indeed a perilous route. I take my hat off to the soldiers who braved this type of danger week in and week out, not only in east Ramadi, but also in other parts of Anbar Province, and indeed all over the country. The risk of driving into an ambush or being struck by a roadside bomb was always present, but the show had to go on and the convoys had to face these dangers throughout their tours in Iraq.

We arrived at Camp Ranger at around 02:00 and I was shown to a bunker room where there were several beds with a number of soldiers sleeping in them. I took out my poncho blanket and a small cammo pillow I travelled with, and rested a while. The next morning I went to the operations room, where I met some US officers and senior non-commissioned officers (NCOs). They listened to my briefing on EWAC's planned project, which was to start across the road from their camp and I produced the necessary official documents.

They were very supportive. They would assist by providing accommodation for some of our personnel until we had erected our own small camp from which to work. They directed me to the operations officer of the 506th Regiment of the 101st Airborne Division (the unit made famous by the TV series *Band of Brothers*), Lieutenant Colonel Matt,[2] at Camp Corregidor. This is where the combat patrols and operations in the area were conducted from.

I caught a ride with some soldiers to Camp Corregidor to have a bite to eat in the dining facility. Once again, I was amazed by how well the US military guys got fed, even close to insurgent combat lines, and with such dangerous roads to have to transport the supplies. Going to the dining facilities in the US camps was the highlight of many PMCs' daily life because you not only got great food, but it was also a place to meet other security personnel, CF members and soldiers.

Lieutenant Colonel Matt was a great guy and I could see that he was a straight thinker who spoke sense, and that he knew what was going on in his area of responsibility. He helpfully provided me with contacts in east Ramadi, west Ramadi and the Al Taqaddum Air Base. I caught a ride back to Camp Ranger, where I would stay overnight. I contacted my security team to plan a private security detail to come and fetch me from Al Taqaddum a couple of days later, when I would compile a report on my progress.

The command element at Camp Ranger helped me to get an appointment the next day with the Iraqi general in charge of the area, General Abdullah. Through an interpreter, I explained to him our mission to construct a new camp for the Iraqi Army. He also offered to help me where he could. He was a gentleman, and we would subsequently have long discussions about politics, Iraq in general and world affairs.

I then made my way to the other side of the road, where there was

General Abdullah (third from left) with our pilot, Cody Purdom,
and Iraqi officers and engineers, December 2006.

a large open field and an old unused warehouse. I took photos, videos
and measurements of the site, and made notes to help me compile a
security plan, which was fundamental to getting the funding released
for the project and to launch it.

My initial mission was complete. I'd made it alive into east Ramadi
and established good contacts with the US military and the Iraqi
Army. It was time to get on a midnight convoy back to Al Taqaddum,
and thence make my way to Baghdad to report back to the EWAC
engineering team and their local construction partner.

I started working on my risk-assessment matrix and security plan
for the east Ramadi project. The greatest challenge would be getting
the truck convoys into east Ramadi, as Route Michigan was the
only road that led to the site. Fortunately, the Iraqi Army had started
running their own military convoys into the area with equipment
given to them by the US military forces. This looked like it might be
a solution for us, as they would run daytime convoys, which suited
our construction team and subcontractors. But it provided me with
two headaches. The first was the security aspect: the Iraqi Army was
going to move in broad daylight along the Hell Run, and they were

not known to be as organised and as efficient in countering the
enemy as the US military were. Secondly, to liaise with the Iraqi
Army, especially where local contractors were involved, was going to
be problematic because of corruption and the distrust locals showed
towards one another.

An alternative solution, raised by our local partner, Sheik FK, was
to get our engineers and security personnel, and weapons, communication equipment and food to the site in short takeoff and
landing aircraft. During the conflict, the use of private planes in
Iraq was not permitted, as the US Air Force and CF controlled the
airspace over the country and it was only for military use, or by
private companies contracted to the Coalition Provisional Authority,
CF and diplomatic missions in Iraq. Back then, Iraq was divided into
combat zones, or 'battle spaces',[3] which were controlled mainly by
the US military and the CF.

Many military operations took place in Anbar Province at the time, so
there were lots of military aircraft (e.g. fighter jets, helicopter gunships,
medevac helicopters and drones) flying around. Careful coordination
and planning were needed to navigate all of these combat zones
without getting shot down by somebody mistaking you for an aerial
suicide bomber – hence the CF did not allow small private planes to
fly around the Sandbox back then. It was clear we would have to get
permission first from the US military and other authorities.

However, if we could get round these challenges and red tape, and
persuade the commanders of the various battle spaces to stop their
ground and aerial fire to allow our plane to fly over their areas of
operation, we figured that using planes would be an efficient way to
deliver our people safely to the site.

Meanwhile, I had to visit our other sites. The project at the
Mahmudiyah Iraqi Army base picked up pace and the construction
efforts went well. There were lots of suicide bombings in the area
and the mortars kept coming at regular intervals, but the team did
a good job keeping everybody safe. The Commando Base projects
in Baghdad were also in full swing. They too remained high-threat

targets owing to their vicinity to the Green Zone, and to the fact that there were numerous attacks on police stations and government facilities around the city at the time.

Getting permission to fly into east Ramadi

At the end of June, I decided to bring Chris Delport, who was working on an EWAC road construction project from the south of the country to Kuwait, back to Baghdad to work with me on the east Ramadi project. I had him earmarked to become the site security manager for the project. He was excited about the prospect because it had been a lonely and uneventful stint for him working on the construction project on the desert plains.[4]

Meanwhile, our local partner, Sheik FK, had acquired two light aircraft – a Pilatus PC-12 and a Pilatus PC-6 Porter. We managed, with great difficulty – both bureaucratic and physical – to land the PC-12 in Basra on a visit to the road construction project. We wracked our brains about what we needed to do to be able to fly personnel to the east Ramadi site. I started making enquiries and was sent all over the country. In the end, I made some good contacts in the CF and was directed to the office in Fallujah that controlled the air space over Anbar, who eventually granted us permission to fly from Baghdad Airport.

We employed a pilot by the name of Cody Purdom, who turned out to be an interesting character. Cody had been a US Marine combat pilot towards the end of the Vietnam War. The story goes that he was shot down over Vietnam and ended up as a prisoner of war. After his plane was downed, the Viet Cong captured him, made him kneel down and shot him in the back of head. Extraordinarily, though, he was not killed and somehow survived. He had a massive scar on his head and a metal plate in his skull as testimony to his traumatic ordeal.

In July I also recruited an old friend and ex-SF buddy, Dries Coetzee, to join us. He had a passion for air operations, was qualifying for his private pilot's licence and was looking to get involved in the Sandbox. The plan was to deploy Dries as the co-pilot in the PC-6.

In November Dries and I travelled to Camp Fallujah to meet with the lieutenant colonel in charge of air operations in Anbar to see if we could get the permission to land the PC-6 on site. He explained the finer intricacies around stopping all ground artillery and air operations in their battle spaces just to allow a private plane to pass through without being shot down – much liaison would be required with all the units on the ground and in the air.

They advised us to consider flying night missions only, as we were almost guaranteed to take small-arms and RPG-7 fire if we flew during the day, particularly before landing and take-off in east Ramadi, where there was a graveyard on our final approach that insurgents used as an area to attack the CF. (The terrorists subsequently did shoot at the PC-6 from the graveyard a few times with PKM machine guns, and an RPG rocket exploded close to the plane once.) We were asked to ensure that our aircraft had the correct UHF/VHF radios with the correct aviation frequencies programmed, and that our pilots could speak fluent English. The G-3 cell would provide the best and safest aerial routes to us, and we were told that our pilots must strictly adhere to them.

It was suggested that we should consider flying southwest from Baghdad Airport towards the Al Taqaddum Air Base and then west over Lake Habbaniyah until we were close to east Ramadi, upon which we would turn north to the landing strip we intended to construct adjacent to the site. This made sense, as the recommended route would take us mainly over an expanse of water, thereby avoiding several military units, and the insurgents were not operating much on water at the time.

The key was to ensure that all the components at the Al Taqaddum Air Base knew about our approach and route past the base. Specific American military flight plans were submitted 24 hours ahead of every planned flight. These would then be sent to Iraq Civil Aviation, who would send them on to the US Air Force to authorise and allocate a unique flight number for each flight.

Eventually I managed to get all the necessary authorisations and informed the relevant entities. We were now set for our first run into east Ramadi in the PC-6.

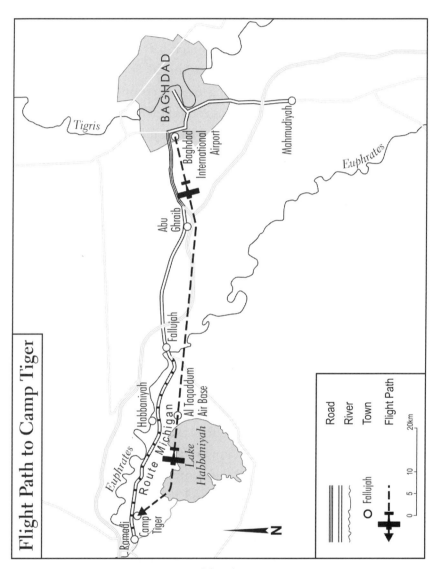

Flight Path to Camp Tiger

BAGHDAD

Tigris

Euphrates

Mahmudiyah

Baghdad
International
Airport

Abu
Ghraib

Fallujah

Habbaniyah

Al Taqaddum
Air Base

Route Michigan

Lake
Habbaniyah

Camp
Tiger

Ramadi

Euphrates

N

Road
River
Town
Flight Path

Fallujah

0   5   10   20km

Map 6

In the meantime, Chris and I started arranging the operational parameters, or, in layman's terms, the mission guidelines and security plans, for the east Ramadi project, which we decided to call Camp Tiger. A week after Chris's arrival at the Dreamland Hotel, our preliminary preparations were done and I applied for a slot for two passengers on the Black Hawk flying to Al Taqaddum, and from there on to Camp Corregidor. The plan was to introduce Chris to the executive officers at camps Corregidor and Ranger. Chris would then return later to Ramadi on his own to start our cooperation efforts with the US military and the Iraqi Army.

During our helicopter flight to Al Taqaddum we were placed in a holding pattern (in safe airspace) for about 20 minutes. This was because an engagement had broken out between US forces and insurgents. The counter-attack from the US included air strikes, so we had to remain in the allocated airspace until cleared to go. From the helicopter we could see rockets and tracers flying in all directions. There was ground-to-ground, ground-to-air and air-to-ground fire. We had an unusual but spectacular view of the unfolding action. Finally a Hornet air strike brought an end to the attack and we could proceed.

The pilots flew 'dark' (i.e. with all lights off and using night-vision goggles) into Camp Corregidor. Even upon landing everything remained pitch black, but we managed to find the quarters of the executive officer, who called Camp Ranger to come and collect us. Introductions were done and we explained our mission. The US military officers pledged their support from both Camp Corregidor and Camp Ranger.

We returned to Baghdad on the same routine flight two days later. Chris then went to east Ramadi to set up communications with our Baghdad office. He also began work on the logistics and force protection measures for our temporary camp and the runway. Chris liaised with Lieutenant Colonel Matt and the other officers and NCOs at camps Corregidor and Ranger, who helped us get the temporary camp built and the project under way. The greatest challenge that we still didn't have an answer to was how we would get our construction convoys, transporting hooches, heavy equipment and personnel, safely into east Ramadi.

After much liaising and coordination, I managed to persuade the Iraqi Army and US forces in charge of the route to allow us to attach a 22-truck convoy to an Iraqi Army military convoy that was going to deploy to the area. At the time, the Iraqi Army could not execute night-time convoys without vehicle lights, and neither could we. Therefore, this shipment – along one of the most dangerous routes in the world – was going to be a so-called white-light convoy, meaning everybody would be driving with their lights on, and would stand out like pimples on a teenager's skin.

The Iraqi Army was also less organised than the US military, and slower, and made lots of noise. Their convoys had been hit hard by the insurgents on the roads around Baghdad, our departure point, and in Anbar Province. I was therefore extremely anxious. Nevertheless, this was an opportunity to move our equipment and supplies.

On 22 August, the security team accompanied me to the Rustimyah Iraqi Army military base south of Baghdad. The truck drivers had been instructed to meet us at the entrance to the base at 18:00, as the convoy was due to depart at 20:30. However, when I got to the base it was evident there was a disconnect between all parties. Firstly, the shift on duty at the gate hadn't been informed that we had permission to join the Iraqi convoy. Then, most of the truck drivers arrived late at the rendezvous point, blaming the Baghdad traffic, as always.

Eventually I managed to persuade the guards at the gate to let me enter the base to go and talk to their command element. I was sent from one office to the next without finding a soul who knew about the convoy arrangements. Eventually, I found an officer who was willing to help, and he made a call to the Iraqi Army division in east Ramadi, where General Abdullah, with whom we had arranged for the convoy, was based. They confirmed that they knew about the arrangements, and we were cleared to tag along.

The initial arrangements had been for our trucks to travel in the middle of the Iraqi Army convoy, as our drivers had no private security escorts with them and neither were they armed (they were civilian truck drivers, not security personnel). However, when the army convoy lined up, they did not want our trucks to be part of their convoy and instructed them to follow at the back.

This almost caused a walkout by the drivers, as they knew how dangerous the route was to east Ramadi via Habaniyah. They were not prepared to chance it without military protection. I tried to persuade them to get on with it, and got our Iraqi managers back at the Dreamland Hotel to call them. I am not sure what was said by phone but they eventually agreed to drive behind the Iraqi Army convoy.

I arranged with one of the army officers to travel in one of their Humvees towards the rear of the convoy, so that I could check whether our trucks were following and that they were safe. Around 22:30 we finally departed, but just after we had cleared the Abu Ghraib area, I got a phone call from one of our Iraqi managers to the effect that one of the trucks right at the end of the convoy had been demobilised by small-arms fire and the driver had fled the scene. The driver of the truck, which was hauling a front-end loader, had been delayed but had promised to catch up. The convoy had to continue and the truck was later recovered – but the front-end loader was missing.

I had to remain with the convoy and carry on to east Ramadi to try to clear up with General Abdullah the misunderstandings about joining the army convoy. Chris had managed to obtain permission to slot our Iraqi Army convoy into a US military convoy, which was due to move past Camp Ranger that night. He had gone on ahead to Al Taqaddum and was waiting when I arrived there.

The stretch of road between Al Taqaddum and Camp Ranger was only 47 kilometres, but it had 17 checkpoints, about half of which were manned by the Iraqi security forces. Good communications and liaison with the US forces were essential, otherwise the chances of arriving at Camp Ranger with a civilian convoy were zero.

The arrangement Chris made was that we would lead the civilian trucks behind the US military convoy in their Humvees, with Chris and I taking up gunner positions on the lead Humvee. At 13:45 the following day, the US military convoy departed from Al Taqaddum. It was a rare sight to have two South African gunners armed with AKs on a Humvee travelling with an American convoy. Our morale was high and we even joked a bit, although that was only a way of diverting our attention from the huge dangers we faced on the second stretch of the drive and to convince ourselves that we would be okay.

The journey from Al Taqaddum took just over two hours. The US drivers had night-vision goggles, but the Iraqi drivers did not, which caused delays, as they were driving blind. I was just very thankful when we arrived in one piece.

The next day, I met with General Abdullah and discussed our situation at length. He assured me that he would do all in his power to help us smooth these problems over, so that the temporary camp could be built and the construction could proceed. I also drafted a letter to various contacts asking for their help because we needed the Iraqi Army to assist us in a more effective manner.

Danger! Convoy protection

The unsung heroes of private security work done in Iraq must surely be the PMCs who rode shotgun on convoys. This was a major part of their duties, and many South African PMCs did this kind of work. After the 2003 war, the US military protected their own convoys, but after the insurgency and guerrilla-style terrorist attacks escalated from mid-2004, the soldiers who had formerly protected convoys were redeployed to fight the insurgents. The US Army then investigated the viability of using private military security companies to escort their military convoys. This form of deployment increased dramatically in 2006 and 2007.

From 2005 to 2008, one of the most dangerous jobs in Iraq was to escort trucks on convoys coming from Kuwait, Turkey and Jordan. During the first quarter of 2007, one of the largest private military security companies involved in convoy protection reported over 300 attacks against their convoys. By then, there were an estimated 25 000 to 40 000 PMCs working in Iraq. Armed PMCs would eventually escort all convoys carrying supplies and reconstruction materials for the CF. According to *The Washington Post*, the US government spent about $450 million in 2007 on protecting their convoys.[5]

Consequently, attacks against PMCs on convoys escalated. Many were killed or seriously injured because the terrorists did not distinguish between military and private security forces. Many of the PMCs who were killed and injured were Iraqis and TCNs because a typical convoy security escort team would consist of a Western expat team leader, with four to six Iraqis and TCNs as gunners.[6]

The vehicles used for convoy escort security were usually armoured gun trucks with a twin cabin that could take four to six people, including the driver, and a gunner, who would normally be upright operating a belt-fed machine gun. Many of these gun trucks had protective plates welded onto sections of the vehicles, and some had wire-mesh screens outside the windows designed to detonate RPG-7 rockets before they could make contact with the armoured windows. These vehicles resembled something out of a *Mad Max* movie, but they were needed to afford the best possible protection to the convoy teams.

Tracking systems were used, so that vehicles could be tracked via satellite feed on large-screen TVs. With these systems, an emergency button was also built into the vehicle for the team to operate should they get attacked. The operations room would then dispatch a quick-reaction team, or contact the CF who happened to be nearest the point of the emergency, who would then scramble squads to assist them.

The Washington Post reported that between May 2004 and June 2007, 132 PMCs died while escorting convoys and a further 416 were wounded. In May 2005, one of the largest private military security companies operating in Iraq at the time received word that one of their convoys had been ambushed and attacked after they had dropped off supplies at an Iraqi police base. Twenty contractors were deployed on the convoy, of whom 12 were killed; seven were severely wounded or were missing. The terrorists went so far as to booby-trap the bodies of the dead contractors to inflict further carnage on the quick-response force they knew would be sent to the ambush site. Fortunately, the team spotted the booby traps. According to some reports, a tank round had to be fired into the pile of corpses to eliminate the threat of the booby-trapped bodies.[7]

Every month there were thousands of convoys moving around the Sandbox, and the PMCs who protected them suffered more than most others in the private military security industry. The majority of South Africans who were killed in Iraq, whose names appear in the Roll of Honour at the end of this book, died while working in security escort teams for convoys.

9

Camp Tiger

Our plans to use the PC-6 aircraft to transport project personnel and some limited supplies to Camp Tiger were taking shape and our next step was to construct the runway. I had pinpointed an area opposite Camp Ranger that would be suited to land the sturdy little tail-dragger plane.

To get earth-moving equipment to the site to start work on the runway, our local partner persuaded a couple of Iraqi equipment owners from the area to make it to the site on their own steam. I am not sure how they managed to do this (probably a couple of greenbacks did the trick and the help of the Iraqi Army), but a water tanker, front-end loader/digger, and a five-tonne truck arrived in mid-August to start the work.

Fortunately, most areas in Anbar Province are as flat as a pancake. All we needed to do was remove the surface shrubs with the front-end loader and level the area slightly. We prepared a 350-metre-long and 50-metre-wide area running in an east–west direction. It was going to be a tricky airstrip to land and take off from, as there were various obstacles in the form of a railway line, power cables and some old buildings to contend with – not to mention frequent insurgent attacks launched from the nearby graveyard. Nevertheless, our pilot, Cody, and his assistant, Dries, were men who could get things done and they said they would make it work.

It took around two days to clear and level the area and then the water tanker drove up and down the runway to wet it to help compact it. Lastly, the truck compacted the sand, as we could not get a roller into the area. After a week we had an area that was flat and hard enough to land the little plane.

We did a test run after getting permission to fly the short hop from the airport to our site in Mahmudiyah, south of Baghdad. It would be the first time PMCs had been allowed to land a small aircraft in an Iraqi Army base. The conditions at Mahmudiyah were similar to those in east Ramadi. The base was small, approximately 300 x 300 metres. Cody had only 250 metres to put the plane down, and the landing area was between buildings and construction materials.

Cody approached from the south, quickly descended over the boundary wall, and put the plane down hard, upon which he immediately put the prop into reverse thrust and braked as hard as he could. We were all covered in dust but it was impressive. Cody had managed to pull the plane to a halt within around 200 metres. This was gutsy flying.

Of course, taking off from a 250-metre runway is not as easy as landing on it, because you have to build up enough forward motion to generate sufficient airflow over the wings for lift-off and, unlike the runway in east Ramadi, there were boundary walls here to be cleared (or crashed into). Anyhow, Cody managed to lift the nose of the plane just in time to clear the wall. Now we just had to repeat this exercise in Ramadi.

Chris and I were under pressure to get another convoy of trailers[1] and construction materials to set up the EWAC camp as soon as possible. During the first week of September there was an opportunity for our trucks to tag along with a large Iraqi Army convoy, in cooperation with US elements, to enter east Ramadi on a night-time, white-light convoy. This time, we got clearance for the trucks to make their own way to Al Taqaddum, where they would link up with the Iraqi Army convoy to east Ramadi.

It was slow going again on Route Michigan but we had no security incidents and no roadside bombs. For once, everything ran smoothly. During the early hours of the morning we arrived at Camp Ranger and Commando (the latter was General Abdullah's army base). Although everybody was tired, we were relieved that the construction materials to start the temporary camp had made it to the site area.

First landing

After expediently constructing our desert dirt runway in October, we got the final go-ahead to fly into east Ramadi. The moment had arrived to fly the tail dragger into serious Indian territory, and we could now start getting the project personnel into the site. They had their work cut out for them: they had to build the camp, and the basic infrastructure and communication systems before the main construction effort on Camp Tiger could even kick off.

I decided to fly in Grobbies and Braam de Beer to augment the security component of the mission. We had to use our air contacts to get authorisation to load our plane with weapons and ammunition. This was no easy feat, as Baghdad has one of the most heavily secured airports in the world, and to march through it with assault rifles and ammunition took a lot of negotiating with various parties.

Around mid-morning we took off, slightly apprehensive, as we knew what the risks were when moving west from Baghdad towards Fallujah, Habaniyah and Ramadi. After a steep, quick-ascending take-off, Cody took the plane to around 6000 feet and we flew west towards the Al Taqaddum Air Base and Lake Habbaniyah. It took around 25 minutes to reach the air base. We then descended and the lake came into view. Cody flew the plane at about just 50 feet above the water level. At this height, one has a better sense of speed. The low-level flight over the lake took around ten minutes and brought us to the south of the dirt runway at our site.

This is where matters got tricky. The plane was kept at low altitude for a while before the pilot had to pull up into a very steep climb to make it over the electricity cables next to the old railway line. Once he had cleared the power lines, the plane was then put into a nosedive, then he banked sharply left in a steep approach to the eastern end of the runway. The plane was put down quite hard, as we could not come in over a long, gradual descent, and once the wheels made contact with the runway, Cody engaged reverse thrust to help brake the plane quickly.

There was a ball of dust and we came to a halt within 200 metres. What an adrenaline rush! The security men on the plane with me were all smiling, but in subsequent trips some Iraqi and civilian project personnel would shout and scream during the rollercoaster manoeuvres that were needed before landing.

This even beat the hair-raising flight I'd had a year before when I flew in a military cargo plane from Mosul to an airfield north of Baghdad. That night, the pilots flew in very low and without any lights on. Before landing, they skewed the plane 90 degrees left and then right in a manoeuvre to evade possible rocket fire. Some journalists who were on the flight started screaming, but I was smiling.

It was a historic day. We'd managed to fly the first commercial, non-CF small aircraft with armed civilians on board into east Ramadi. The whole team was elated and a lot of intensive work had come to fruition. The way was now paved to fly project personnel and security guards to the site to get cracking on building Camp Tiger.

Shortly after the first landing, we started shuttling construction and security personnel to the site. The trailers were moved into position and connected to the power grid. A generator was put in place and the water and sewerage pipes were connected to the frail infrastructure of the abandoned buildings around the site. Chris and I worked continuously with the US military authorities to try to get a third large convoy to the site. At the end of November, we managed to arrange one with more materials and supplies. Our temporary camp got built and the project manager and construction personnel did well under testing circumstances, and with very few resources.

The team who were on the first flight to Camp Tiger in November 2006: from left, ex-Recces Dries Coetzee, myself, Braam de Beer and Grobbies Grobbelaar.

The US military folks were very helpful despite having to deal with serious security problems in their immediate area. From Camp Tiger, we often heard the contacts and explosions, and on a number of occasions had to rush to the bunkers when incoming fire was directed at the US camps. The insurgents hit US patrols almost daily, and we would hear the medevac choppers fly in frequently to pick up the wounded soldiers. In 2006 many servicemen paid the ultimate price in Ramadi. That year the insurgents and terrorists ran amok in the Ramadi/Habaniyah/Fallujah corridor of Anbar. Deadly attacks in Baghdad would often be planned and launched from this area.

The locals in the province were majority Sunni Muslims. After the 2003 war, they had initially sympathised with the ideals of the Sunni insurgents and AQI, who were opposed to the Americans and the Shiites who were then running the country. However, the US forces had a change of strategy and started interacting more with the local Sunni groups in Anbar. This approach was called the Awakening Movement, or the Anbar Awakening. The idea was to win the hearts and minds of the locals, train the tribesmen in basic warfare, arm them and then pay them a salary to fight against the AQI insurgents and terrorists.

The effort started in mid-2006, but gained momentum in November when family members of a prominent sheik and tribal leader in the Ramadi region were murdered by Sunni insurgents and terrorists. The sheik joined the Awakening Movement and started cooperating with the US forces. This moment marked a turn in the fight against AQI in Anbar. Members of the Awakening Movement became known as the Sons of Iraq.

This model was then exported to other Sunni-dominated areas in the north of the country and proved to be effective. In 2007 the US government increased the overall number of servicemen in the country to around 181 000 troops – the maximum number of US soldiers during the entire Iraq campaign. This is referred to as the 'surge', when the numbers of US troops were bolstered to fight AQI. From mid-2007, the violence levels in the province started subsiding considerably. At this point there were more private contractors in Iraq than US soldiers. The number of contractors, which included drivers, maintenance crews, construction workers and security personnel, was estimated to be around 183 000.

Snipers

We got to know some of the US soldiers at camps Ranger and Corregidor, talking to them over meals in the dining facility. Speaking to the guys who operated in this area gave us a better sense of the security problems on the ground. We heard some stories about a SEAL[2] sniper who was doing great work neutralising insurgents who operated in the area. We were told that this sniper was particularly effective and had had many kills, and that the enemy was wary of him.

Many years later, I read *American Sniper*, the autobiography of US Navy SEAL sniper Chris Kyle, which was made into a movie. Kyle worked out of west Ramadi. The sniper whom the soldiers at Camp Corregidor told us about was more likely to be a counterpart of Kyle's who operated from Camp Corregidor. But we saw the Hummers with the 'Punisher' logo in the camp from time to time – this was the squad that Kyle served with.

Chris Delport and me at Camp Corregidor in east Ramadi in 2006.

We were introduced to a group of men who mainly kept to themselves; they turned out to be the Navy SEAL team in Camp Corregidor. By all accounts, these soldiers did sterling work to suppress and neutralise the enemy under the most dangerous conditions.

One day in the dining facility, a lieutenant, the team leader of one of the SEAL teams in the camp, asked if he could join Chris. He was curious about this guy with an AK-47 and a Glock pistol, who spoke with a foreign accent. The soldiers there thought that Chris must have been with the CIA or some other intelligence unit.

After that first discussion with the lieutenant, Chris would join them often at their table and they would share stories. Some of the SEALs had read Eeben Barlow's book, *Executive Outcomes*, and said that they had huge respect for the South African military contractors. By now they had found out that Chris was a qualified sniper trained with the South African SF, and they wanted to share his ideas on how to counter the persistent sniping attacks their patrols faced around Ramadi. Over the weeks, they gained mutual respect, showing how soldiers from the special forces tend to have the same mind set regardless of their nationality.

The sniping attacks continued day after day. Chris had to visit Camp Tiger frequently to assess the security around the camp, where the EWAC engineering and construction teams were due to be doing the construction work. He had to be sure the engineers and workers would be safe from sniper fire, and spent a lot of time there observing the surroundings. On more than one occasion during these assessments, he took incoming sniper fire.

While visiting the camp, Chris became friendly with a major from the Marines, who was based there. This officer gave Chris great Intel on sniper attacks and direct threats to Camp Tiger. It turned out that he was also reading Eeben Barlow's book and had many questions about South African SF soldiers and the work they did in Africa. Chris told him about an incident in southern Angola in the 1980s during which I had been hit by a grenade. The 40 mm high-explosive round had come from the M79 launcher that Braam de Beer was carrying.

The incident happened when we had gone down for a rest after various contacts with enemy forces and we were evading artillery fire. The launcher was strapped to the side of Braam's backpack, and a strap on the backpack accidentally caught the trigger and the loaded device went off.

I was just a few metres from Braam when this happened. The projectile did not detonate because the arming distance for those 40 mm rounds was between 6 and 7 metres. I suffered a broken finger and broken rib, though, where the grenade hit me but it could have been much worse. Lady luck smiled on all of us that day. There had been no error on Braam's part – it was just one of those freak accidents.

In 2006 EWAC decided to employ a company of Georgian ex-soldiers as TCNs. It had become commonplace to deploy TCNs as auxiliary security personnel and in other support functions. As mentioned, there were several advantages to hiring TCNs. Firstly, as foreigners they had no political affiliations, like the Iraqis. Furthermore, they did not have the pressure of having families in the theatre of operations, so they could not be coerced to cooperate with the insurgents and/or militias if their families were threatened. TCNs could stay on the base or site location 24/7, as they did not have to travel to and from their homes, as was the case with the Iraqis (which posed logistical challenges and security risks). Most ordinary working-class Iraqis cannot speak much English, whereas most of the TCNs were recruited from countries where English was spoken or was at least taught at school. The TCNs were also paid much lower salaries than the usual expats.

In the beginning there were some misunderstandings and animosity between the Georgians and the South Africans, mainly caused by language and cultural differences but, after a while, everyone began to work together. The Georgians helped with the security at our hotel; we also deployed a contingent to the Mahmudiyah site and prepared another squad to be on standby to deploy to the east Ramadi site once things were set up.

By the end of 2006, we had made good progress with the temporary camp in east Ramadi, and the Mahmudiyah and Commando Base projects were also progressing well. The road construction project in the south was also nearing completion. I continued with training on Fridays at Commando Base 11 in Baghdad, which had a shooting range where we practised private security officer, contact and counter-ambush drills. We also kept our combat shooting skills sharp.

The Georgians started blending in a bit better with the other expats and Iraqis, and I felt the combined security team was in good shape.

A serious warning to us all

Between early 2004 and 2010, Iraq became notorious for kidnapping, hostage taking and the execution of hostages. Around 200 foreign hostages, and thousands of Iraqis, were kidnapped during this period. The terrorist organisations mostly kidnapped and executed foreign hostages for publicity, and to instil fear among the local people. They also tried to use hostages to force governments to withdraw their troops, but this never worked. Sometimes the kidnappers would try to arrange prisoner swaps for the hostages; this failed too.

The militias, on the other hand, tended to conduct kidnappings to extort a ransom. In December 2006, we were shocked to hear that four South African contractors had been kidnapped at a makeshift rogue checkpoint in Baghdad – André Durant (team leader), Johan Enslin, Callie Scheepers and Hardus Greeff, who worked for security firm Safenet. That day they were supposed to escort a convoy of trucks taking critical supplies and equipment to Kirkush.

They were almost out of Baghdad when their tracking unit showed that they had been stationary for a while. This did not raise a red flag immediately, as they were close to a checkpoint and they were in early-morning heavy traffic. But, minutes later, the company operations room received a call from an Iraqi security officer from another team who was on his way to work, who informed them that the team had been stopped at a bogus Iraqi checkpoint. The operations room immediately tried to make contact with the South African team, but could not get through to any of them.

In the PMC circles, everyone tried their best to get any kind of information and we all tasked our Iraqi employees to keep an ear to the ground for any clues that could be passed on to the authorities. On 12 December we were told that the five Iraqi guards who had also been taken hostage with the team had been released. But there was no news of the South Africans.

Then, on 21 December, André Durant made a call to his wife using one of his captors' phones. That was the last anyone ever heard from the four men. There was no ransom note; no contact was made with the abductors. Many locals claimed that they had information about the incident or the abductees, but nobody could produce any real, tangible evidence. The men were officially declared dead five years later.

All security companies sharpened their drills after this incident. All Iraqi checkpoints henceforth had to be treated as potentially hostile. Where possible, a team of Iraqi security personnel would now travel ahead of the expat team to determine if a checkpoint was legitimate, and whether the security personnel manning the checkpoint displayed any suspicious signs or behaviour.

All private security teams ensured that the doors of their vehicles remained locked, that they used tracking units, and particular care was taken when using soft-skin vehicles and when they worked low-profile. For a while after this incident, as we approached checkpoints I used to draw my pistol, which was always cocked and locked, and would keep it hidden under my leg, pointing towards the vehicle door. This was a problem, though, because most checkpoints were legitimate and presenting arms could be construed as a hostile action towards the Iraqi security personnel, so great care and discretion had to be taken to avoid an unnecessary shoot-out with the local security forces.

Revs

During my time in the South African Defence Force, the SF guys had a slang word for an enemy attack. When you got 'revved', or a team was in a 'rev', it meant that you were being shot at or your team or position was under attack. In east Ramadi all military bases and posts got revved – and very often.

From mid-September to the end of November alone, Chris reported more than four occasions in which their positions had been revved. During one particular mortar attack, Chris had just entered the office to meet General Abdullah when a mortar landed right on the bonnet of his Nissan Patrol. His vehicle was blown to smithereens.

Even the portable toilet and showers at Camp Ranger got hit by mortars several times. Chris had the toilet repaired and moved to another part of the camp. After the attack, Chris was the only one who would use this toilet. He placed a padlock on it and maintained it as his own personal WC.

The soldiers had to make the short journey down the road to Camp Corregidor at mealtimes. The insurgents knew when the soldiers in east Ramadi ate and this was the most dangerous period, as the dining facility got hammered with mortars and rockets while everybody was eating.

A few months after the toilet incident, Raymond Archer, an ex-SF colleague and friend with whom I had worked in Haiti and who came to the Sandbox in 2006, was helping the team in east Ramadi when, during one of his lunchtime visits to Camp Corregidor, the camp got mortared. Raymond was incredibly fortunate. He had parked his Jeep next to a metal container, got out of the vehicle and walked away. Moments later, a 60-mm mortar landed on top of the container and exploded. He was shaken but not stirred; luckily, no shrapnel hit him. When he arrived back at the temporary camp, he remarked drily how 'the fuckers had tried to spoil his lunch'.

During this period, I once had to stay over in east Ramadi for a couple of nights to visit the project. By now the main camp was functional and sometimes our pilot and co-pilot stayed over before flying the PC-6 back to Baghdad again. We had managed to get a Jeep Cherokee to the site with one of the convoys. Early one evening, Dries and I took the Cherokee to fill it with fuel. We pulled up to the pump area and, the next thing, we heard serious gunfire coming from the southwest perimeter of the base and saw tracer rounds coming from behind us and flying overhead. During this dangerous commotion, Dries nevertheless managed to crack a joke: 'Maybe we should turn the car around, so that at least we don't get shot in the back of the head.' As I was laughing, I manoeuvred the Jeep around, so that we could see the direction the gunfire was coming from. The shooting continued for several minutes; it was probably a harassment attack against the perimeter of the base (which was a common occurrence at the bases in east Ramadi). We filled up the tank and made our way back to our camp. I have never forgotten Dries's dry humour in all these years.

Camp Corregidor probably took the most hits of all the bases in the area, and the combat outpost near Camp Corregidor got attacked the most overall. Many US servicemen lost their lives or were wounded at the outpost, or while moving between there and the bases. Either way, during 2006 you could rest assured that you would be revved, sooner or later, if you hung out in east Ramadi.

Towards the end of the year, Chris tendered his resignation.[3] Although I was sad to see a good security operator and manager go, I was pleased for him that he was undertaking a new business venture with his father, who was developing a golf estate in Mozambique. I now had to find a replacement to act as security manager for the east Ramadi project. I asked Grobbies and Raymond to go to east Ramadi, and I wanted to expose Braam to the project and site. Our main contact and ally at Camp Corregidor, Lieutenant Colonel Matt, was also finishing his tour and he introduced us to his successor and new executive officer, Lieutenant Colonel Dave.

A new company is established

During the previous months, in between setting up the mission in east Ramadi and arranging permission to use the aircraft, we managed to register the new security concern both in the US and in Iraq with the necessary authorities. The security company would be owned and subcontracted by the EWAC group and their local partner, Sheik FK. This was easier said than done, as the Ministry of Interior had by then really turned the screws on private military security companies, regardless of whether they were foreign or locally owned.

To protect our Iraqi partners, I will call this new company Skywave Services. To register it, I used the services of a legal consulting firm that helped companies set up in Iraq. But even with their help, the process was not moving as fast as we wanted it to. It was frustrating as there were endless amounts of paperwork, but I finally managed to get over the hurdles.

The biggest challenge was meeting the Ministry of Interior's criteria and undergoing their close scrutiny. This powerful arm of the Iraqi government was rife with corruption. The department allowed militias with hidden agendas to operate death squads from within its ranks. Favouritism and cronyism were the order of the day. And the earlier incident in April, when the men from the Ministry of Interior raided the house where our standby team were staying, had not helped us at all.

I received an instruction and final warning from the Ministry of Interior through the legal firm to report to their HQ in downtown Baghdad to explain why our application was incomplete. I smelt a rat. Had they connected the dots and found out about our link to Sheik FK's family, whom they had targeted before? I had five days to see them. At the Ministry of Interior I had to wait a long time before a major called me into his office. Through an interpreter I learnt that our application was apparently incomplete. This was bullshit, as I had made sure to file all the necessary documents, pledges, registrations and a mountain of other papers, just as our lawyers had instructed me to do. I sensed that it was a delaying tactic on their part.

Eventually, the exercise of registering the company would keep us busy for the next two years and took much wheeling and dealing on my part.

End of the Saddam era

Towards the end of 2006, a special tribunal of the Iraqi government found Saddam Hussein guilty of the 1982 murder of 148 Shia Muslims in the town of Dujail, north of Baghdad. Prime Minister Maliki announced that he had been found guilty and would be executed by hanging on 30 December. Various human-rights advocates and NGOs voiced their opposition to the death sentence but they were ignored. A member of the execution group secretly filmed the hanging and the video was circulated even before Saddam's corpse was cold.

Saddam's death heralded the end of an era in Iraqi politics. Many ordinary Iraqis hoped that the new Shia government under Maliki would improve the standards of living and governance in the post-war and post-Saddam era. Afterwards, there was much celebrating in the streets of Baghdad by those Iraqis who had been brutally suppressed by the former dictator. However, there were also discontent among a large portion of the Sunni population, who had seen Saddam as their champion. Many of his former Baath Party officials and members would go on to join AQI, fuelling the conflict.

When Saddam was hanged, I was on leave in South Africa. My family remarked that I looked tired. They were right; it had been a long year. What I did not discuss much with them was the fact that I was really tired of the pain I was constantly suffering from. I was taking more painkillers and drugs than the human body could safely handle. I took cortisone steroid injections into my damaged shoulder each time I went back to South Africa.

My feet had been aching since 1986, when I injured my heels during my military days. I had had unsuccessful surgery on both heels in the early 1990s. This, coupled with the severe pain I felt in my shoulder after injuring it in the 2004 ambush (at the time I did not realise that the shoulder was dislocated: I put it down to a bad sprain), caused me to be in chronic pain in multiple places. I also suffered back pain from a bulging disk that pressed on some nerves.

My solution was to keep increasing the dosages of painkillers, and to make concoctions of various scheduled medicines to fight the pain. Early in 2007, I got hold of Tramadol Hexal vials, which can be injected intra-muscularly for rapid relief of pain. This is a class of opioid, a substance that acts on the body's opioid receptors to produce morphine-like effects.

When I was at the hotel and had some down time, I would first try natural remedies, such as ice packs, an infrared lamp and hooking myself up to a TENS machine (a small portable battery-operated device that is worn on the body and transmits transcutaneous electrical pulses to the body that feel like small electric shocks). These all ease the pain for a while, but the problem with these measures is that the result does not last as long as the injections. Also, I did not have the time or the means to use this kind of natural pain relief while I was on the move between the sites or when I stayed over in east Ramadi. The short-term solution to staying operationally capable was therefore to take lots of painkillers and injections. But the medication started getting to me and I could feel the side effects in my system.

There were some mornings when I hurt so badly that the only way I could get myself going was to inject Tramadol Hexal into one thigh, and a mix of vitamin B6 and B12 complex into the other. It was a survival mechanism, but it did the job and I was able to get my work done. I was also aware that the stuff was highly addictive and that I was treading a very dangerous line. Later, I learnt that a large number of deaths in America are attributed to opioid painkillers, often prescribed by doctors for chronic pain. In April 2016 the musician Prince died of an opioid overdose, and in 2017 some states in the US declared this kind of addiction a public health emergency.

10
Feeling the heat

Although the first half of 2007 was bloody, the US and CF started turning the tide against AQI and other terrorists in the second half of the year. The Awakening Movement was working well – the Iraqis started taking charge of their own destiny, and the training and support the US forces gave them made them much more effective.

In the first few months of the year we were operating on five reconstruction projects in hostile areas of Iraq. The projects progressed well despite security problems and attacks in these areas. I would move around from site to site to ensure that the security personnel were supported to the best of our ability, and to get a feel for the security situation on the ground.

The road project in southern Iraq was nearing completion; the Iraqi Ministry of Defence (MOD) base in Mahmudiyah was over halfway finished; and renovations at the two Commando bases in Baghdad were just about completed. But the construction of the new Ministry of Defence base in east Ramadi remained the biggest challenge, and I had to focus much attention on this project. Braam took over as the site security manager when Chris left, and the temporary camp was occupied by our engineers and security personnel early in 2007.

Personnel were shuttled on regular flights to east Ramadi in the PC-6; limited supplies, such as electronic goods, some food and sensitive equipment, could also be flown in. This little workhorse plane could carry a load of up to 2 tonnes, but because of our short dust runway the pilots tried to limit it to 1 tonne. But it remained a challenge to transport heavy materials and supplies by road.

Personal pressures

After more than two years in Iraq, I'd started noticing that the pressure on PMCs who worked away from home for extended periods increased exponentially the longer the deployments got. The guys with younger children seemed to suffer more than the ones with older kids. Sometimes you could hear the younger kids crying for their fathers when they spoke to them on video calls.

This often influenced my decision-making when I had to choose guys to go on high-risk missions. I preferred to send the single men on such tasks, or the older warriors whose kids were grown up. Right or wrong, I always thought it would be harder to break bad news about the death of a father to a young family.

It also takes a special kind of wife or girlfriend to cope with this kind of life. I realised this early on in my life when I saw the high divorce rate that prevailed in our armed forces, particularly in homes where the husbands served in combat units that took them away from their families for very long periods. These problems can be compounded by the fact that PMCs earn good money, and some wives, in their loneliness, turned to retail therapy to comfort themselves. When the guys got home, expecting a fat bank balance, they sometimes discovered to their horror that it had been blown. I am blessed to have a modest, genteel wife who works and pays her own way and did not rely on my income.

In addition, loneliness sometimes led to affairs, both back home and in the Sandbox. Then there would follow divorces, which could get messy when it came to the distribution of assets and cash that had been earned through blood, sweat, tears and dust. Moreover, these circumstances affected the emotional state of the PMCs and this could make them lose focus. Therefore, as a manager or leader of security personnel, these personal and marital developments had to be carefully monitored and taken into account when I composed teams.

One should also bear in mind, however, that not all the PMCs who worked in the Sandbox earned big money the hard way. Many ended up in cushy jobs where they worked mainly in the Green Zone, or at some forward operating base, and never really had to brave the dangers of the conflict other than ducking and running for the mortar bunkers from time to time. In their case there was big money up for grabs without too much of the blood, sweat and tears part. In these instances, the old adage would sometimes apply: easy come, easy go. I had seen too often how colleagues would blow all their money on a high lifestyle back home without investing or saving it wisely. In the past I was slightly guilty of this sin myself, but I have since learnt my lesson.

Another issue I had to contend with was the phenomenon of clingy wives who cannot leave their husbands alone for one day and stick to the scheduled times for making phone calls to their loved ones. And, of course, there are those men who cannot function without constantly contacting their wives. With the advent of the smartphone from 2007, this problem worsened. Instant messaging and video calling became the in thing – wearisome wives and lonely husbands had a new tool with which to stay in constant communication with their partners.

A few years later, in the 'new Iraq', from about December 2011 onwards, I often observed situations in which PMCs would be contacted by their wives by text message while they were on a mission. If he did not reply within a short period of time, he got called or was bombarded with more messages. I had to bear this in mind when composing and managing teams, because a sharply focused team can mean the difference between life and death.

The men in my team weren't allowed to drown their sorrows in drink. Most private military security companies allowed moderate use of alcohol for their personnel when not on duty, and in a secure environment. My policy was that team members had to stay dry when on contract or when deployed, and could only drink alcohol on controlled and approved occasions.

I gave up alcohol in 2000, but because I had been an avid follower of Bacchus for the previous two decades, I know it is impossible to keep grown men from alcohol for long. On Thursday nights, the team braaied and relaxed because Fridays were quiet, as the Iraqis took time off to go to the mosque and spend the day with their families. The team were allowed a couple of beers on these nights, after they had ensured that all the guards were at their posts and that the machine-gun positions around the hotel were manned. We always had constant radio contact with the security personnel.

On braai nights we always invited the engineers and any other personnel who were around to join us. Now, in South Africa having a braai is a national pastime, and we take it very seriously. Most South Africans know how to make a decent fire and how to prepare steaks, ribs, lamb chops, sausages and other delicacies with spices, sauces and all kinds of secret flavourings. All the guys on the team enjoyed chipping in and helped to prepare the meat and braai it. We had some spectacular cook-outs and it was good for morale.

The EWAC security team and clients at a Friday braai at the Dreamland Hotel, late 2006.

Former Special Forces operators (from left) Braam de Beer, Mark de Wet and me.

I usually retreated early in the evening and left the men to chat over a couple of beers. This was permitted as long as nobody was going on mission early the following day, in which case they had to stop drinking 12 hours before the deployment. Anyway, I knew that my team members would adhere to the two-beer rule after I'd gone to my room – although it hardly ever happened that they stuck strictly to the rule!

One night one of our team members,[1] was as happy as a lark after braai night. He decided to watch a movie in his room afterwards. Not long after the guys heard a commotion on the radio and upon inspection found Mac trying to talk to an action hero character through his radio …

In December 2006 there was a shooting incident in the Green Zone. A foreign private security contractor killed an Iraqi guard while inebriated. The company he worked for had to pay compensation to the guard's family, but this could and should have been avoided by having a dry policy. If private military security companies do allow their employees to drink, then it should be tightly controlled, particularly regarding the rules concerning firearms. As the saying goes, firearms and alcohol don't mix.

We often heard about fights that had broken out between contractors when too much alcohol had been consumed. In an incident in 2009 in the Green Zone, an inebriated British guy shot and killed two fellow contractors, and wounded an Iraqi guard after an argument. He was sentenced to 23 years' imprisonment in a tough jail in Baghdad's Sadr City. His family tried numerous times to have him extradited, but the fact that he had wounded an Iraqi probably did not work in his favour and their requests were refused. I cannot imagine the conditions he must endure in that particular jail, but he did kill people in cold blood.

Many PMCs have also been fired because of alcohol abuse while at work. In my view, there is no place for drinking in an operational and dangerous environment, as it blunts your edge.

The key to access

A PMC, or any other civilian contractor, could not operate in or move around the Sandbox without the right 'badging'. Initially in 2003, the only official badge that contractors who worked on US government contracts, or civilian companies contracted on such contracts, could obtain was the DoD card. However, by the end of 2006 a new type of access card had been brought in. This was referred to as the MNF-I card (Multi-National Force – Iraq) and was issued by an office in the Green Zone that was run by the CF. Without an MNF-I card, PMCs could not enter the Green Zone or US military installations and would not be able to go on US military flights or have access to the combat hospitals and dining facilities.

Some of the access cards I had to carry with me over the years.

It was a mission to obtain these access cards – and with good reason, because the US and CF had to prevent terrorists from getting their hands on such badges. You had to prove that you worked on a US government contract, and a lot of paperwork accompanied the application.

Early in 2007, the US government temporarily stopped issuing DoD cards in Iraq to non-CF citizens. The only way to get them during this period was from a DoD processing office at a US military base in the States or selected US bases in certain countries. As EWAC worked on numerous projects funded by the American government, and the expat security team members needed to be able to move around freely through checkpoints to the respective project sites, these cards were essential and we investigated where we could obtain them. We discovered a US Air Force base in the UK that could assist us.

In February I arranged with the EWAC head-shed to fly to England to secure the cards. I prepared the necessary documents and obtained a point of contact at the base. As I was waiting for my contact, a staff sergeant, to issue the cards to us, he asked me about Iraq and the security situation on the ground. I told him about what we as PMCs did there.

'Thank you for your service to our country,' he said.

I was quite taken aback by this unexpected compliment. In my mind, we were the ones who had to thank the American government for allowing us to work on contracts funded by them.

At the same time we also started applying for the new MNF-I badges. This was a cumbersome undertaking – even just getting an appointment with the issuing office in the Green Zone was not straightforward. There were different kinds of MNF-I badges, colour-coded according to the different levels of access and privileges they allowed.

We also had to ensure that we carried in-house company ID cards, accompanied by an in-house weapons card. The weapons cards had to be accompanied by an MNF-I special document (called a FRAGO order) that gave your security company permission to use the weapons you listed and declared to the interior ministry. In May I also had to reapply for my US embassy access card, as the one I'd been issued with the year before had expired.

So, a PMC ended up having to be in possession of an armoury of different identification cards, a letter of authority/identification and FRAGO orders. Without these documents you could not pass through checkpoints, enter CF installations or bases – and you might even be arrested.

At the beginning of 2007 I also decided that I would attempt to get an Iraqi residency permit. This would help me with various legal processes regarding the new security company we had to get off the ground. It might also ensure more favourable treatment by Iraqi government institutions, I figured. I approached some Iraqis in the security forces who had contacts in the government to take me to an office in the downtown Karada district of Baghdad for an interview to apply for a residency card.

Bear in mind that this was during a dangerous period when the kidnapping of Westerners was a very real threat. After some deliberation, we decided that I would pretend to have been in exile in Jordan, but now wanted to return to Iraq. I did not have an Iraqi birth certificate or other relevant papers but, fortunately, my connections had some 'friendly' contacts in this particular office. The most difficult part would be to get around the fact that I did not speak fluent Arabic, and would not be able to answer the questions during the interview they would conduct with me. We thought long and hard about this and came up with the idea that I should pretend to be deaf and mute. On the day I went to the office, I was wearing jeans, a long-sleeve shirt (to hide my tattoos), a pair of sneakers and a shemagh. I had a boot knife concealed by my shirt in the small of my back; two of my companions carried concealed pistols.

The interview was tense. My Iraqi contacts answered on my behalf, while I mumbled unintelligibly a couple of times. Thankfully, the application process seemed to go down successfully. We were particularly alert as we left the office in case someone who suspected I was a foreigner 'pinged'[2] me. A number of weeks later, one of my contacts informed me that my application had been approved and that I could fetch the residency card from the same office. A similar

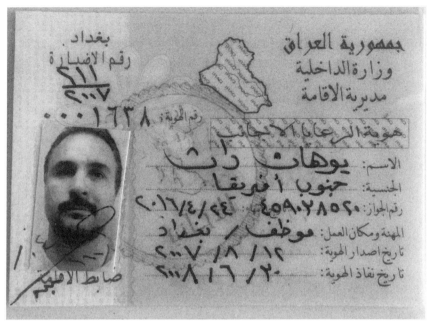

The Iraqi residence card that I got early in 2007.

undercover operation was conducted, but this time it was easier, as I only had to sign for the card and then we could leave.

In pursuit of certain goals

In 2007 the Skywave Services security licence also finally came through. Our next step was to arrange for vehicles, weapons, radios, body armour, uniforms and other security apparel to fit our security needs. Until then we had used four old Jeep Cherokees that were up-armoured to level B4 (to withstand small-arms fire) for our short runs around the hotel and to the Green Zone, and we used the Blue Hackle private security detail teams for the long-haul trips.

These Cherokees were a big headache for the security team and me, as they continually broke down. Moreover, they were very cramped inside after the up-armouring. The bigger guys in the team battled to get in and out of these vehicles, especially in body armour and tactical vests. We eventually got some B6 armoured Land Cruiser SUVs and Ford F350 double-cab bakkies with machine-gun turrets on top, which was a big step up from the Cherokees.

I went to the Green Zone and some hotels around Baghdad where I looked at Kevlar helmets, body armour (bulletproof vests and plates) and other webbing to purchase for the new Skywave Services security team, which would comprise all our expats, including the Georgians, and the Iraqi guards. Skywave Services was now the in-house security division of EWAC and had a security force of over 500 personnel. During these buying trips, I encountered many vultures who were out to make a quick buck from inferior or written-off gear they had scored somewhere. Fortunately, there were also legitimate suppliers and I managed to get the items we needed.

Soon we were ready to start operating under our new umbrella company. We expected that we would be treated fairly, like other security companies, by the Iraqi Ministry of Interior. That turned out to be wishful thinking ...

My workload increased, as I was not only wrapped up in getting the new company launched, but also had to visit all the project sites regularly, which involved a lot of travelling in dangerous areas. In addition, there were endless visits to the interior ministry, who demanded mountains of documents that seemed to be very repetitive and unnecessary.

I drove myself harder and harder to ensure success for the company, and, in doing so, started neglecting my health. When I get busy and have goals to achieve, I do not stop until the job is done. This may sound like a positive thing to someone wishing to hire my services, but I learnt that it can also be a flaw. You need to know when to retreat tactically today to enable you to fight again tomorrow. This is captured well by an anonymous quote I once read: 'The pursuit of certain goals might destroy you entirely.'

During this period, Awie came into my office one evening and reminded me to eat something, as they hadn't seen me in the restaurant for a few days. That was when I realised that I had not had a proper meal in a while and had been living on energy bars and energy drinks. It dawned on me that I was in fact hungry and tired. I joined them for supper that evening, but the intensive work continued and it started taking its toll.

Sometime in March I had to get to east Ramadi to visit the project there. For technical reasons, the PC-6 was grounded at the time, so I booked a flight on a Black Hawk from Landing Zone Washington in the Green Zone to the Al Taqaddum Air Base, where I would spend the night and try to arrange a lift to east Ramadi on a helicopter the next day. The following day I was told that there was no space for me on a flight that day, but that I had to come back in the evening to see if there was a no-show or cancellation. I then walked to the other side of the base where they arrange the midnight convoys to see if I could catch a ride on one, but that also turned out not to be an option.

I walked back to the overnight trailers. I was exhausted; I had walked for miles across the base. I was on my own in the containerised housing unit, which was great, as I would not be interrupted while taking a rest. I turned the aircon on and switched the light off to ensure a cool, dark environment before reaching for my pillow and blanket in my E & E bag. I set the alarm on my phone for 15:00, so that I would have time to walk back to the flight area where passengers report for the night-time chopper flights to east Ramadi.

I drifted off. But then, suddenly, I felt an electric shock running through my brain. It felt as if my skull was sizzling, as if electrical wires were frying my brain. When I came around, I was on the floor and couldn't see anything for a few moments. When I gathered my wits, I was sweating and my pulse was racing. It felt like a bolt of lightning had struck me and I could not get up. I lay down flat in the dark and took deep breaths.

After about three minutes, which felt like a lifetime, I was able to get up slowly, while holding onto the bunk bed's iron leg for support. I felt absolutely exhausted. I lay down again on the bed for a good ten minutes. I then managed to get up, first swinging my legs off the bed, like an old person, and sitting for a while before rising slowly and taking a few small steps. I was steady and could walk at a snail's pace.

My head was pounding more than when I'd had a blinding hangover in my youth.

I made my way to the Marine field hospital, which was fortunately not too far away. I reported to the entrance desk, showed my DoD card and explained what had happened. A short while later, a doctor arrived and walked me into a large hall, which looked like a medical exam room. The doctor asked me what had happened and took my blood pressure and pulse (both high at the time). An assistant helped him to draw blood, they then turned me on my side and placed a square object underneath my torso, which was an X-ray device or scanner of sorts.

He asked me about my medical history and the medication I used. Once he heard about the amount of chronic pain medication that I was on, he asked me what I had had for breakfast and whether I took these meds in the morning. I then realised that I'd skipped breakfast and had taken a bunch of pain meds, as I was hurting badly from the travels of the past week.

The doctor then asked me about my work hours, how many days a week I rested, and how many tours I had completed in Iraq. I explained that I worked seven days a week, 12 to 16 hours a day for 90 to 100 days at a time, and that I had been in the Sandbox for over three years. After about 20 minutes, the doctor produced results from the blood tests and scans. I was dehydrated, my electrolyte levels were low, my blood-sugar level was low, and the amount and combination of pain meds I had taken might have caused a seizure and blackout, he explained.

They then proceeded to X-ray my skull to ensure I had not injured myself when I blacked out and then ran an intravenous line into my arm to hydrate me and to raise my sugar and electrolyte levels. The examination and treatment took around an hour.

As I was lying on the metal gurney, the doctor came over and in a friendly manner recommended that I get some rest, reconsider my diet and take fewer painkillers. Lastly, but most importantly, he said I should quit working in the Sandbox, as this kind of stressful environment over such a long period of time is not good for one's health, he pointed out. He told me that I could leave once the contents of the drip were in my body, but that I should go and rest. I thanked him politely, smiled and closed my eyes as I mulled over his words.

It was not the first time a medical practitioner had advised me to leave Iraq. Early in 2006 my general practitioner in South Africa had advised me to quit the job as he was injecting cortisone steroids into my aching left shoulder. 'That place will kill you,' he used to say to me. I have always found it incredibly sad and indicative of how bad the crime situation is in South Africa that, ironically, he died before me. He was hijacked and killed by thieves on a road outside Johannesburg. I guess my home city is another kind of war zone. His death made me realise that, regardless of who you are, and where you are in this world, when your number is up, your number is up.

Despite his wise words, the only thing I could think of saying to the American military doctor was, how could anybody even suggest that I should quit working in the Sandbox? This is my life! This is what men like me do.

I waited for the fluids to disappear into my arm, and then got up, put my shirt and boots back on, thanked the medical team and left. It was getting late and I had to get to the helicopter pad to see if they had space for me. I felt slightly better now; some energy had returned. I made a mental note that I should infuse myself with dextrose intravenous fluids from time to time to get some extra oomph, so that I could work harder.

At the helicopter flight office, I was told that there still wasn't room for me that night. For once, this suited me fine – I could do with a good night's rest. I had a proper meal before retiring to my hooch. Later, I could hear music playing, my kind of music. I decided to go check it out and was amazed when I got to the source of the sound. There, in the middle of the air base, was a rock band on a stage playing for a group of soldiers. If I had not feel so groggy I would have joined them in the head-banging. Once again, I was astounded by the lengths the US military will go to entertain their soldiers.

And it made me reflect – here I was, in the Al Taqaddum Air Base, in the heart of the insurgency in Iraq, rocking with fellow soldiers.

What a good life this is! I thought. There was no way I was going to give it up now.

This feeling was reinforced by another experience I had on the night-time Black Hawk flight on my return from east Ramadi to Baghdad. As I was waiting for the helicopter to arrive at the landing zone behind Camp Corregidor, I leant back against my E & E backpack and did some stargazing.

When the helicopter had landed, some soldiers got off and I was informed that the pilots would make one stop at a landing zone close to Fallujah before heading on to the Green Zone in Baghdad. I was led to the chopper in the dark by a ground safety officer. I jumped into the belly of the bird and slung my weapon with the barrel facing down (a safety drill). The rotor revs picked up and the door gunners got into position.

As soon as we cleared the northern side of Route Michigan, I spotted tracer rounds below. I could not tell if it was a ground attack, or if the chopper was being targeted, but I kept an eye on the tracers in case they came close to the helicopter, in which case I would have lain down flat on the deck, as the underbelly of the Black Hawk is designed to withstand small-arms fire.

The pilots flew the chopper hard and fast on that dark night. It felt good. I was hyper-alert and my senses sharpened. I smiled as the cocktail of adrenaline, testosterone and endorphins flowed through my veins. In that moment, I realised that as long as I could remember, I had wanted to be a soldier, even if it was now in a private capacity. Despite what the doctors had said, in my heart of hearts I knew that I would not have made such a success of my life had I become a banker, a lawyer or some administrative or pencil-neck type. This was the life for me!

A short while later we landed outside of Fallujah and a few more soldiers jumped into the chopper, then we took off again for Baghdad. Around 15 minutes later, the pilots deployed as countermeasures high-intensity white flares that burn at a high temperature to attract heat-seeking missiles. The idea is that any missiles aimed at the chopper will (hopefully) go after the flares, and not the heat generated by the engine.

Jakes and some Iraqis were waiting to collect me and take me back to the hotel. The flight was late and it was after midnight when we crossed the bridge over the Tigris and approached checkpoint 14, which would take us out of the Zone. The checkpoints around the Green Zone closed down at midnight and reopened at 06:00 the next morning, but they would occasionally let vehicles pass through.

On this particular night the soldiers at the outgoing checkpoint indicated that their lane was shut down, but that we could sneak over into the incoming lane, against the traffic. We headed off but the next moment we heard the crack of gunshots flying over our vehicle. Clearly, the soldiers at the other checkpoint point thought we were a potential threat and opened fire. We stopped dead, turned the headlights off, the interior light on and held up our DoD cards and a small American flag that we kept in the vehicles for exactly such occasions.

The shooting stopped and we informed the soldiers about our status and mission. It was clear that there weren't any comms or coordination between the two checkpoints. We were given the go-ahead to exit the Green Zone. I cannot help wonder where those bullets landed and whether they injured or killed somebody. So many innocent Iraqis must have been killed over the years by all the stray bullets that seemed to be forever flying all over the place.

Superstition

Many times I have been lucky to have escaped serious injury or death. Here I have to confess that I have a small superstition when it comes to my personal safety.

In our Special Operations Forces community, all operators who are airborne qualified celebrate the festival of Saint Michael each year in September. This tradition was apparently started in World War II by members of the US 82nd Airborne Division, and it is believed that the Archangel Michael is the protector of airborne soldiers. There is a prayer to Saint Michael and a motto, 'Saint Michael, Patron of Paratroopers, Protect Us' being the most common version. There are also reports that mariners around the Mediterranean would pray to Saint Michael for protection as long ago as the 8th century.

In 1987 when I was a young corporal in 1 Reconnaissance Commando, I got a silver pendant with the Saint Michael logo that depicts an angel standing on a globe, with a parachute canopy in the background. Around the edge of the silver design are the words 'Our Lady, Queen of Angels, Defend us in Combat'. Whoever designed this limited edition clearly thought it would be better for our protective angel to be a woman.

My Special Forces (left) and St Michael pendants.

I keep this pendant laced around my neck with a piece of string. For the past 30 years, I have never left my house without my St Michael around my neck, and I would never deploy or go on a mission in a high-threat environment without it. I remove it only at night, when I usually keep it on a bedside table, or when I'm out in the field, hang it over the front sight of my assault rifle, which always stands next to my bed. When I get up I immediately place it around my neck.

As Murphy would have it, one morning before a mission with

our no. 1 client, Sheik FK, I could not find the pendant. I looked everywhere but to no avail. The team were calling for me on the radio but I would not budge. I was convinced something bad might happen to us that day if I left without it. I searched high and low. Finally, I found it between the headboard of the bed and the wall. There were a few long faces when I finally made it to the motorcade, but I wasn't concerned about that. At least I was secure in the knowledge that our patron, Saint Michael, would be travelling with us that day.

Sometime in 2007 Mark de Wet, a former South African SF operator who was on the team with us, asked a jeweller to make a limited run of gold badges for the South African ex-SF operators bearing the official insignia of the unit – a dagger and a laurel wreath (see photo). I ordered one and attached it to the string alongside my St Michael.

I believed I had now doubled my protective forces and have worn these two pendants for over a decade. It is my wish to be buried with these pendants around my neck so that I will also be protected when I move on to the next world.

The end, version 1

Even though Chris Delport had left the Sandbox, he and I stayed in regular contact. Before he left, he had asked me if I would like to join him in his new venture in Mozambique, but at the time I could not leave behind my responsibilities in Iraq. In April 2007 he asked me again if I might be interested in assisting him with certain aspects of the project, including the security planning and set-up.

Although I loved my work, there were moments when I contemplated a life beyond the Sandbox, especially after the blackout episode at Al Taqaddum. The military doctor's words of advice had stayed with me. My pain levels were beyond explanation and I was using even more painkillers. I kept pushing my physical and psychological limits. Furthermore, I was growing alarmingly distant from and out of touch with my family, whom I didn't see for long periods.

Deep down I knew something had to give. Perhaps it was time to move on and explore different things. In the end all of these factors steered me to join Chris and call it a day in the Sandbox. It wasn't an easy decision to make but by June I'd made up my mind. Even though I was on top of my game and had an exciting career ahead in Iraq, I decided to try something new and give the opportunity in Mozambique a go.

After more than three years in the Sandbox, I typed my resignation letter to Sheik FK and others in the top management of EWAC. Over the next six weeks, I handed over as country security manager for EWAC and the newly formed Skywave Services to Jakes.

On 1 July members of my team took me to the airport after I had said goodbye to all and sundry at the Dreamland Hotel, from the chefs and cleaners to support personnel, the EWAC engineers and managers, and finally my old team. When the plane took off, I felt slightly emotional. It was the end to a busy but enriching chapter in my PMC career. But at least I was pleased with what I had achieved, especially getting the security approved for the projects to start at Mahmudiyah and east Ramadi.

11

A break from the Sandbox

Two months after I left Iraq, a serious shooting incident in September 2007 by employees of a private military security company in Baghdad made world headlines. It would have serious consequences for the members involved, and for the industry as a whole.

On 16 September, PMCs from US security services firm Blackwater Security Consulting opened fire on Iraqi civilians in Nisour Square in the Mansour neighbourhood of Baghdad, not far from the Green Zone. The team involved perceived a possible threat against their convoy, which led to the shooting. Seventeen Iraqis were killed and another 20 wounded.

On the day of the incident, a convoy escorted by Blackwater was passing through Mansour. When they approached Nisour Square, they observed a white Kia vehicle occupied by a woman and a male (her adult son). The vehicle ignored an Iraqi policeman's warning to stop. When the Kia continued to approach the convoy, it was seen as a hostile action. (Here, one has to bear in mind the context – one of the terrorists' preferred tools of attack, and the most devastating, were suicide car bombers. During that period, many convoys attached signs to the rear of the last vehicle, which read in large print: 'Warning! Stop! Stay 50–100 metres away – convoy ahead.')

According to the PMCs, the Kia proceeded slowly towards the convoy, ignoring hand signals to stop, upon which a warning shot was fired, followed by more shots, which killed the woman and her son. However, an Iraqi policeman who was following the car on foot was also killed. When other Iraqi policemen saw that their colleague had been shot, they apparently opened fire on the convoy.

This was, in turn, construed as a hostile action by the PMC team and they then opened fire on a crowd of unarmed civilians in the

A warning sign on the back of the last vehicle in a convoy.

square. The shooting left 14 civilians dead and at least 17 wounded.

As I have explained, terrorists, insurgents and militias often used police and military uniforms as a disguise. Some accounts indicated that there was an explosion, possibly from a mortar, and that at least eight attackers were shooting at the convoy. Normally, the first action a PMC team will take when under attack would be to announce the action by shouting, 'Contact! Contact!', followed by the direction it is coming from. The drivers in the convoy will then attempt to get away from the X-mark[1] and drive out of the contact area, in the opposite direction from where the hostile action is coming from. When you break contact, the gunners and security personnel will respond with suppressive fire towards the attackers.

It was claimed that when the team moved out of the contact area, another vehicle with armed passengers tried to block them, which was seen as part of a supposed bigger attack. A quick-response force element was dispatched to assist the convoy team, but they were delayed by the Iraqi police and dense traffic, and arrived only half an hour later.

There are many different reports and witness accounts of what happened that day. Some seem to corroborate certain versions of what happened, whereas others contradict the official reports completely.

All PMCs who have worked in hostile environments and conflict zones understand that one should be proactive rather than reactive, and that prevention is better than cure. Of course, this approach does not warrant shooting at perceived threats without good reason. You can only do so if you believe your life, the life of those you are protecting, or the lives of your teammates are in imminent danger. Something must have triggered alarm bells with members of the security team. I certainly do not believe that so many people could have been killed and injured without there having been a perceived threat to the contractors.

This incident made the news headlines. The next day the Iraqi government revoked Blackwater's right to work in the country, and demanded an investigation into the incident, upon which various investigations were undertaken, including one by the FBI. The Iraqi prime minister asked the US government to suspend Blackwater's contracts in Iraq and demanded that the security officers involved be held accountable, and that compensation be paid to the victims' families.

Up until then, foreigners working for private military security companies were guided by the CF's rules of conduct and use of force. The press and various human-rights groups criticised the US government's lack of oversight of private military security companies working in Iraq and Afghanistan, and in general.

Shortly after this incident, the US started implementing tougher accountability laws that meant that PMCs could be charged for unwarranted shootings and other actions, and even end up in jail. In addition, in October 2007 the UN released a report stating that although most PMCs working in Iraq were hired as security officers, they ended up performing paramilitary duties and could therefore be classed as mercenaries.

The report found that the use of contractors such as Blackwater was 'a new form of mercenary activity' and illegal under international law. However, the US is not a signatory to the 1989 UN Mercenary Convention banning the use of mercenaries. Nor is it a signatory to the 1977 additional protocol to the 1949 Geneva Conventions, of which Article 47 specifies that mercenaries are civilians who 'take a direct part in the hostilities' and are motivated to take part in the hostilities 'essentially by the desire for private gain'.[2]

After this incident the Iraqi people grew even more hostile towards foreign PMCs, and the media were at times also very critical of the industry.

In addition, the Iraqi government and its interior ministry started to very heavily regulate security companies. It is understandable that they needed some kind of regulation for PMCs working in their country and to make them accountable. Now all private military security companies had to submit mountains of paperwork when they renewed their security licences each year and the Ministry of Interior made it difficult to obtain new licences. In this context, more Iraqi security companies sprang up. Mostly government officials, ex-generals and wealthy individuals well connected to the Iraqi government owned these licenses.

In December 2008, five PMCs were taken to court by the US government on 14 charges, including murder, over the incident at Nisour Square. A US magistrate judge dismissed the charges saying that the testimony against the PMCs was 'improperly' built in exchange for immunity. Then, in April 2011, after severe criticism by the Iraqi prime minister and other political figures, charges were reinstated by a US federal appeals court against four of the PMCs.

In January 2012 Blackwater settled a lawsuit filed on behalf of six of the family members of the victims for an undisclosed sum. On 22 October 2014, a federal district court jury convicted one of the PMCs of first-degree murder, and three other guards were found guilty of voluntary manslaughter and using a machine gun to commit a violent crime. The PMC who was convicted of murder was given a life sentence, while the other three guards were sentenced to 30 years in prison.[3]

After I left Iraq, I tried to set up a new business venture with Chris in Mozambique. We registered a new construction company and a security risk-management consultancy for the planned golf estate in

Mozambique. During this period we also worked as personal security officers in Mozambique and South Africa.

We launched the property sales for the golf estate in August 2008, shortly before the world financial markets crashed towards the end of that year. Our line of credit was stopped by an international bank that almost went under, and this hampered our progress. We poured private funding into the project but it was not enough. Eventually the project floundered.

Chris and I then got involved with VIP protection for the 2010 Fifa World Cup in South Africa, but after that we went our separate ways. I did short-term protective and consulting work in the Democratic Republic of Congo and Nigeria, and I also assisted with extractions of contractors from Libya and Tunisia after the Arab Spring uprising, which began at the start of 2011.

Even though I was busy exploring other opportunities, I was in regular contact with my old team members and various other contacts in the Sandbox. I often thought of my time in Iraq and stayed abreast of political developments there and what was happening on the PMC scene. For instance, in January 2008 the Iraqi security forces took over the security of the Green Zone. This was a significant and symbolic event marking the handover of power from the US military to the Iraqi government. The Iraqi security forces used the opportunity to vent years of frustration with private security companies and made it really difficult for them and other private-security-related vehicles and personnel to enter, and sometimes even exit, the International Zone (the name the Green Zone gradually acquired from around this point).

From the end of 2007, and during 2008, the US military and CF started gaining the upper hand in the fight against the insurgents and terrorists. President George W Bush's troop surge and the strategy of cooperation between the US military and the Sunni tribes in Anbar Province were paying off. There were still frequent attacks across the country, but their incidence was much lower than in the preceding three years during the height of the civil war in Iraq.[4]

A broken-down vehicle and a close shave

Although the situation had become slightly less dangerous in Iraq, there were a number of hair-raising incidents among the PMC community. One of them involved Martin Smith, an old friend and former South African SF colleague. Sometime during 2008, Martin and his team ran into trouble south of Baghdad. I've included his story here because it's a good example of how PMCs, and specifically South Africans, often managed to survive serious scraps quite miraculously.

Martin and a number of other ex-Recces were working for security joint venture OSSI-Safenet, operating out of Saddam Hussein's old palace in the Green Zone. One day Martin and his quick-reaction force were called to go and help a team who were experiencing vehicle problems on the main supply route that runs from the Kuwaiti border in the south to the Turkish border in the north.

Martin's team were in two GMC Suburban vehicles and a minibus, all low-profile (i.e. unmarked vehicles similar to those used by the local civilians). He and a team member nicknamed Bloubul (Blue Bull) were travelling in the minibus. The first GMC was manned by Adriaan (Eier) Myburgh and Sammy Moll, who was the medic. In the second Suburban were Iraqi guards and a South African mechanic.

The team lost comms with their HQ when they approached the broken-down vehicle approximately 70 kilometres from Baghdad. Even the satellite phones were not working. The vehicle was under a flyover bridge. When the convoy arrived, the second Suburban was instructed to pull in front of the broken-down vehicle and hook it up with tow straps, so the mechanic could try to identify the problem.

The first Suburban, with Adriaan and Sammy, was sent across the road facing the oncoming traffic to give cover to the team's rear. Martin's team in the minibus stopped around 50 metres behind the broken-down vehicle to give the team cover to the front.

The mechanic did a few checks and decided it must be poor-quality fuel that was to blame. He was in the process of cleaning out the fuel supply system when an ambush was sprung on them. A group of insurgents had obviously noticed the broken-down vehicle and knew that a recovery team would be sent out. They had enough time to plan an ambush and position themselves for an attack.

The ambush was initiated by a drive-by shooting on Adriaan and Sammy's Suburban. The vehicle was shot up pretty badly by the assailants but the occupants were miraculously not wounded.

The main attack was then sprung from some palm trees to the right of Martin and Bloubul's minibus. The mechanic and the Iraqis working on the vehicle were pinned down behind the vehicle. In the minibus Bloubul was desperately trying to cock their PKM machine gun but it jammed. Martin jumped out, ran to the side of the vehicle, opened the door and grabbed the PKM. He jumped on the cocking lever with his boot and managed to clear the jam.[5] He gave the PKM to Bloubul, who then let loose on the attackers.

In the meantime, Sammy and Adriaan had followed the classic drill used by private security details and managed to drive their vehicle out of the killing zone. They had only gone a short distance when they took a fresh round of incoming fire as they headed towards the rest of the team looking for some cover. Unbeknown to them, they were actually moving into the main killing zone.

Approaching the broken-down vehicle, Martin could not see or ascertain what exactly was going on and instructed the mechanic and his team to get the tow straps hooked onto the vehicle so they could try to get away. The team took heavy fire while they were placing the tow straps on the vehicles, but eventually they were done, and the mechanic and a team of Iraqis were ready to head off towards Baghdad.

Martin tried to establish comms with the second Suburban manned by the Iraqi guards, as they could not see where it had disappeared to after the initial contact. They were unsuccessful and their cellphones had no signal, so they couldn't make contact with their operations room in Baghdad either. They drove off and about a kilometre from the ambush site they managed to make contact with the second Suburban via radio and learnt that it had been shot to pieces and was immobilised. The main team did not know exactly where their pinned-down colleagues were, as they could not see them.

Martin told the mechanic to tow the broken-down vehicle to Baghdad, while he and his crew would go back to look for their colleagues. After the team in the minibus had gone some 300 metres towards the area where they had last seen their colleagues, they spotted the Suburban while taking a fresh round of incoming fire. Bloubul managed to lay good fire on the ambushers with the PKM. Martin learnt on the radio that the stricken Suburban's wheels were shot out but that Adriaan and Sammy were not wounded.

In all this confusion, another vehicle pulled up in the road about 40 metres in front of the minibus. The car had two passengers but it was unclear what their intentions were. Martin waved at them, motioning to get out of the way, but to no avail. Then, all of a sudden, one of them got out and started walking towards the minibus. Was he a suicide bomber? The question flashed through Martin's mind.

When the Iraqi was around 10 metres from the minibus Martin fired a warning shot over his head but he did not bat an eyelid and kept walking towards the team. When he was around 3 metres from the minibus, a warning shot was fired into the road in front of the Iraqi (a civilian, it turned out) and then he finally got the message, promptly turned around and walked back to their car.

Martin then told Adriaan to put the Suburban into four-wheel drive mode to try and drive it towards the team in the minibus. The vehicle managed to get going by driving on the rims, which were crumbling on the asphalt road. They managed to get to the minibus where they quickly cross-loaded their weapons and remaining ammunition and boarded the minibus. While this was going on, Martin grabbed the PKM and halted the Iraqi civilian's vehicle, which approached them.

By now it seemed as though the ambushers had left the area and the team were not taking incoming fire any longer. After the cross-load, the team set fire to the shot-out Suburban, which was common practice to deny the enemy the use of a vehicle after an ambush. The minibus took off towards Baghdad, and when they had cellphone reception they called the mechanic and his team, who reported that they were almost in Baghdad. The team also reported the incident to their HQ.

Around 2 kilometres from the ambush site, the minibus took more fire, this time from men in a BMW to their right. Adriaan shot at the attackers with the PKM and, after a short exchange of fire, the attackers were neutralised and fell silent.[6]

It was a miracle that nobody died or was wounded during these incidents. Sadly, not all PMCs were that lucky, though. Many never made it home or left the Sandbox badly wounded.[7]

By 2009 the security situation in Iraq was much more stable than in the preceding years. There were still bombings and killings, but the graph below, showing the number of deaths in the period 2003–2011 shows how much the situation had improved between 2007 and the end of 2011, when US military forces left the country.

In June 2009, the US military completed their withdrawal from Iraqi cities and ceded control to the Iraqi security forces. At the end of that month, Prime Minister Maliki declared 30 June 'sovereign day' and turned it into a public holiday.

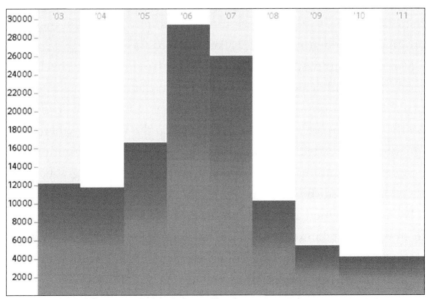

This graph, based on US military figures, clearly illustrates the spike in violence-related deaths in Iraq during 2006 and 2007.

Late in October two massive suicide bombings in Baghdad killed 155 people and wounded over 700 in the deadliest attacks in the country in almost two years. Islamic State in Iraq (ISI), the successor to AQI, claimed responsibility for the bombings. Yet 2009 was the first year since 2004 that no South African contractors had been killed in Iraq.

In December that year and in the weeks running up to the elections in early 2010, ISI were behind many bombings, resulting in more than 100 deaths, with over 400 wounded. Observers were of the opinion that the terror group wanted to destabilise the elections and create fear among the population in an attempt to stop them from voting.

In 2010, I was travelling between Mozambique and South Africa, working on planning the personal security operations for VIPs who would be visiting South Africa for the Fifa World Cup that year. In January, my old team and the company I'd helped form, Skywave Services, got raided and seriously harassed at the Dreamland Hotel. Once again, rogue forces within the Ministry of Interior were responsible. After I left Iraq, there were times when they were under surveillance by elements within the local security forces, who were seething about the drubbing they had got when they raided the hotel where the security team was staying.

This time around, they ransacked the hotel and auxiliary buildings, vehicles and even the dog kennels. They confiscated all weapons and security equipment, and helped themselves to some good expensive electronics too. They even broke down walls with sledgehammers to gain access to rooms that were locked. This time the US military were not around to assist us and the raiders rocked up in larger numbers than they had during the 2006 raid.

Fortunately, our client, Sheik FK, and the then country security manager, Jakes, were out of the country, because the raiders were looking for the owners and manager of Skywave Services. Jakes left André Swanepoel in charge with another five South African security contractors, some Georgians and a large number of Iraqi staff. The members of the interior ministry confiscated the expats' passports without giving any explanation, which created a big problem. The team got outside assistance and eventually their passports were returned to them, but these were tense times.

The raiders managed to succeed in partially shutting down the Skywave Services operations, and forced many changes and disruptions. Their vengeance was served icy cold and with no flavour.

From 2012 onwards, the Maliki government alienated the Sunnis in Iraq even more through exclusion in Parliament and by going after prominent Sunni leaders, businessmen and role players. They were obsessed with dishing out revenge for the Saddam years. In so doing, they unleashed a monstrous new set of problems that created a fertile environment for terror. When militant Sunni terror groups began recruiting young and hate-filled Sunni Muslims from western and northern Iraq a few years later it would be the start of ISIS.

In an attack reminiscent of the 2005 Al Hamra attack, on 25 January 2010 terrorists targeted three hotels around Baghdad that were frequented by foreigners and contractors. At 15:28 the first bomb struck the Sheraton in downtown Baghdad, a hotel that is located close to the notorious Palestine Hotel. Three minutes later, the second bomb detonated at the Babylon Hotel in the upmarket Jadriya neighbourhood. The third bomb exploded six minutes later at the Al Hamra Hotel, which was round the corner from my old location at the Dreamland Hotel, and where Jakes and the Skywave Services security team still resided and worked from.

These were massive bombs, but only 36 people were killed and another 70-odd injured. The death toll would have been exponentially higher if the bomb targeting the Al Hamra had made it into hotel building itself. It detonated outside at the security checkpoint in front of the entrance to the hotel. The Dreamland was shaken hard and window panes, doors and access gates were blown out.

By this time Grobbies had left the Skywave Services team and joined another international private military security company. He was in the Al Hamra during this attack. He was standing on a balcony when he saw the fireball, and then the blast waves hit him. Grobbies was thrown back through the open sliding door into the room, and was floored by the destructive power of the explosion. Luckily, he was not injured.

In January 2010, during a routine trip from the Dreamland to the International Zone, one of our South African expats, Ferdie Heynemann, ran into some trouble. At a checkpoint, a beady-eyed officer detected that there was one digit on the documents they were carrying that did not correlate with the engraved vehicle identification number. Over the years we'd learnt to check every single document each time the Iraqi government or interior ministry issued new ones, as they often made mistakes that cost the operators on the ground serious problems at checkpoints.

Ferdie, as the custodian of the vehicle, and the only expat in it, was taken into custody on suspicion of vehicle theft. He was sent to the cells at the notorious 56th Brigade's counter-terrorism unit in the International Zone.

Jakes and the team sent some of the senior Iraqi personnel to go and reason with the officers of the 56th Brigade, but initially this was to no avail. He then contacted another former SF officer and friend, Josiah (JoJo) Bruyns, who at the time was the chief of security for Motorola Services. JoJo had an Iraqi contact with enough clout to get him access to the jail, so he could deliver some food to Ferdie. (The jailers were known to not provide food to inmates.) Meanwhile, the team back at the Dreamland tried all their contacts to see if they could help.

It was a seriously problematic situation for a number of reasons, least of all because Ferdie was due to fly out on leave to get married. About a week before his wedding, he was still locked up in an Iraqi jail, his family blissfully unaware of his precarious position. (In jail Ferdie happened to meet the British guy who in 2009 shot and killed two other British contractors and wounded an Iraqi guard in a drunken brawl.)

Then somebody, somehow persuaded the authorities to let the South African go if they retained his passport. Finally, Ferdie was released and taken back to the Dreamland. But, without a passport, how was he going to make it to his wedding?

South Africa does not have an embassy or consulate in Iraq. The closest diplomatic support was in Amman, Jordan. Jakes then used some contacts and convinced somebody at the British embassy to issue a temporary passport and travel document for Ferdie to get to Jordan, where the South African embassy could assist him. I do not know whether it's because South Africa is a member of the Commonwealth, but the British embassy in Iraq has always been incredibly helpful towards South Africans in the Sandbox.

Ferdie managed to make it back to South Africa, if slightly skinnier, the day before his wedding. He decided that since he was now a married man he had new responsibilities and would not return to the Sandbox.

The graph above shows that 2010 and 2011 saw the lowest number of violence-related civilian deaths in Iraq since the 2003 war. Nevertheless, there were still about 4000 deaths attributed to violence and terrorism during these years, which at the time was one of the highest rates globally until the Arab Spring uprisings.

Another highlight of 2010 was that one of Saddam Hussein's right-hand men, Ali Hassan al-Majid, known as 'Chemical Ali' (Saddam's Minister of Interior and Intelligence Chief), was hanged for his role in the deaths of thousands of Iranians and Kurds in attacks where the Iraqi Army used chemical weapons. He was also held responsible for the execution of a number of Shia and Kurdish opposition group members who rebelled against the brutal Saddam regime.

The Iraqi elections were held in March 2010, but there was a much lower voter turnout than in the 2005 elections. The US-aligned Ayad Allawi surprisingly beat the incumbent prime minister, Maliki, but he did not secure enough votes to win an outright majority in Parliament. In May, Allawi negotiated with Maliki to form a coalition government, but by August these talks failed, leaving Iraq without a formal government.

Some senior parliamentarians, notably Sunni leaders, warned the Obama administration that Iraq was not ready to take over all security roles after the planned 2011 withdrawal of US troops. A senior Iraqi Army general warned that the Iraqi Army would not be ready to safeguard Iraq for another decade. Many believed Maliki had hoodwinked Obama about the readiness of the Iraqi security forces to keep the country safe from insurgent and terror groups.

In August 2010 Obama had announced that Operation Iraqi Freedom, which had started in March 2003, would come to an end and that the systematic withdrawal of US troops would begin. The date for the final withdrawal of US troops from Iraq was then set for December 2011.

In late December, ISI detonated nine car bombs and six roadside bombs, killing close to 70 people and wounding over 200. The bombs targeted Shiite markets, restaurants and public spaces in an attempt to fuel the sectarian hatred between Shias and Sunnis. These kinds of attacks served as a stark reminder that the Sunni insurgency was not entirely suppressed and that they could still strike fear into and terrorise the population at large. ISI also systematically stepped up attacks against Christians and Yazidis (a religious minority group), particularly in the north and west of the country.

By 2011 violence levels in Iraq were at an all-time low since the start of the war. Although a number of terrorist attacks were staged, there were fewer than during the previous eight years. There were also fewer attacks targeted at PMCs. The last serious attack on PMCs happened in June 2011. This incident involved a massive roadside IED or EFP attack on a security convoy in central Baghdad, close to the infamous 'Assassin's Gate', or Checkpoint 1, outside the International Zone. Two South Africans were seriously wounded and the armoured vehicles they were travelling in were destroyed.

The most important development of 2011 was the final withdrawal of the US military in December. However, before that happened one other noteworthy event occurred, which points to how regional politics, or rather religious loyalties across country borders, still influenced an already complex situation in Iraq.

In the 1980s, a facility called Camp Ashraf was created for Iranian dissident exiles in Iraq who were opposed to the Ayatollah Khomeini's rule since 1979. The camp was about 60 kilometres north of Baghdad and had a population of around 3 500. Over time, the camp started to resemble a small town and even had its own infrastructure. Camp Ashraf was attacked on more than one occasion by Iranian Air Force bombers in the early 1990s after the Iranian regime accused the camp's residents of being behind attacks on oil pipelines and infrastructure in Iran.

After the 2003 war, the US coalition government took the responsibility of protecting the camp. When the US forces handed over power to the Iraqi government in 2009, it asked them to pledge to continue protecting the exiled dissidents. While the Iraqi government seemingly agreed to do so, it obviously had an issue with the Iranian exiles, as the Shia politicians in Baghdad were closely aligned with the Iranian regime. In July that year, Iraqi forces raided the camp and attacked the dissidents in a move that was widely condemned. Nine people died and 400 were injured. It was a blatant turnaround on the Iraq government's deal with the US to protect the dissidents.

Then, in April 2011, the Iraqi Army raided the camp again, and on this occasion 34 people were killed and around 320 injured. The UN got involved and arranged for the exiled leaders to meet with Iraqi parliamentarians. The exiles expressed their need to be registered as asylum seekers with the UN and to be relocated to other countries. The Iraqis then presented a plan to move them from Camp Ashraf to a transitional facility closer to Baghdad. The camp leaders expressed serious concern for their safety should such a move go ahead. The UN negotiated with the Iraqi government to grant them refugee status, but Maliki rejected this request and ordered Camp Ashraf to be closed down.

In late 2011, a delegation from the European Parliament was sent to visit Camp Ashraf to ascertain how the European Union could help the exiles. One way was to register them as refugees with the UN Refugee Agency, which would give them the status of asylum seekers, and they could then be taken in by countries sympathetic to their cause. However, the Iraqi government refused permission for the delegation to visit the camp, and not enough momentum was created to get the UN to support this motion.

Towards the end of the year, there was a change in the UN leadership in Iraq and the new representative for the organisation was convinced by the Maliki regime that the Iranian exiles were 'terrorists'. The exiles were then moved to Camp Liberty, adjacent to Baghdad International Airport. Camp Liberty formed part of the US and CF larger Victory Base complex in Baghdad, which borders the airport area. This was used by the US military and CF as a forward operations base and logistical centre after the 2003 war.

Most of the exiles were relocated to Camp Liberty during 2012. The conditions at Camp Liberty were described by observers as akin to a detention centre, unlike the functioning community that the exiles had created at Camp Ashraf. Some of the exiles stayed behind in Camp Ashraf, though. The following year, in September 2013, men wearing Iraqi security-force uniforms raided Camp Ashraf and killed 52 residents. Maliki ordered an investigation into the raid but concluded that no members of the security forces had been involved. This is possibly true because Shia militias in Iraq often wear military-style uniforms and fatigues. They could have been responsible for the raid, with the backing of their puppet masters in Iran. Obama and other US senators campaigned for seven Camp Ashraf residents who had been taken hostage during the raid to be released.

From early in 2015, one of the most powerful militias, the Badr Brigade, started operating out of the then empty Camp Ashraf in their fight against ISIS. The previous year the latter had started invading the northern and western parts of the country. In late 2015 Camp Liberty was attacked by a barrage of rockets (see Chapter 16).

After the 2003 war, at the height of the fight against the insurgents, the US had around 170000 to 180000 troops in Iraq. From 2008 onwards, they slowly started demobilising their troops as the Awakening Movement and US military surge of 2007, when the largest number of US troops were sent to Iraq, started taking effect in eradicating AQI, ISI and other militant insurgent groups. Maliki also applied pressure on the US to withdraw its troops.

When Barack Obama became president in 2008, he followed through on his campaign promises to get the US troops out of Iraq as soon as possible. It was agreed that the last US troops would withdraw no later than December 2011. By 18 December, the last US troops had left the Sandbox and full control of the country was handed over to the Iraqis.

Many observers believe the withdrawal was too hastily expedited and that it opened the door to the rise of militant Sunni insurgent and terror cells, while also giving rise to the powerful Shia militias, who had the backing of the Iraqi government and the Iranian regime.

More Sandbox photos

The sun sets over Baghdad, with the Babylon Hotel on the right.

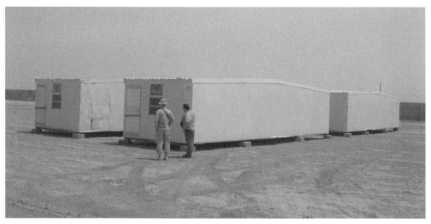

Our 'cattle truck' hooches at the Musayyib Power Plant.

A 107 mm rocket shell turned into a vase, Al Kasik military base.

Daytime temperature in Iraq – a searing 58,4 °C.

Staff Sergeant 'Coop' was part of the team on one of the midnight convoys to east Ramadi, November 2006.

Former SF operator Raymond Archer and me at Saddam Hussein's old parade ground in Baghdad in 2007.

The initial EWAC security team in January 2006.

The EWAC security team at the Dreamland Hotel in Baghdad in June 2007.

US soldiers hold communion prayers.

A reunion with old friends in 2012: Grobbies Grobbelaar (left rear), me (right rear), Dick Venter and Naseer.

Making new Iraqi friends (bird hunters) in the Gharraf Oilfield area, 2015.

The Ali Baba monument in downtown Baghdad.

12

The 'new' Iraq

Early in 2012, while I was based in South Africa, I was contacted by my old colleague and friend Grobbies, who wanted to know whether I would be interested in a short-term opportunity back in Iraq. I was very interested. I had roamed Africa for five years after our construction effort in Mozambique did not come to fruition. I had worked short stints in Mozambique, Nigeria, the DRC and Zambia, and assisted in hot extractions[1] in East and North Africa. But none of these gigs were long term, and I was ready to go back to the Sandbox now, as that wretched place had in fact been quite good to me. Even though I had decided to leave, I always felt I still had a lot to offer and to do there.

Besides, during those five years in Africa I almost kicked the bucket several times. In May 2008, I was involved in a scuba-diving accident in Mozambique, in which I almost drowned. (I'd swallowed so much water that I blacked out and had no pulse for close to a minute, after which I was revived on the boat.) During this incident my already bad left shoulder dislocated again and the arm was rendered useless.

I had reconstructive surgery on the shoulder but it took two years of serious rehabilitation to get the left arm to function again. Later that year, I was involved in a car accident on the highway between Mozambique and South Africa, and my car almost landed up under the trailer of a 40-tonne truck.

Then, in August 2009, I contracted swine flu (H1N1) in a period when over 20 people died of the disease in South Africa. I bled from both lungs and had to be in intensive care for eight days. To top it all, I fell off a ladder that failed and broke a couple of ribs, and almost my neck, too.

So, when I announced to my family and friends that I was heading back to Iraq, they were to a large extent relieved, as they agreed that I might actually be better off and safer there.

Overall, I was in better shape too. Fortunately, by 2012 my shoulder had recovered and, since my workload was less, my feet and back didn't hurt as much, so I was able to cope with less painkiller medication.

Sandbox, version 2

So, in early May 2012, I was off to Baghdad where I had been hired to stand in as security manager at the Baghdad International Airport Hotel. I was pleased to learn that, by then, a number of commercial airlines were flying into the city. When the Emirates Boeing started descending, I took up a spot at a window to have a look at the city I had left five years before.

I could see nothing new, except for some greenery on Route Irish. Even the airport still looked exactly the same from the outside. And when I stepped out of the plane, I registered something else that was familiar – the smell! Baghdad still smelt like an open sewage plant. Some things never change …

Grobbies and a team of Iraqis met me at the airport and took me to his employer's villa in Jadriya, which was close to the Babylon Hotel. One of the first things I noticed, other than the lush green grass that had been planted along Route Irish, was the absence of US and other Western soldiers. There were also very few checkpoints in the city now.

There was a bustle in the air and many Iraqis were out in their vehicles and walking on the side of the road. I also noticed that the drivers did not swerve to avoid papers and debris lying on the road, as we used to in the old days, when any such item could conceal the trigger mechanism of a roadside IED. I could tell instantly that things seemed safer and more relaxed in the 'new' Iraq. It made me think about the role the US and CF had played in creating a safer environment for the Iraqi people.

When we entered the city and drove into Jadriya, I also noticed many street cafes selling food and drinks, and several supermarkets.

This pleasantly surprised me because such commercial enterprises were few and far between in the old days. It used to be far too dangerous to hang out on the streets. Now just about any Western brand of toiletries, food, sweets and other items could be found in supermarkets and stores. Pharmacies were also aplenty and stocked some quality medicines from Switzerland, the US and the UK (alongside other cheap and fake brands originating in the East).

Gone were the days when a foreign contractor had to fly into the Sandbox with a large suitcase full of essential items that could not be found in Baghdad, or in the US military's PX stores. Instead, travel bags could now be filled with nice stuff, such as home-made biltong, South African spices and other things that you crave – and this made a 90-day rotation more bearable. There was even the odd ATM inside banks and at the airport where you could draw cash if you had Visa or MasterCard.

Life in the Sandbox had changed for the better, at least from an international contractor and wealthy Iraqi's point of view.

New start-ups

The US company that Grobbies now worked for, and that had contracted me, was in partnership with a local Iraqi, as most foreign companies were now compelled to have a local partner. I shall refer to this outfit as Night Security. It started operating in 2011 and was on an expansion drive. They had landed the security contract for the airport hotel, which is where I would stand in for a month while the site security manager was on leave.

I was first introduced to the Iraqis, then Grobbies and Neil Reynolds (an old colleague and friend, and now the country security manager for Night Security) gave me an orientation tour of the villa where they stayed, and which also served as the company offices. After the tour and meeting the personnel, I was accompanied to the Baghdad International Airport Hotel, where I underwent another orientation and settled in. Everything seemed pretty straightforward. The hotel is situated within the greater Baghdad airport zone. The International

Zone and the airport zone were considered the two safest areas in Baghdad.

The hotel complex consisted of a series of ground-level prefabricated buildings around a kilometre from the airport terminal buildings. There was a small security office near the foyer, from where the security manager coordinated the hotel security and protection operations. There was only one entrance to the hotel complex, where we had a couple of guards to perform entry control measures. The contract also involved supplying guards to man the entrance to the Iraqi Airways building, which was close to the hotel. This was the easiest and safest job I'd ever had in the Sandbox.

An Iraqi supervisor and me at the Baghdad International Airport Hotel in 2012.

Revisiting Iraq, I was amazed by how many new security companies had sprung up since I'd left five years previously. Most of these were owned by influential and rich Iraqis, who were close to government, and in particular to the prime minister's office, the Ministry of Interior and the Ministry of Defence – all state institutions that were involved in granting security operating licences.

Many of the foreign security companies from before were now nowhere to be seen. I was told that foreign companies that were still around from the early days could still get their operating licences but the Iraqi government was systematically making it more difficult for them. The government wanted most security contracts to be awarded to Iraqis. This may have been good for upliftment and job creation, but it presented a few challenges.

Firstly, in my opinion, the sense of discipline among younger Iraqis was not as strong as the job required. Secondly, most Iraqi companies employed personnel along family and sectarian lines, much in the way the government and military were run. This caused many problems, which I'll describe in more detail later. Thirdly, Iraqis are influenced more by changes in the local environment. For instance, if there are road closures due to military operations or enemy actions, then locals cannot get to work, whereas foreign PMCs stay on site 24/7 for the duration of their tour. Iraqis can also be easily blackmailed by terrorists or militias, as their families are in the firing line.

I believe the ideal team is made up of a combination of experienced, foreign PMCs and Iraqis, as both elements are needed if a security team is to be strong, fulfil all functions and overcome challenges. However, it became clear to me that the Iraqis in power just didn't want foreign PMCs around any more.

Getting back into the game

Once again, I decided to acclimatise myself to the heat by jogging (still with badly aching feet) a couple of times a week over my lunch break. Temperatures were already in the 40 °C range and I built up a proper sweat running along the roads in front of the hotel.

One day after a run, I was approached by some of the guards, who wanted to know how old I was.

'I'm going on 45,' I told them.

They shook their heads and told me I was crazy. I was then told that, in Iraq, a man is considered old when he reaches the age of 30, and 'very old' if he makes it to 40. I had suspected this for a long time because Iraqi men are not known for their propensity to exercise, and they chain-smoke from a very early age. Life expectancy for Iraqi men is lower than the world average, and my guess is that after 2003 it might have fallen even lower owing to the exodus of qualified medical personnel, the decline in hospital standards and the overall danger of living in a war-torn country.

Some of the young Iraqi guards simply couldn't understand why someone as 'old' as me would risk their health further by running around in the heat of the day.

During the month I was there, I went to Baghdad on two occasions to look up old contacts and friends. I arranged to be escorted into the new US embassy in the International Zone to visit an old EWAC contact, and was amazed by the size and modern set-up of the embassy compound. The compound covers 42 hectares, which is almost the same size as the Vatican City, and approximately 15 000 people work at the embassy. It is the most modern and expensive embassy in the world and also one of the most endangered embassies globally, hence no expense was spared to ensure maximum security measures (figures of between $800 million and $1 billion were rumoured in Baghdad circles). I was impressed.

I had a chance to visit the PX store, which, much to my disappointment, had changed a lot. Now it stocked very limited supplies of tactical gear, no knives and little in the way of electronics. The shop now mainly catered for essential items, such as clothing, food and beverages. There were quite a few hadji shops[2] in the compound selling the usual memorabilia and junk. I bought a couple of items, and later had a meal in the dining facility – at least nothing had changed there: the food was still outstanding.

On my second trip into Baghdad, I hooked up with my old friend Jakes Jacobs, who had just started working for one of the largest US specialised security firms around.

An old Iraqi friend called Naseer also came to the hotel to see me.

We reminisced about the good old days and he reminded me how he used to pray for me each time I took off for east Ramadi. He had been in charge of logistics at the time, and we worked closely together to get the first convoys to the site area. Naseer tapped ceremoniously on his knees to show how often he prayed for our safety. I suspect it might have been more a matter of him praying that all the goods reached their destination rather than having to explain to Sheik FK, the CEO of EWAC Iraq, why the convoys had not made it to east Ramadi …

My month-long stint with Night Security flew by. Once I arrived back in South Africa, in June, I started sending out my CV to contacts in Iraq. Night Security then informed me that they had a spot open for a personal security detail team leader for missions around Baghdad. I accepted the position and flew back to the Sandbox in August. This time I was based at the Night Security villa in Jadriya, where I stayed with, among others, Grobbies and Neil Reynolds.

Between August and December our main task was to conduct personal security detail runs from the airport to the city, and to take various clients from the International Zone to government departments in the city, notably the Ministry of Oil, because the country's oil industry was picking up with great speed.

On these trips we had to wear suits and ties, which was a first for me in Iraq. The last time I'd had to work in a suit was when I worked in the protection unit for the president of Haiti. One of our main clients was a major Russian oil company whose VIP personnel we would meet at the airport and escort to the oil company's villa and HQ in the International Zone, and from there to meetings at the Ministry of Oil.

Black gold

The Ministry of Oil is the biggest, and probably one of the busiest and most important, government agencies in Baghdad. More than 95 per cent of the county's revenue is derived from the oil and gas sectors.[3] The ministry is located in central downtown Baghdad in an immense labyrinth of buildings, including a ten-storey high-rise, where apparently 5 000 people work.

On our trips to the ministry, the oil firm's in-house country security manager would always travel with our teams to ensure our clients' safety. The going was slow, as we always encountered heavy traffic in this busy part of town, which had many checkpoints, blocked-off streets and one-ways. Previously, this was a part of town where many serious roadside IED bombings and other attacks were carried out. Fortunately, more than a year had elapsed since July 2011, when the last contractor had been killed or wounded in an armed attack in Iraq.

The impressive Ministry of Oil building in Baghdad.

Our trips with the managers from the Russian oil company would usually involve a slow drive in two or three B6 armoured Land Cruiser SUVs from the International Zone to the oil ministry. Our Iraqi drivers would drop us off at the main building and then I would escort the client and their country security manager into the building. Once we reached the office or meeting room, we would conduct a security inspection before positioning ourselves outside the door until the meeting was concluded.

I used to wear with my suit a pair of black, almost knee-high, leather

CAT boots. When you stand up, it looks like you are wearing black shoes, but when you sit down you can see that they are boots. Once, while I was waiting outside a meeting room, Ahmed K, one of the country security managers, spotted that I was wearing 'biker boots' with my suit. This amused him incredibly. So I showed him how these boots could comfortably accommodate a decent boot knife, and a small cellphone for emergencies, such as when you lost comms in an ambush, or perhaps had to hand in your official cellphone when entering a government building, or if you were arrested. He smiled and shook his head, but agreed that boots could indeed hold quite a lot of contraband.

We also conducted a number of long-haul private security detail runs from Baghdad to the Badra Oilfield, which is east of Baghdad on the border with Iran. We would drop expat oil engineers at the drill rigs where they worked for various companies. The trip took anywhere between three and five hours, depending on the traffic in southern Baghdad, which is bad at the best of times, and the hold-ups at the checkpoints.

However, I enjoyed these trips, as they got us out of the city. The Badra Oilfield, an area of roughly 165 km^2, lies on the Iranian Zagros mountain range and consists of sandy hills and rock formations. It is one of the areas in the Middle East with the most landmines. During the war between Iraq and Iran from 1980 to 1988, Saddam's forces purportedly laid millions of mines in this area to prevent the Iranians from crossing the mountains into Iraq.

Iranian forces also laid mines when they made it across the border into Iraqi territory. A 2008 report by the Iraqi government to the UN suggests there are at least 20 million anti-tank and anti-personnel landmines mainly in border areas and around the southern oilfields.

However, because the survey was conducted in only 13 out of 18 Iraqi provinces, and the fact that the figure of 20 million mines is based only on what the Iraqi Army placed, it seems likely that there are actually far more unexploded mines in Iraq than this. There were four active oil drill platforms as of the end of 2012, and the field was earmarked to expand fast, as it holds a vast reserve of oil deposits.

A drilling rig in the Badra Oilfield.

A warning best heeded in the Badra Oilfield.

During this time Night Security appointed a new country manager, an American, Ted McAuslin. We also moved premises to a new and larger building, also in Jadriya. Two more expats joined the team during this period, Diederik (Dick) Venter, an ex-Taakie,[4] and another South African, Stephen Swanepoel, a medic who had gained personal security detail experience in Afghanistan. In August we were tasked to assist with the demobilisation of one of the last US military forward operating bases, which was in central Baghdad.

Generally, things proceeded smoothly until one day in November, when Stephen had to go to the International Zone on a mission for the oil company. At the checkpoint one of the officers spotted an Afghan stamp in his passport. Stephen has dark hair and a dark complexion, which made the officers suspicious of his identity. The Iraqi forces viewed any links with Afghanistan and the Taliban as a threat. They took Stephen into custody and he was put into cells controlled by the intelligence officers of the 56th Brigade (where Ferdie Heynemann had been held years before). One of the local team leaders with whom he was travelling was also arrested. The other locals in his team alerted us to the situation. Ted, Grobbies and I had to act quickly.

Firstly, we got hold of our contacts within the government and other influential Iraqis to see if they could assist. Ted also sent an Iraqi lawyer to represent Stephen. The Iraqi intelligence officers came up with all sorts of crazy stories to explain why this South African citizen was treated as a Taliban terrorist.

Stephen was placed in a cell with four suspected al-Qaeda terrorists, one of whom was wounded in the hip and leg when he was apprehended by the Iraqi forces. These were hard-core terrorists and they immediately closed in on Stephen. They intimidated and assaulted him once they realised he couldn't speak Arabic. At one point he had to fight three of them off. They indicated that they wanted to sodomise him.

Later that day our Iraqi team member was released but Stephen was still held, presumably because they wanted to make money out of this foreign prisoner. We arranged for food and water to be sent to Stephen. He was going to spend the night with these terrorists in this cell and he knew that it would be a very long night, as he would have to stay awake to keep an eye on his cellmates.

Nevertheless, as he was a paramedic Stephen tended to the wounded terrorist after he asked for his help. This act of goodwill might well have helped him to survive the night. The next day, he was moved to the police station cells in the International Zone where he was held in a larger cell with around 12 people but who seemed to be more neutral towards him. We kept sending food and water to him, and the lawyer engaged in negotiations with the officials in charge of the jail.

Eventually, after five days, the lawyer managed to get Stephen released; it helped that she presented a good number of 'Washingtons'.[5] Stephen was tired and bruised, but smiling. We were all hugely relieved that this unfortunate incident had a good ending.

Towards the end of 2012, Night Security was awarded a new security contract for the China Petroleum Pipeline company (known in Iraq as CPP), which was due to kick off early the following year. I was appointed as the assistant country manager, and Ted and I started planning the security for this mission. In November I flew home for a rest and recreation break following my first full three-month rotation after returning to the new Iraq.

13

Building villages from scratch

When I arrived back in Baghdad in February 2013, I was deployed to initiate the new CPP project at the Badra Oilfield. The Chinese were going to build a new camp at the entrance to the oilfield from where they would create a network of pipelines leading to the nearest city, Kut, from where more pipelines would be constructed to run south.

When I got to the site, I realised that the camp still had to be erected. The Chinese engineers were staying at a camp nearby until the hooches, generators and construction materials arrived. I stayed with our team in a building resembling a hotel in Kut, about a hundred kilometres from the site.

The road between Badra and Kut was in a terrible state and had witnessed many road accidents. Because of the road, the number of trucks using it and the checkpoint outside Kut, the travel time was long. We had to be at site at 08:00 each morning, and left around 17:00 in the afternoon. This meant that we had to leave Kut by 06:00 in anticipation of delays, and at night we arrived back at around 19:00. It was winter, so we were in the dark on both legs of the trip. I was not pleased. I didn't particularly want to die in a car crash, which can be largely avoided. Fortunately, this only went on for two weeks until the hooches arrived for the use of the security team.

The Chinese had a very different approach to security, I noticed. It was the first time I had seen the client station the security team outside of their own camp. Most clients wanted their protection officers as close as possible to where they stay. Our hooches were outside the front gate of the camp on the main road that runs from the village to the oilfield. We were outside the blast walls and therefore exposed. I addressed this with Ted and the client, but there was a big language barrier. Most of the Chinese could barely speak English. In the end, we had to accept that the plans for their camp were final and that they would not let the security team stay inside the camp.

People tried to reassure me that this was the new Iraq, and that security contractors no longer got shot, that there were no longer bomb attacks or rocket fire. Nevertheless, I was uncomfortable with the situation because I believe one should always plan for the worst. Rather have a gun and not need it, than need a gun and not have it. I got the Chinese to at least erect a berm outside the row of hooches on the side facing the road to provide some security. The height of the berm was around four to five feet – sufficient to give a person cover against shrapnel and small-arms fire, that is, if you survive the initial assault and hit the deck in the rooms quickly.

The CPP camp in Badra under construction.

After a month, a number of the Chinese engineers could move into the site while the rest of the camp was being constructed. I arranged further force-protection measures, such as positioning Jersey barriers at the front gate and installing CCTV and pan/tilt zoom cameras. We also erected a large steel gate at the entrance, and smaller ones at the side and back as alternative escape routes.

Two dining halls were built, one for the Chinese workers and a smaller one for the Iraqis and our security team. The food we were served was truly shocking – it was like food one would expect in a jail in a developing country (and I should know, because I had been – wrongfully – locked up in one in the DRC the year before). They offered me a place in the main mess hall, but I could not accept this, as I couldn't subject my security team to second-class food while I was upgraded.

I thought about the matter and decided to tell the Chinese managers about the UN minimum standard of food served to workers. I don't think there is such a thing, but it didn't matter, as it seemed to have the desired effect. The quality and quantity of the food improved slightly after my intervention.

We started escorting the Chinese engineers and managers to the main camp and we took them on visits into the oilfield. I was called out to the first site area sometime in March because there had been a small explosion under the wheels of a construction machine. It must have been a small anti-personnel mine or a detonator of sorts, and there were no injuries.

Hand-drawn demining map for Badra from 2013.

Although the explosion was not big, the problem was that it happened in an area that had been supposedly cleared by a demining company,

Jasper was a loyal companion on the CPP project in Badra.

and now people were worried that there might be other (bigger) explosive devices that had not been cleared. The area had to be checked again and declared safe, and a few days later the earthworks could proceed.

During this time, a policemen who worked at one of the checkpoints inside the field walked a few paces from his post to urinate when he stepped on an anti-personnel mine. His lower leg was blown off but he survived. This was a stark reminder to all to stay on the roads, paths and safely designated areas, as the oilfield was littered with mines.

Early in the project, I came across some puppies living wild among the sand plains in the camp. I gave them some scraps of food, as they must have been starving. One of the dogs was larger and stronger, a male and obviously the alpha of the pack. We took a liking to each other. I called him Jasper. He slept under my hooch and would follow me around the camp. On one of our trips to Baghdad, I managed to buy immunisation injections. He looked like a German shepherd, but with a thicker coat. I grew very attached to Jasper.

A new opportunity in the south

I had just started on the Badra Oilfield project when Jakes contacted me about a potential position as the security project manager on a site where a port was going to be built in the Persian Gulf in southern Iraq, near Al Faw.[1] The company he worked for was in the process of tendering for it. The compensation was better and, as I had never been involved in a port security project before, I was keen. The new position would be with US company Triple Canopy, or TC, one of the largest and most reputable firms in the business.

In April 2013, TC got the green light to secure the port construction project, and I was recruited. In the first week of May, I spent some time with the team at their hotel in Baghdad, so that I could get up to speed with the company's standard operating procedures, the workings of the operations room, logistics, finances, human resources and other support sections. I enjoyed the new setting, and always liked working with the Americans. I could tell that this was a seriously professional and proud company.

Tuffy Joubert (left) and me at the eastern breakwater pier in Al Faw,
a few months into the project.

I had to put together an eight-man team of expats. It was crucial to select the right men for the job. Fortunately, by 2013 there was a good supply of security personnel with over a decade of experience of working in Iraq and Afghanistan. I got hold of JoJo Bruyns, who had vast experience in the Sandbox, and he joined us as assistant project/ operations manager. I asked André Swanepoel, my colleague from my EWAC days, to be the team leader of the personal security detail. Tuffy Joubert, another former SF officer (from the waterborne 4 Reconnaissance Regiment), accepted the position of maritime commander.

I organised the security equipment that had to be taken to the site – armoured level B6 Suburban vehicles, weapons with mags and ammunition, complete body armour sets, radios, trackers, GPSs, medical bags and other 'contraband'. I got a team of experienced Iraqis who knew the Basra area and could assist me with the recruitment of other Iraqi team members down south. They would also help me to get around Basra and to the site to liaise with the client, Archirodon Overseas Construction (ARCO), and to get the show on the road.

In our military days, the SF operators often forgot about the role played by the support personnel to make our deployment on operations possible. It was calculated that at least seven personnel from the logistical, human resources, finance, maintenance and other divisions were needed behind the scenes to support us. The same is true in private military security companies – without support personnel, a mission cannot be completed successfully. At TC we had excellent support. I received solid backing from the level of the regional security director in the company's American offices (who also happened to be a South African ex-SF man), all the way down to the mechanics and storemen on the ground in Baghdad. I looked forward to this mission, but little did I know of the challenges awaiting me.

ARCO, a large Greek company, had had a presence in Basra and Al Faw, the southernmost town in Iraq, since the end of 2012. I made contact with the ARCO managers, who stayed in a villa in Basra, to introduce myself and to discuss the security processes that had to be arranged. We had a cordial meeting, I reconnoitred the villa, and they arranged for me to visit their place in Al Faw and meet their personnel stationed there.

There was a lot to do. I had to find a villa to set up a branch office in Basra and furnish it before it could be inspected and accredited by the interior ministry. I also had to recruit Iraqis for the security teams in Basra and Al Faw, and I had to start working on the initial standard operating procedures, emergency and evacuation plans, Intel briefs and security induction training for the clients.

I interviewed Iraqis for positions in the personal security detail team and as static guards at the villa. Our current Iraqi team members interpreted because the locals could not speak much English. We went around town to look at buildings and negotiate the rent.

In all of this, it was very important for me to have an understanding of the Iraqi Arab culture. The Iraqis, and Arabs in general, will seldom give you (especially if you are a foreigner) a straight answer when you ask them what something costs, or how much they need to be remunerated for a service, even something as small as the price of a haircut. When you ask what the cost is, you will often get an answer like 'as you wish' or 'as you see fit'. But you have to be careful not to offer an absurdly low price because this might be construed as an insult, which creates a completely new set of problems.

Most costs, including rent, are negotiated in a bartering process. The idea is that you should get the person offering the product or service to lower the price. In the eyes of many older Iraqis, you are weak if you simply agree to their initial price. However, many inexperienced foreigners, especially larger companies with deep pockets, and particularly in the years immediately after the 2003 war, agreed to whatever price the locals offered them. This meant that rent, security and other essential services were hugely overpriced.

Al Faw

The southern tip of Iraq has around 300 kilometres of coastline on the Gulf. The country has two main ports – Basra (a river port) and Umm Qasr, a medium-sized port southeast of Basra and close to the Kuwaiti border. However, there was a need for a large deep-water port with container terminals, an oil pumping capacity and other facilities.

One of the main challenges of constructing a new port on this part of the coastline near Al Faw, which lies about a hundred kilometres south of Basra, was the presence of mud and silt beneath the water. This is because the Tigris and Euphrates converge in a large water body called Shatt al-Arab, causing mud and silt to drain into this part of the Gulf.

The engineers decided that the first phase would entail building a breakwater pier on the eastern (Iranian) side of the port, which would run 8 kilometres into the Gulf. During phase two, the western breakwater pier, running 14 kilometres into the Gulf (on the Kuwait side) would be constructed. ARCO was going to construct the eastern breakwater pier (the contract for the western breakwater had not yet been awarded).

We brought JoJo to Basra at the end of May, which was a great help, as I was incredibly busy. He took care of the daily operations and helped with getting the new personnel's paperwork to Baghdad and issuing them with uniforms, radios, weapons and other security items.

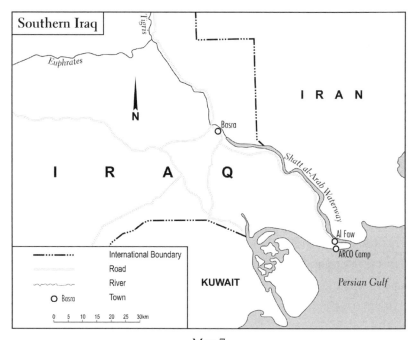

Map 7

We also travelled to the temporary camp that ARCO had constructed at the entrance to the Al Faw port area. We soon found how dangerous the trip from Basra to Al Faw was on the narrow two-lane road, which witnessed many serious vehicle accidents.

The Shatt al-Arab, which lies east of Al Faw, forms the natural southern border between Iraq and Iran. The people inhabiting the area are traditionally fishermen and traders because the town is situated near the borders of four countries – Iraq, Iran, Kuwait and Saudi Arabia. The locals are referred to as Marsh Arabs. For centuries, all kinds of smugglers have been attracted to this area because of its location, coupled with the fact that it is sparsely populated and there is no coast guard. In centuries gone by, the area was considered a key opium route to distribute drugs from Central Asia, notably Afghanistan, to the Persian Gulf countries.

Al Faw has been the site of many battles over the past few decades. In 1986, during the Iran–Iraq War (1980–1988), the Iranian Revolutionary Guard overwhelmed the Iraqi Defence Force in Al Faw and occupied the peninsula for a while. The Iranians also used the area to launch missile attacks against both Iraq and Kuwait. During the war the mainly Sunni Kuwait supported Saddam in his fight against Iran.

In April 1988, Saddam attacked the Al Faw Peninsula with sarin chemical weapons and deployed an Iraqi force of around 100 000 in retaliation for the occupation. Within 48 hours Iraq had taken back the area and captured a vast amount of equipment from the Iranians.

During the 1991 Gulf War, the area was heavily bombed by the US and British forces to shut down the Iraqi shipping route, and to prevent access to the Shatt al-Arab, which runs northwest towards the hub of Basra. The area was also captured by US Marines and other CF units during the 2003 war in an effort to secure the oil refinery, oil installations and pipeline network that fed oil and gas to and from Iraq via an undersea pipeline.

The turn-off to the oil storage area in Al Faw and the new port was at the Al Faw checkpoint, which was manned by police and intelligence officers, and this would become a problematic checkpoint for the next four years. Further on there was another checkpoint manned by the Iraqi Border Police.

ARCO's temporary camp, which occupied a very small area, was crammed with as many hooches as they could fit in. On the day of our first visit, JoJo and I introduced ourselves to the management and it was agreed that TC would take over the security contract from 1 June. We were given a very small hooch, where JoJo would stay to keep an eye on the guards on site and the villa in town. I proceeded to find and furnish, and initiate the registration for, the company villa and offices in Basra, and to keep an eye on the guards at the client's Basra office.

The main ARCO camp was 18 kilometres from the temporary camp and the Al Faw checkpoint, and about a kilometre from where the new breakwater pier would be constructed. The entire area was infested with mines and unexploded ordnance – we even found mines on the muddy beach when the tide receded. Before anything could proceed, the area had to be demined. Underwater mines and other unexploded ordnance were destroyed.

The main camp area had to be raised by four metres, as it was below sea level. This, and the construction of the dirt roads to the breakwater pier, involved a large earth-moving operation. When JoJo and I first went to reconnoitre the site, I was impressed to see at least 200 diggers, trucks and other earth-moving machines. I realised that this was a major project, undertaken by a serious and capable company. ARCO also built a small office area close to where the breakwater pier was going to be.

I started planning the force-protection measures for the camp and vehicle checkpoint, and presented my plan to the ARCO management specifying the types of fences, guard towers, bunkers and security offices we needed. I researched which types of patrol boats would be suitable, and the permissions that would be required for them, as this was the first time that maritime security patrols would be deployed in Iraq by a private military security company. It turned out that none of the Iraqi government entities that deal with private military security companies knew what kind of paperwork was needed, as they had never had such a request.

I liaised with the Ministry of Interior, the Ministry of Defence and the Navy in Basra Province, and helped them develop a new type of procedure, so that we could move ahead. As usual, there were officers who saw this as a new way to extort bribes, but we prevailed and eventually got everything sorted out. The maritime security teams were not due to deploy until September, and the immediate priority was to get André into the country, as the private security detail team had to start with client transportation.

The date for our takeover – 1 June was approaching fast, and we had to deploy static guards to the temporary camp and ARCO villa in Al Faw. With the help of a contact at the Ministry of Interior in Basra, I managed to transport the weapons that we would need to our site just in time. In the previous weeks, JoJo and I had interviewed a large number of people from Al Faw, from among whom we were able to appoint only a small number of guards. The problem was that this town had no experienced security guards – there had been only one project in the area before and it had needed only a few security personnel. A further concern was that not many of them spoke English and we needed a certain number of English-speaking watchkeepers and supervisors. We therefore ended up employing teachers, taxi drivers and other young Iraqi men without much work experience, let alone security experience. We would have to start a comprehensive basic guarding, patrolling, communications and weapons training programme soon.

The locals who had been unsuccessful in our recruitment drive were upset and started hanging around outside the camp gates every day. We also had a visit by representatives of the town council, including the head of security matters for the town. We were instructed to inform the town council about all appointments we made, and were told that these required their approval. We were also told that the council would supply us with CVs for future recruitment of guards and that the council would 'make life easier for us' if we followed their guidelines.

I realised that they were trying to influence our appointments along tribal lines. In a normal world, it would have been seen as outright intimidation, but this was our reality. Tribal rivalry and factionalism have existed from the early days of Islam when rival tribes competed for the title of caliph, the ruler of the Muslim caliphate, or kingdom (more on this in Chapter 15). We realised we had to be careful not to be seen to favour one tribe over another. The restive crowd at the gate grew larger every day, demanding to be employed. Problems had to be sorted on an almost daily basis.

I drafted my first serious incident report the third week of June. I was threatened by a supervisor who worked at the ARCO villa in Basra, whom I fired for insubordination. Over the years, completing such reports would become a regular aspect this project. In the second part of 2013 alone, we had 21 serious incidents and 2014 would be even worse.

Setting up in Basra

Basra was not the cleanest of towns.

Basra is the third-largest city in Iraq, and the capital of this southern-most province of the same name. The Shatt al-Arab flows past Basra as it makes it way south to the Gulf. After the 2003 war, Basra, which has a network of canals, fell into disrepair. When I arrived there, the city was incredibly dirty, and basic services, such as power, water, sewerage and rubbish removal, were non-existent. The canals are littered beyond description

In Baghdad you might have power for two-thirds of the day, but in Basra it would never last for more than 12 hours, and sometimes only four. Without a decent generator, you are screwed. On the roads you have to dodge potholes and the many unfinished construction projects dot the city like discarded carcasses on a battlefield. The smell of sewage reminded me of parts of Baghdad.

After an extensive search, I found a smallish but suitable villa in Basra, not too far from the roads to the airport and Al Faw. The owner of the villa was an elderly, British-educated Iraqi, Mr Jamal. He helped me a great deal to set up the villa, taking me to markets to buy furniture and office equipment. He also introduced me to the officer in charge of the private security company section in the interior ministry, Colonel Oda, whose office was responsible for issuing licences and documents for the personal security detail teams. Oda was also an older gentleman and we got on from the start. His English was not good but Mr Jamal helped to translate. Over the next two years, Colonel Oda and I became good friends, and he showed an interest in the history and politics of South Africa. Mr Jamal also introduced me to Brigadier General Walid from the police. A year later my friendship with these two officers would stand me in good stead.

Basra Province is a hub of Shia militias, who were supported by Iran. In the past, many soldiers and PMCs lost their lives or were maimed there by roadside EFPs and IEDs originating in Iran. After the US withdrawal in 2011, however, the area became fairly safe, as the few Sunni insurgents and terrorists left in the country were more active in the northern and western parts.

However, occasionally a terrorist slipped through the checkpoints

A rubbish-filled canal in Basra.

and escaped the security forces' net, and would launch an attack in the south. One such occasion was on 16 June 2013, when two car bombs detonated in the city, killing a police general and several civilians. This attack, coupled with a few earlier ones in May and June, was the first in a while. Thereafter the security forces and the personnel at the checkpoints were on high alert.

Checkpoint chaos

We needed a special kind of movement authority from the Basra Operations Command (BaOC). This command deemed itself to be a completely different entity from the Ministry of Interior in Baghdad. I was told that the province aspired to become an autonomous region, akin to Kurdistan. I could not get my hands on these movement letters until the Ministry of Interior in Basra had inspected and approved our villa, and this was not a quick process. This created a grey area in the interpretation of the guidelines for our movements. Our movement letter that was issued in Baghdad every 15 days indicated the national routes the company's private security detail teams were allowed to travel on, which supposedly included authority to move around in Basra Province.

However, the checkpoints in Basra Province insisted that we needed permission from both the Baghdad and Basra authorities. Therefore, without an accredited office and their own version of this documentation it was difficult to get through the checkpoints in the province. A sad reality of the new Iraq was that the government, and particularly the Ministry of Interior, tried their very best to make life difficult for private military security companies through their goons at the checkpoints countrywide.

In June I had my first run-in at the Basra Gate checkpoint, which is between the airport and the city. The first issue was that we had not received our Basra Operations Command letters, as the office inspection had not yet been completed. Secondly, the Iraqi drivers I had brought from Baghdad (this was before I could recruit a local team) were not listed under the correct names on our movement letter.

Furthermore, the interior ministry had made a mistake in the listing of one of our weapon numbers on their weapons approval form – a single digit did not match the number on one of the rifles. To add insult to injury, I was told that the 5.56 mm guns we had were illegal, as they were classed as weapons of war. It turned out that we were the only (foreign) PMCs who were still being issued with 5.56 mm assault rifles after the US military's withdrawal. I was especially annoyed by this because, in my opinion, the AK-47 assault rifle is deadlier that the 5.56 mm. The officers also said our tinted windows were illegal. A new law apparently decreed that these had to be clear glass, so that guards could see who was inside the vehicle.

An ex-Delta Force PMC I had worked with in southern Sudan used to call impossible situations a 'clusterfuck'. This was turning into a cluster very quickly! I was detained by the officers. I immediately contacted our office in Baghdad, who got our Iraqi lawyer involved. After spending about an hour and a half on the phone, including to Mr Jamal, who, in turn, called Colonel Oda, we got released. To rub salt into our wounds, a slimy young intelligence officer informed us the problem could have been sorted very easily with a couple of Washingtons. I told him it was against company policy to pay bribes. He smiled wryly and left us alone. I contacted the project manager on another project of ours, who was stationed not too far away in Basra, and asked him to take the weapon with the wrong number and keep it because I still had more checkpoints to clear on my way to Al Faw. By the time they hooked up with us, many hours had passed and it was getting late. What I did not realise was that this episode had flagged us – we now had a big bull's-eye painted on our backs.

We finally headed off again, but shortly afterwards had to stop at the checkpoint leading out of the city. When a bunch of policemen descended on our convoy I knew something was wrong. They wanted to inspect our papers and to see our weapons. When I asked them why this was necessary, I was told they had to make sure our weapon numbers were correctly indicated on our papers. I then realised somebody at the previous checkpoint must have tipped them off about our woes with our documents.

What they did not know was that the weapon with the wrong number had been removed. They turned the vehicle inside out and became irate when they realised it was no longer in our possession. They repeated the charges of their colleagues at the first checkpoint, saying we had the wrong type of assault weapons and that our dark-tinted windows were illegal. We were detained again. We were taken to a police station nearby where they held us for over an hour.

Once again, I contacted the company lawyer and Mr Jamal, who drove out to where we were to speak to the officers in charge. After a lot of toing and froing, I had to sign something in Arabic to the effect that I understood that if I were ever again caught with tinted windows, or anything else that was out of order, they would lock me up. I had little choice but to sign. When we left the checkpoint, we were reminded by one of the police officers that our problems could very easily go away if we just followed the advice of his colleague at the first checkpoint – show them some money.

Wrongful enemies

Over the next few years, we and many other PMCs would be treated with hostility and aggression by the police, and in particular by the intelligence officers, not only at checkpoints but in general. Although this surprised us, it was probably to be expected. When the US military had been present, PMCs could move around the country fairly easily and enjoyed a close relationship with the US military and CF. When the Iraqis took over, they wanted payback for what they saw as the preferential treatment PMCs had received at checkpoints under the US military and CF. Some PMCs also abused their power by shooting at civilian vehicles, pushing the locals off the road and throwing objects, such as water bottles, at them.

Furthermore, Iraqi generals and politicians with security licences wanted to get their hands on the work that the foreign PMCs were doing. Greed and corruption drove government officials to make life difficult for us, and they tried their best to find any problem to be able to extort money from you. Many private military security companies paid bribes after they got tired of battling wave upon wave of issues to ensure that their operations continued uninterrupted. This created a precedent, and the companies that did not pay bribes were even more unpopular.

It was now time to start rolling out the expat team. André, who had arrived in mid-June, ran the personal security detail missions, experiencing great difficulty at the checkpoints, and JoJo was point man on operations. André and I commuted from Basra to the site in Al Faw every morning, as there was only one room available at the temporary camp, which JoJo occupied.

Tuffy arrived in the country in July to manage the maritime team. In September André's brother Johan (Swannie) Swanepoel joined us as kennel master for the canine explosive detection team. He had to ensure that the explosive-detection dogs were retrained on a regular basis. Swannie had been a dog handler in the police.

I offered the job as guard force commander to Willie de Klerk, who also had much experience working in the Sandbox. The only other position that still had to be filled was a maritime skipper to assist Tuffy, and for this we recruited Pieter Haasbroek, a veteran of the Rhodesian Bush War, who had been shot in the leg in 2003 in Iraq.

Ramadan

Ramadan is a major part of the Islamic faith but many Westerners are unfamiliar with it. After arriving in Iraq, we had to learn to respect this Muslim tradition. In 2013 Ramadan was from 9 July to 7 August, shortly after we started working in Al Faw and Basra. There are many reasons why this month has great significance for Muslims. For one, it is the month in which the Holy Quran was revealed. Also, Lailat-ul-Qadr, a night worth a thousand months, comes in Ramadan. The Prophet Muhammad, the founder of Islam, stated that all the gates of paradise open during Ramadan and stay open throughout the month while all gates of hell remain closed.[2] During Ramadan, Muslims fast from Fajr (the dawn prayer) to sunset, as ordained by Allah. Fasting during Ramadan is one of the Five Pillars of Islam. The conclusion of Ramadan brings about the joyous occasion of Eid al-Fitr (the festival of breaking fast), a three-day celebration, during which Muslims feast and give gifts to family and friends.

In the wild old days of Iraq (2003 to 2008), the insurgents and terrorists would launch more concentrated attacks at the onset and the end of Ramadan. This was mainly because of the belief among the insurgent forces that fighting a foreign occupation force during Islam's holy month would put a believer especially close to God and ensure a greater reward in heaven.[3] For instance, on 26 October 2003, the first day of Ramadan, suicide bombers drove carloads of explosives into five buildings in Baghdad – the headquarters of the International Committee of the Red Cross and four police stations.[4] During Ramadan the US military and members of the CF were attacked with more intensity each year.

We also had to adapt our approach to our Iraqi guards and other employees during this time. Firstly, one had to understand that Ramadan was a holy celebration, a period of rejoicing, of kinship and humanitarian deeds that were made as a sign of your commitment to God. It was a time to be with family and friends. Managers and team leaders had to adapt the guard duty rosters to ensure all Iraqis had equal time off work, particularly after sunset when they were allowed to eat and celebrate until first light.

One also had to make concessions for guards who turned up tired for the day shift because they often celebrated Ramadan until the early hours of the morning. They would often also be irritable and weak, especially later in the day because they were not allowed to eat or drink during daylight hours. We also had to be careful not to eat or drink in front of the locals, as this would show disrespect to those who were fasting.

In 2013 Ramadan fell during the hottest time of the year, and in

Two of the Iraqi guards who worked at the ARCO camp during its construction.

southern Iraq it is extremely hot. The northern end of the Gulf also experiences extreme humidity. This combination was so bad that the health and safety officers on site had to halt work when the temperature exceeded 50 °C and the humidity 60 per cent. During Ramadan workers started keeling over like bowling pins, and some fainted owing to a combination of the extreme conditions and the fact they hadn't eaten. Productivity would decrease, but we couldn't do anything about it. Often it also made the Iraqis on the security team act rather irrationally, and a lot of patience was required.

Building a small village

Soon the new permanent camp started taking shape. When an international company decides to erect a camp in the desert of Iraq, there is absolutely no infrastructure, such as roads, power lines, water, or sewerage systems. It is like building a small village from scratch and it requires first-rate planning and execution. Despite numerous logistical challenges and issues, ARCO's main camp progressed well.

The proposed fencing, guard towers, Hesco barriers and mortar bunkers that I had asked for were trucked in and I oversaw the erection of these force-protection measures. More hooches arrived at the site and one unit was given to the security team. Tuffy volunteered to move to the new camp while it was still under construction to supervise the guards there and at the breakwater construction site. We now had five sites with guards and they kept us very busy, as there are always issues with the guard force members.

I also oversaw the construction of the vehicle control point, where Swannie and his dog team would search all vehicles entering the site. The first order of business at the vehicle control point was to build kennels for the dogs, complete with training and grooming areas. Small supervision cubicles were installed in all work areas. Two brick-and-mortar dining facilities were built inside the main camp, which were to cater for a force of around 500 people of various nationalities

Three generators the size of buses were trucked in and electricians laid the electricity grid for the camp. The IT guys created a network

André Swanepoel (left), me and JoJo Bruyns at the ARCO camp site, June 2013.

The ARCO camp under construction.

of cables and Wi-Fi points and connections, and the sewerage, water tanks and pipe systems were built.

More of the ARCO personnel moved out of the temporary camp and into the new main camp. The office sections for the ARCO engineers, the quality-control company and the security offices were completed by the end of October.

André, who was still experiencing problems at the checkpoints (our branch office in Basra had still not been inspected by the interior ministry), helped me to get the villa ready according to the guidelines of the ministry. Among other things, we had to set up an operations room, install CCTV cameras around the villa, put in place a secure strong room to lock up our weapons and ammunition, and build a secure parking lot for the armoured vehicles.

We had everything in place towards the end of October and informed the ministry that we were awaiting their inspection. They twiddled their thumbs. I got the impression that certain elements were waiting for their palms to be greased to speed up the process. But, eventually, the committee came to inspect our premises and they issued the branch licence in November 2013. We could apply for our movement papers, as we were now officially a Basra-based private military security company.

14

Caught up in tribalism

The withdrawal of US forces, together with the Arab Spring uprising in 2010/2011 and the subsequent civil war in Syria, emboldened Sunni insurgents and terrorist groups in both Iraq and Syria to start a new insurgency and terror campaign. These actions mainly targeted the Shia-led Iraqi government.

In April 2013, a government raid on protesters in Hawija, west of Tikrit, resulted in the deaths of 42 people, while more than 150 were wounded. The protesters were mainly Sunni Arabs. In the wake of this, violence levels between Sunnis and Shias picked up dramatically after a period of relative stability. The following month, a number of car and suicide bombs, including attacks in Basra Province, rocked the country, and in July there were a number of coordinated attacks.

One late afternoon in July, André and I were on the roof of our villa discussing security measures when, for the first time since I had returned to Iraq, we saw a massive fireball, followed by the bomb blast. A big car bomb had gone off just under a kilometre from our villa. Fortunately, the insurgents mistimed the detonation and there were few bystanders around at the time of the explosion. Nevertheless, eight people were reported dead and another dozen wounded.

In July there were more attacks countrywide, and more explosions in Basra too. We had to ensure that the way in which we did our planning and operational orders kept our movements confidential. We also had to be aware of areas where attacks were more likely to occur, to avoid being at the wrong place at the wrong time.

The province of Anbar was particularly restive, with areas such as Abu Ghraib, Fallujah, Ramadi and Haditha flaring up badly. Areas north of Baghdad, where Sunni tribes formed a big part of the population, also flared up. The Shia militias vowed to take action and, through their

Popular Mobilization Forces, they went all out for blood and revenge. The escalating violence showed the same trends as during 2005 to 2007, when the civil war between the Sunnis and Shias was at its worst. The withdrawal of the US forces definitely created a security vacuum and contributed partly to the chaos that would ensue.

Uprisings and riots among the local workforce

By September a few more caravans had arrived for the security team, and unlike with the Chinese oil project at Badra, we were now strategically positioned inside the camp, close to the main gate and security offices, and in the vicinity of our clients, the bunkers, gates and other defensive positions. JoJo joined Tuffy in the main camp, while André and I continued to commute and worked from the villa in Basra.

The patrol boats were purchased in Dubai and shipped to our site on one of ARCO's fleet of barges, which were towed across the Gulf by tugboats to deliver their machinery and construction materials to site.

JoJo and I recruited a number of guards, most without any security experience, and our guard force grew as the client rented two more villas in Al Faw to house all the skilled labourers they had to bring in while the main camp was under construction. Members of the local town council, as well as individuals in our guard force, tried their best to influence who we hired. In this process, we experienced first-hand the local tribalism and factionalism.

The groups of locals who turned up at ARCO's Al Faw villa and at the temporary camp to demand work grew louder and rowdier by the day. In early September there were demonstrations at the client's villa, with groups of up to 100 young males threatening the guard force, trying to breach the building and demanding to see the project managers in a desperate bid to get work. Tuffy had to get the local police to disperse the crowd.

When I left Baghdad for Basra, the Iraqis who came with me warned me that the locals in Basra were 'less sophisticated' than those in Baghdad, and that there were serious tribal rivalries in the south.

When I was in Basra, and the Iraqis there heard I would be working in Al Faw, I was told the people in those parts were 'very tribal and unschooled'. It seems that the further south you go in Iraq, the greater the likelihood that you will encounter tribal feuds. Luckily, given my SF background and because I had worked extensively in Africa as a PMC, I had some experience of tribalism.

There were three main tribes in Al Faw and more outside the town. By now, ARCO had befriended some officials on the town council, and in good faith accepted the council's recommendations for drivers, cleaners and other Iraqi applicants who could be employed. But, it turned out that all these new local employees were from the same tribe and they, in turn, would lobby for their relatives and friends to be employed as the operation grew. This caused discontent among rival tribes.

One night towards the end of October, the guard force of around 30 cornered Willie and me inside the temporary camp. They surrounded us and locked the gates to the camp. One of the supervisors, who acted as their spokesman, told me that they were tired of wearing body armour, that Willie disciplined them too much and that they wanted me to fire him. They also wanted to work out their own shift roster, and insisted that we should relax the search procedures on locals who entered the camp and work area.

I was fuming but kept calm. I knew that if I let rip it could lead to a confrontation. I also wanted to disperse the crowd as quickly as possible before the client was drawn into the debate. They handed me a list of their demands and I was told that I had 48 hours to react to them or more action would be taken.

This was the first time since I had worked in the Sandbox that my own security force had turned on me and my fellow PMCs. Before, this would never have been tolerated and the whole lot would have been fired. But, although it might have been possible to fire a bunch of guards in Baghdad and replace them, we were at an isolated site, with one small town close by from where all our workers were recruited. To top it all, everyone, from our drivers to the top officials in town, was related and working in unison to undermine us.

I memorised the faces of the chief troublemakers and antagonists, and decided to change our strategy. From now on, I would start to box smarter. First, I moved Willie to André's personal security detail team. Then, I decided that no expat security team member would discipline an Iraqi guard any more, regardless of how difficult the situation. From now on, the Iraqi supervisors would address all issues and discipline their own compatriots. We used the supervisors we had also identified as troublemakers to execute the bulk of these disciplinary actions. We hoped that this would create friction between them and other troublemakers in our guard force, which would have the effect of 'neutralising' the leaders.

We also made sure that all warnings and disciplinary actions were carefully documented, so that we could fire the offenders after three fair warnings, and be able to prove to the city council that the correct procedure had been followed. This way, we started getting rid of the worst offenders.

By now we were learning which tribes were dominant in the area. We started appointing replacement guards from different tribes to ensure there was a balance in the guard force. This created ill feeling towards the expats, and me in particular, from factions within the town council, police and other officials because their sons, cousins and other extended-family members were slowly but surely being weeded out.

I had a few run-ins with some of the drivers too. They were extremely cocky and tested the security measures constantly. Towards the end of October, I received a message through some of my supervisors that I had to tread carefully and not drive into town on my own, and that I had to ensure that I wore my bulletproof vest all the time. I was also held at the Al Faw checkpoint, and often taken to the local police station, simply to make life difficult for us.

On the evening of 9 November, things took a turn for the worse when I received a call from the acting ARCO deputy project manager, Andreas Christidis, asking for immediate assistance at the temporary camp. He was being threatened by the local employees and believed his life was in danger. JoJo also sent me a message to the effect that some of the locals had told him Andreas should leave the area – and the country – because some people were baying for his blood.

When I investigated the matter further, I learnt that they were accusing Andreas of having assaulted his driver on the way to the camp one day. This could mean serious trouble – even though I suspected it was a set-up. I heard what had actually happened from JoJo, who was at the temporary camp. While they were en route, it seems Andreas had handed his phone to the driver, so that he could pass on a message to someone in Arabic. When the conversation was over, he took the phone out of the driver's hands. However, the driver claimed the phone had been ripped out of his hands, and this was construed as an assault.

By that time Andreas had serious doubts about the tribe whose workers dominated the workforce, and others who were contracted to supply various goods to the project, in particular diesel. As mentioned, the Al Faw Peninsula was a notorious smuggling route and it turned out that the area was home to an elaborate fuel-smuggling network. At night, inferior fuel was smuggled in from Iran by boat and sold at discounted prices across the border in Iraq.

Although Iraq is swimming in oil, it does not have many refineries that can produce fuel, and there is often a shortage of diesel, especially in remote areas. Andreas suspected that ARCO was receiving illegal and inferior-quality fuel that was being supplied by elements who were now embedded in our workforce.

He asked me to look into the matter and I started a sensitive under-cover investigation into the fuel-smuggling network. I uncovered a lot of skulduggery but kept it as quiet as I could. Andreas was in the process of looking for alternative suppliers of not only fuel but also other products and services, such as catering and construction materials. Needless to say, this would pose a huge threat to the income of certain tribe members and groupings in the village. They had to get rid of him as quickly as they could and I believe this is what triggered their plan that evening.

Another fact that pointed to this being a set-up is that a large and angry crowd had gathered outside the temporary camp within just 15 minutes of the so-called assault. Given that the village was a few kilometres away and that most demonstrators did not own vehicles and had to rely on taxis showed that this demonstration must have been planned if they were able to gather so quickly.

There was also absolutely no sign on the driver's face or body that he had been assaulted. Calls were made to ARCO's regional HQ in Dubai, and the decision was made for Andreas to be withdrawn from the project out of concern for the safety of all expats working on the project. I thought this was a mistake because it would set a precedent and might well encourage other troublemakers to do the same to serve their own crooked agenda. I shared my views with the management team, but it was too late – the troublemakers had spooked the ARCO higher management.

André's team collected Andreas just as the rioters were about to break down the gate and enter the camp. One of the engineers and I went to Andreas's room to quickly pack some of his personal gear when we noticed that his door had been broken open. Somebody had gone through his belongings. This had to have been an inside job because our guards on the perimeter had locked down the main camp as soon we heard about the trouble at the temporary camp.

Andreas caught a flight to Dubai the next day and never returned to the project. This indicated to us that there was a serious problem brewing within the workforce, and that underhand activities to protect a money-making racket would be fiercely protected.

When I started conducting my confidential investigation, I spoke to very few people about it. But, as with all intelligence-gathering exercises, I had to rely on sources and I suspect one of them might have informed others of Andreas's suspicions. My inkling was confirmed months later when one of my sources would unwittingly leak that I was compiling a 'file' on the smuggling networks and crooks in our midst. This leak would come back to haunt me.

The Festival of Ashura

For Shia and some Sunni Muslims, Ashura marks the climax of the Remembrance of Muharram[1] and commemorates the death of Hussein ibn Ali, the grandson of Muhammad, at the Battle of Karbala in AD 680. During the battle Umayyad tribal members attacked and killed Hussein and his companions, and this played a role in the consequent split between Sunni and Shia Muslims. Muslims, particularly Shia Muslims, commemorate Hussein's death with sorrow and passion.[2]

I became more aware of the significance of Ashura in the new Iraq, particularly after I started working in the south, as this is a staunch Shia area. In 2013 the Festival of Ashura started on 13 November. We noticed flags were flying around Basra, along the route to Al Faw and even in our camp. Many of these would portray photos of Ali with blood smears around his head, representing his martyrdom.

Large numbers celebrate the occasion. When Ashura starts, thousands of revellers flock to Iraq and visit the shrine to Hussein in Karbala. Globally, many Shiites engage in acts of self-mutilation during this period to prove their commitment and self-sacrifice to this holy martyr.

Ashura marchers by the roadside in 2014.

We saw hundreds of pilgrims making their way to Karbala (a pilgrimage that, from the southern parts of the country, can take about a month). There were women with baby strollers and young children. Many young men carried large flags mounted on poles that were held in place by a leather pouch fastened around their waists.

Women and children make their way to Karbala during the Ashura festival.

Next to the road locals provide pilgrims with free tea, water, food and even tents in which to sleep. This is an inherent part of the charitable deeds one is supposed to perform during the festival. During the Karbala pilgrimage, you had to keep a careful eye out because of all the people on the roads.

Sunni insurgents and terrorists usually increased their attacks on Shias during the Festival of Ashura. At the height of the civil strife in 2006 and 2007, numerous deadly attacks were carried out against festival-goers. On 14 November, we received reports of an expat PMC who had been severely assaulted north of Basra after he removed an Ashura flag from the armoured vehicle he was travelling in upon his client's request.

Fortunately, JoJo and I had asked our security team members not to mount any flags on our vehicles, as this would mark us out to Sunni insurgents, who would then know that we did not have any Sunnis on the team. They understood our rationale and in subsequent years we made sure that our vehicles remained flag-free during Ashura, even if it wasn't always easy, and the camp would become littered with flags.

During the festival, on 16 November, I was called by the ARCO project manager to respond to a threat they had received from 'officials' in the village who claimed that a large group of rioters were mobilising to march to both camps and burn everything down. This threat came after a meeting at the town hall, where a group of locals conveyed their anger that the company was not handing out enough jobs to certain factions, and because they hired Indians and other nationalities instead of Iraqis.

It was a serious threat and the client had rightfully turned to the security team. It wasn't an option to use armed action against the rioters – we could only do so if they first shot at us, which didn't happen during such riots. In any normal country, one could go to the police to ask for their help, but this was no normal country. The crowd at the town hall made these threats in front of officials and the police. I knew that these officials were part of the smuggling networks that were the cause of the problem and had no interest in intervening for calm.

I therefore decided to approach the governor of Basra's office through my friend and owner of our Basra villa, Mr Jamal. In Basra I met a colonel who worked in the governor's office and asked for his help, as this was a national key-point project in their province. I was again reminded that nothing in Iraq comes for free. It was agreed that they would help us, with the understanding that I introduce them to the project personnel for them to possibly take over the logistical supply that was the root of the problem. I agreed, but warned them that I was in no position to influence ARCO decisions in this regard.

The next day, the colonel from the governor's office arrived on site with armed bodyguards. By then, word had spread that I had gone to get reinforcements from outside the local tribal lines. This did not sit well with the villagers, regardless of the fact that the governor's office had more authority than the local town council. It was seen as a threatening move, which had been orchestrated by me.

However, it had the desired effect, because a full-scale riot was averted and the threat was contained. The troublemakers realised that we had the support of a higher authority and that the security team would not sit back and allow them to run riot. Still, it created even more animosity towards me from elements within the workforce, and from town council officials and police officers.

Vehicle control point and maritime patrols

Dog training at Al Faw in October 2014.

In the meantime, the dog kennels and the vehicle control point had been built, and Swannie escorted the dogs from Baghdad to the site. We interviewed potential dog handlers from the village, but it turned out that they had no prior experience, so Swannie selected some candidates and started training them.

We began searching all vehicles that entered our camp and conducted on-duty training with the locals. On a number of occasions the explosive-detection dogs picked up the scent of vapour from explosives and sat down, the sign that they had detected something. As mentioned, the dust, and particularly the mud in winter, contained traces of explosives. This was not surprising, as the area was littered with mines and unexploded ordnance. These traces would trigger positive responses from the dogs, and in such cases the area would be cleared of personnel and the vehicle thoroughly searched. If the kennel master was satisfied that the vehicle did not contain explosives, he would send it to be thoroughly cleaned. In most cases, the vehicles passed the second sniffer-dog inspection.

The maritime area became busy with barges, tugs and other vessels arriving from the UAE, and with local subcontractors working on construction of the 8 000-metre-long breakwater pier. We were still waiting for the patrol boats to arrive from Dubai but, meanwhile, Tuffy and Pieter Haasbroek organised a fleet of boats that they hired from locals (yes, from the same tribe that had provided everything else thus far) to be used for our maritime patrols. Many locals had grown up as fishermen and knew the local maritime conditions well, so Tuffy recruited two teams of 'marines' to conduct the day- and night-shift patrols.

One of the patrol boats used by the team.

Winter was approaching and conditions in the Gulf were getting rough, with serious windstorms and high swells. It had started raining. During the last two weeks of November and the first week of December, we had heavy storms and rough seas that tossed the boats around like rubber toys. One vessel landed on top of the breakwater area, a patrol boat capsized and a huge barge broke loose from its anchoring and ended up many kilometres away up the shoreline. The site became one big mudbath.

When a camp site turns into a mudbath …

Towards the middle of December, I took my usual break. My first full year back in the Sandbox had been filled with challenges. But these weren't the kinds of challenges that I had been used to in Iraq, where I'd had to outfox an enemy, but challenges characterised by administrative battles with the authorities, legal issues, trouble with our own workforce and tribal disputes. I preferred the good old days, when we knew who the enemy was, and had the support of the US military and the CF. But at least the country was much safer now for contractors and PMCs.

15

Reinvigorated evil

By early 2014, the security team, me included, had moved into the new main camp, which was now in its final construction phase. André remained in the Basra villa with his personal security detail team to keep an eye on our office and the ARCO villa close by.

The vehicle control point and dog teams were running on all cylinders, and the maritime patrols were going smoothly. At the end of the previous year, I had asked Neil Reynolds to join us, as we needed a second team leader on the personal security detail team. Neil also had the advantage of having a commercial skipper's licence, so we could deploy him as a backup skipper if required.

Our armoured vehicles were taking a beating on the 18 kilometres of bad dirt road leading to the main camp. And the tar road between Al Faw and Basra was not in good shape either, so we had to regularly send our vehicles for repairs and maintenance.

On 24 February, I happened to be at the villa. (From time to time, I would stay over at the villa to attend early-morning meetings with the authorities in Basra to ensure that we had the documents authorising us to operate legitimately as a security entity.) At 21:30 we heard a loud explosion outside. The blast cracked windows in the building.

The guards told us that two young males on a motorcycle had set off a grenade of sorts in the street. We remained behind cover for about ten minutes to ensure there were no secondary explosions or follow-up attacks, but the area was quiet after the explosion. We maintained an armed overwatch from the roof of the villa while Neil went out to investigate the scene.

Neil found a lever that turned out to be from an offensive percussion grenade. Such devices are typically used by security forces to control riots or to stun the occupants of buildings before entering and executing room-clearance drills. Iraqis called them sound bombs, as they caused a loud bang. Some incidents involving these small incendiary devices had been recorded around Basra during this time. They tended to be used to intimidate and harass people rather than to kill them.

I was unsure about the motives for this attack. It had occurred, though, during a time when I had received regular threats and attempts at intimidation from the crooks in Al Faw and their cohorts in Basra. After the assault saga with Andreas, I had become the main target of the fuel-smuggling gang because I had assisted Andreas in the investigation and attempts to stop their activities. But an Egyptian shipping and freight-clearing company had offices on the opposite side of the road and it may have been set off by a disgruntled ex-employee of theirs.

By now, I had reduced the number of trips I made to Al Faw, and travelled in an armoured vehicle when I had to go and see the town council's security representative, Hadji Hussein.[1] Hadji was a pleasant character and we got on fairly well. Nevertheless, he was on our case each time we fired a guard. When guards were dismissed, they usually came up with all sorts of bullshit stories about how we had mistreated them in an attempt to claim unfair dismissal. Fortunately, we followed due process and documented all verbal and written warnings. We also tried our best to 'counsel' the offenders.

Seeing how their brothers and cousins had succeeded in getting Andreas removed, some of the guards got so cocky that they thought they could follow their own agendas as they saw fit. Over time, we managed to weed out the rotten apples and replace them with new employees even if they were all somehow connected to one of the local tribes, who saw our project as a cash cow that could be milked without end.

One of the accusations I faced from disgruntled fired guards was that I was employing Jews on my expat team. I have nothing against Jews, but I was savvy enough not to employ them in a country with such an endemic anti-Jewish sentiment, and which has enacted laws that prohibit the conducting of business with Israel. It is probably one

In Iraq, even a dovecote can be used to express anti-Israel sentiments.

of the only places on earth where you will find swastikas painted on buildings. In the south, this anti-Israel stance is fuelled by Iraq's neighbour Iran.

The anti-Semitic accusations were levelled against Tuffy Joubert, who has one of the best beards in the business and resembles a member of ZZ Top. But, in the eyes of these Iraqis, the big beard made him not an American rock star, but an orthodox Jew. Tuffy is actually a devout Christian but I had to swear in the town council's office that neither he, nor any other expat on the team for that matter, were Jews, and that I would never employ Jews on the project. During one of the interior ministry's inspections of our Basra office, they found a field dressing in a medical bag that happened to be manufactured in Israel. Our next challenge was to search for and 'sanitise' all our equipment to ensure we had absolutely nothing that originated in Israel.

The Iraqi immigration and customs authority refused to issue work visas for personnel who had Israeli immigration stamps in their passports. They would then have to apply for new passports in their countries of origin.

On 1 March, JoJo was the acting team leader for the personal security detail team when he was detained at a checkpoint in Al Zubair, a town to the west of Basra. They accused the team of not having the correct paperwork. JoJo and his team were taken to a police station where JoJo, thankfully, managed to talk their way out of the situation. The harassment and intimidation never seemed to stop.

Bats out of hell

Between August 2013 and February 2014, more than 80 people were killed in road incidents between Basra and Al Faw. The road was now extremely busy with trucks hauling construction materials to our site. The truck drivers were paid per delivered load, so they raced their heavy trucks back and forth along the road. This road was also busy with taxis, as many locals did not own cars. Iraqi males drive as fast as they can and seem to be infatuated with being first. Taxi drivers were predominantly young men with a cavalier attitude and no training. They raced along this road like bats out hell, often overtaking into oncoming traffic and barely making it.

Many people died in accidents on the narrow road between Basra and Al Faw.

Our teams often had to brake hard and move off the road to avoid collisions. On one particular day in March, JoJo and his team were almost involved in a head-on collision when a truck that had sped past another truck burst a tyre and was on a collision course with our convoy. The overtaking truck was so close to our vehicles that it sheared off a wing mirror. They were lucky that day. It was the first mission in the Sandbox where the team prayed for protection from other road users, as opposed to from the enemy.

A few months later, our personal security detail team were incredibly lucky to survive a serious road accident. Teddy Toma, a Fijian who had joined earlier in the year, and his team were on their way to the main camp after they had collected clients from Basra Airport. An oncoming taxi attempted to pass a truck but ran out of road space and headed towards our convoy. A head-on collision seemed unavoidable. The taxi swerved off the road, but it was too late. Our front vehicle slammed into the side of the yellow taxi. Our armoured Suburban vehicles have very strong bull bars mounted on the front and the rear, designed to absorb a lot of kinetic energy in car crashes or to ram vehicles out of the way in an ambush. Sadly, the small taxi was hit with such force that the impact killed three passengers, while another and the driver were seriously injured. Our vehicles were still mobile and Teddy had the good sense to move away from the scene, as a mob of people gathered quickly. However, he sent a local team member to wait at the scene for the police and an ambulance.

We had learnt that it does not matter whether you were the cause of the incident or not – the Iraqis will always demand justice from expats and foreign companies if there is loss of life, injuries or material damage. Around a week after this accident, I got a call from Hadji Hussein asking me to come and see him. At the meeting he asked me how the company would compensate the families of the deceased, the injured driver and passenger. I was not surprised by this and had my answers ready. I told him that our company's legal people were carefully studying the evidence and facts, and that they might consider financial compensation if wrongdoing could be proved on our part.

There was of course no such an investigation, but he bought it, albeit reluctantly. He would continue to phone me about this incident for two years, as the families of the deceased stayed on his case to harass us for money. Ironically, even the reckless driver, who had caused the accident, now wanted compensation from us.

The road carnage continued, and we would often hear of entire families who had been wiped out in minibus taxis that had collided with trucks. For a short while, the mayor and town council of Al Faw prohibited trucks from using this road; the only alternative was a bad dirt road that ran to the port area. This was a longer route and the trucks had to drive much more slowly, so the drivers lost time and money. Consequently, the ban did not last long: the trucking companies and drivers bribed local officials to let them use the tar road again, regardless of the lives that would be lost.

Maritime activities

Maritime construction machinery photographed in 2014.

The construction of the breakwater pier was now in full swing. It was an impressive operation, involving a fleet of over 50 barges, tugs and support boats. Big barges with construction machines and cranes laid enormous rocks on the seabed. These had to be shipped across the Gulf from the United Arab Emirates. Construction crews worked 24/7, so we had day- and night-shift marine patrol teams on the water.

Our patrol boats often observed speedboats in the distance, which were probably used to smuggle drugs and light weapons. In early April, one of our marine patrol teams heard gunfire and the crack of bullets flying overhead. They replied with a volley of fire in the direction of one of the speeding craft, after which it disappeared. We weren't sure if our guys actually hit something, but the crooks got the message – do not mess with our teams.

After this incident, I had to write extensive reports for our lawyers, which they would take to the Ministry of Interior, as every bullet spent by private military security companies in the new Iraq now had to be accounted for. I found this galling, as locals shoot millions of rounds into the air when celebrating and nothing comes of it, but if we were to fire one round in self-defence they were on our case.

Our skippers were doing a sterling job training Iraqis how to operate the patrol boats. The team endured long hours on the water in severe conditions and extreme heat throughout the year. In the meantime, we had recruited another skipper, Martus Visagie, an ex-parabat[2] from South Africa, who had extensive experience as a maritime skipper in Africa. It was his first deployment to Iraq and he was enthusiastic and energetic. It was good to get some new blood. Martus started picking up all kinds of strange occurrences, mainly at night, and mostly when the tugboat that transported the diesel for the construction machinery and other craft made its appearance.

It became obvious that a number of people were on the take. At the height of the operation, around 200 000 litres of fuel were consumed each day on the operation and a lot of money could be made on the

Skipper Martus Visagie (centre) and Iraqi guards on patrol.

black market by rackets selling watered-down fuel. I built a complete picture, using an organogram, of the supply networks that were involved. I was not surprised to discover through my sources that the fuel syndicate had help and cover at various levels of government, regionally and nationally. My sources feared for their lives, so once I had a good picture of who was involved in the smuggling racket I stopped debriefing my sources in order to protect them.

A new kind of terror

On 10 June 2014, we received reports that a group of insurgents had crossed from Syria into northern Iraq and were executing attacks in and around Mosul. Most people in the industry thought it was merely another small group of jihadists committing hit-and-run terror attacks. Little did we and most observers know that this action would give rise to a new Muslim extremist movement that would change the face of global terrorism.

More than 10 000 men from the Iraqi Army abandoned their positions in Mosul and the insurgents took control of Iraq's second-largest city of around 1.2 million people. They stole almost half a billion dollars from financial institutions in the city and are said to have taken another half a billion dollars' worth of gold reserves. Overnight, ISIS became the richest terrorist group in the world. They also took over all the abandoned Iraqi Army and police assets, including armoured vehicles, tanks, rocket launchers and weaponry and ammunition, most of which had been given to the Iraqi Army by the US military before they left the country.

A bunch of jihadist thugs now had the money and the military equipment to fight very effectively for their cause. They called themselves Islamic State in Iraq and Syria, although some referred to them as ISIL – Islamic State in Iraq and the Levant (the ancient name for Syria). A new terror had come to Iraq.

In 2014 Ramadan was celebrated from 28 June to 27 July. On 5 July, Abu Bakr al-Baghdadi, the leader of ISIS, attended a religious service at the Grand Mosque in Mosul. There, the militant Sunni Islamist announced himself to be the new caliph. A caliph is a political and religious leader who is a successor (caliph) to the Prophet Muhammad. He leads the caliphate, and his power and authority are absolute.

Al-Baghdadi also stated that the group had formed a caliphate, or Islamic state, that stretched from Mosul in northern Iraq west past Tal Afar and Sinjar, and over the border into northern Syria to the city of Raqqa, which they declared their capital. The last caliphate was the Ottoman Empire, modern-day Turkey, which existed from 1517 to 1924. Before that, there were several official and unofficial caliphates, dating back to AD 632, the year of Prophet Muhammad's death. (For a short history of the first four caliphs and caliphates, and the religious factionalism that is still prevalent in the region today, see Addendum B.)

After his death, Muhammad was laid to rest in Medina in what is now the Kingdom of Saudi Arabia. At the inception of the first caliphate after his death, there was fierce rivalry about who the rightful caliph was. The exact lineage of the successor caliph was not clearly defined. Furthermore, Arabs have large extended families, which gave rise to various claims to the blood lineage by cousins and other tribal members.

Muhammad had only one surviving child at the time of his death, a daughter, Fatimah, who married her cousin, Ali, the son of Muhammad's brother Abu Talib. They had two sons, Al-Hasan and Al-Hussein, the Prophet's only grandsons. When the Prophet died, his son-in-law took responsibility for burying his body. The next day the community chose a non-family member, Abu Bakr, as their caliph, but Ali did not approve of him. Although he remained silent, in the years to come some tribes would force him to reconsider his position on this matter.

Some Muslims still believed that a caliph must be a direct descendant of the Prophet. This belief led to the eventual split between Sunni and Shia Muslims. According to Sunni Muslims, the first true caliph was Abu Bakr, followed by Omar, then Uthman (Osman) and finally Ali. However, Shia Muslims believe that Ali, the Prophet's son-in-law, should have been the first caliph, and was chosen by the Prophet as his successor. So the initial split between these two Muslim groups goes back nearly 1400 years.

Al-Baghdadi called for a war on the Shias, who number around 120 million, or 10 per cent of the world's Muslim population. ISIS also want to exterminate and persecute other non-believers, including Christians, Jews and groups such as the Yazidis from northwestern Iraq. Al-Baghdadi instructed his soldiers to 'greedily drink the blood' of non-believers.

After the war in 2003, al-Baghdadi became a founding member of the militant group Jamaat Jaysh Ahl al-Sunnah wa-l-Jamaah and served as the head of the group's sharia committee.[3] When this group joined the Mujahideen Shura Council in 2006, al-Baghdadi also served on the council's sharia committee. After the Mujahideen Shura Council was renamed Islamic State of Iraq in 2006, al-Baghdadi became the general supervisor of its sharia committee and a member of the group's senior consultative council.[4]

Al-Baghdadi was arrested by the US military on 2 February 2004 near Fallujah, and detained first at Abu Ghraib and then at Camp Bucca, another notorious detention centre, in southern Iraq. At the end of 2004, he was released and considered a 'low-level prisoner'.

In 2010 al-Baghdadi became the leader of ISI (also known as al-Qaeda in Iraq because of its affiliation with Osama bin Laden's group, al-Qaeda). He was thought to be responsible for planning the bombing of the Umm al-Qura Mosque in Baghdad. Between March and April 2011, ISI claimed responsibility for 23 attacks south of Baghdad, all allegedly carried out under al-Baghdadi's command. In May 2011 al-Baghdadi vowed revenge for bin Laden's death at the hands of US forces.

In 2013 al-Baghdadi shifted ISI's operations to Syria and announced the formation of ISIS. Apparently, al-Qaeda's new leader ordered al-Baghdadi to abolish the newly formed group and to limit his operations to Iraq. However, in January 2014, ISIS, deploying many fighters recruited from al-Qaeda's Syrian front, engaged in large-scale fighting with the Syrian government forces of Bashar al-Assad.

Then, in June that year, they entered Iraq, attacked Mosul, and on 29 July declared a new caliphate, with al-Baghdadi as the new caliph, a claim that was rejected by the majority of Muslims worldwide.

Hot extractions and emergency evacuations

After Mosul was taken by the terrorists, foreigners and private military security companies had to evacuate their locations in the city, and northern Iraq in general, very quickly. The ISIS invasion rapidly spread south towards Baghdad. In Anbar they spread their tentacles across the province to Fallujah and Ramadi.

Skywave Services, the company I had got off the ground and which Jakes had nurtured into adulthood, had the contract to secure Mosul Airport, but they also had to evacuate in June 2014. Similarly, Reed Inc, another security company, had to evacuate and extract their clients from the Baiji oil refinery, when ISIS ferociously attacked and took over the facility. Our friends and ex-colleagues from Sallyport Security Services, who were stationed at an airfield north of Baghdad, had to evacuate their US clients, who were working on the F-16 fighter aircraft maintenance programme when ISIS started moving south. Olive Security also sent a South African ex-Recce team leader, Martin Lennox, with a team of Iraqis to evacuate people north of Baghdad. The South Africans and other PMCs did excellent work during these emergency evacuations while on the back foot.

When I started working on the ARCO project the year before, I had compiled a critical response and emergency evacuation plan. It was now time to upgrade this and to practise emergency-evacuation drills with the client, as there were fears that ISIS might spread to the southern parts of the country. We also had to keep in mind that we were close to the Kuwaiti and Saudi Arabian borders – both Sunni-majority countries that might be sympathetic to the Sunni insurgents.

Nick Petitt, ARCO's health, safety and security officer, and I made the necessary preparations for our evacuation drills and organised security planning and briefing sessions with the security team and the ARCO managers. We were in the best position to evacuate from the country, as we were in the far south and furthest away from the threat. In addition, we were the only company with a private fleet of maritime craft, which we could use in an evacuation to get to either Iran or Kuwait (or remain in international waters until help arrived).

Nevertheless, it would be a challenge to evacuate multiple sites. We had the staff at the Basra and Al Faw villas, and around 500 people at the main camp. Serious coordination would be needed. After numerous planning sessions, it was time put into practice the evacuation of the camps and other working areas to the breakwater pier. At this point, the pier was 4 kilometres long, making it possible to board small boats that were moored to it, from where we could then shuttle the evacuees to the larger barges and tugboats.

We practised this drill on a few occasions, normally on Fridays at around 18:00, when the day shift returned and before the night-shift workers started, to ensure all personnel were involved. Younger, able-bodied men would walk the 2 kilometres to the pier; the older men and the ones with aches and pains would be taken there in vehicles.

We briefed the personnel on how to pack a small E & E bag with the bare necessities, such as passports, travel documents, medication, laptops and hard drives, a jacket and protection against the sun, wind, dust and seawater. We placed food supplies and water in containers for personnel to take with them.

JoJo and I embarked on several overland trips from the port area to Umm Qasr, and further afield to Safwan, near the border between Iraq and Kuwait, in the unlikely event that we would not be able to evacuate by sea. We scouted dirt roads that had not been used for many years. During these trips we observed numerous dirt mounds that looked like huge anthills with sloping sides. We learnt that these structures had been constructed in the Saddam era after the war with Iran. They were made for artillery pieces and tanks. Saddam's engineers worked out the angle at which their munitions would have to be fired to target key points on the border with Iran.

We also saw an old fertiliser plant near Camp Bucca and the Kuwait border, where al-Baghdadi had been detained in 2004. Apparently, chemical weapons used to be manufactured at this plant. We mapped out routes and pinpointed hospitals and clinics that we could use if required during an emergency. The greatest challenge of an overland evacuation, though, would be to find enough vehicles to take over 500 people to safety. Using our vehicles, it would take two to three runs to evacuate all the personnel under our protection.

I also investigated the feasibility of aerial evacuations using a large military cargo aircraft, such as the Russian-built Ilyushin IL-76. This is a rugged plane that can lift 20 tonnes of cargo or transport up to 250 passengers. It can land on dirt runways and a fairly short strip. There were some 20-metre-wide dirt roads in the port construction area. I took photos and worked out the trajectory of possible approaches and take-offs. I contacted charter companies in the UAE and found two that could arrange these scarce transport planes. It could be done but it would have to be executed in daylight hours and in fairly stable weather conditions. But as least it was another option.

Arrested for terrorism

Our security efforts, particularly the work done by the marine and canine teams, had been making life increasingly difficult for the smugglers.

There was extensive night-time maritime patrolling, which hampered the attempts of the smugglers' tugs to come close to our area of operations, while on land we intensified surveillance of the fuel-storage facility and searched all vehicles with renewed intensity.

For a year there had been efforts to intimidate me, and in July it finally came to a head. At 05:00 on 11 July a contingent of about ten members of the Border Police entered our camp unannounced. They were in desert camouflage uniforms and armed with various types of weapons, ranging from pistols to AK-47 assault rifles and PKM machine guns.

They acted quite aggressively and asked the guards at the gate where they could find the security manager. JoJo spoke to them. They insisted that he take them to my room without explaining why they were looking for me. JoJo phoned me and told me the Border Police were looking for me. When I opened the door, my hooch was surrounded by police.

I was told through an interpreter that they were arresting me under Article IV of the Terrorism Act on suspicion of being a foreign terrorist. This is a serious charge – it carries the death penalty in Iraq. They ransacked my room, allegedly for illegal weapons, and took my laptop. One of the officers wanted to handcuff me but Major Sadik, the officer in charge, said it was not necessary. They escorted me to a bakkie; there was an armed police officer on either side of me. As the convoy headed out of the camp, I could only wonder what this was all about and what my fate would be.

JoJo decided to follow us at a distance with a driver and one of our supervisors, who could act as an interpreter. They drove me to the Al Faw Border Police command, which was just outside the town. I had previously met the major who was leading the investigation and some of the other officers at the command centre (in connection with the permits to deploy armed maritime teams).

Major Sadik apologised and said he was only following orders. I knew this was a set-up by crooked elements within the security forces who were also part of the smuggling syndicate. They obviously wanted to take me out of the picture, as I was heading the security team that made their unlawful activities difficult.

I was then questioned by Sadik. He asked whether I had been to Kuwait, Saudi Arabia or Qatar in recent times, or had any contacts in these countries. My reply was no. I was told that the order to arrest me had come from the Basra Intelligence section via the Basra Operational Command Centre and that I would be transferred there for further questioning. I was taken to the BaOC, but the officers on duty said they had no knowledge of my case. But, as there was a warrant of arrest for me signed by a magistrate, they had to do something, so they decided to put me in a holding cell until the matter was resolved.

I was kept in a cell with seven other young Iraqi men, who I guess were also accused of being ISIS terrorists. Seeing these young terror suspects eyeing me reminded me of Stephen Swanepoel's arrest two years earlier, when they wanted to rape him, so I prepared myself for confrontation. I found an unoccupied corner where there was a metal bed and a very dirty, thin mattress.

The heat was unbearable and I could feel that I was dehydrated, as I had been given very little liquid. Fortunately, JoJo had earlier managed to hand me my pain medication. Thankfully, they did not confiscate this or find the small emergency cellphone that I had concealed in one of my boots before they entered my room. I set the phone to silent and sent SMS messages to JoJo, who contacted the security firm's office in Baghdad, who dispatched the company lawyer to help me. Jakes tried to get hold of somebody at the South African embassy in Kuwait, but to no avail, as it was Friday, the day of prayer.

The heat and stench in the cell were overwhelming, and I took off my shirt and boots. The inmates watched me beadily, but I avoided making eye contact with them. I do not know if the fact that I was bigger than them and in good physical shape caused them to leave me alone, but they did. They seemed amused by my heavily tattooed upper body and arms, and maybe this, together with the fact that I was clearly pissed off, held them at bay. Still, no matter how tired I felt, I didn't dare fall asleep in case they tried to overpower me.

At around 18:00, I was given some seriously rotten-looking rice with a sauce of sorts and some water in a dirty plastic jug. I was hungry and very thirsty and consumed all of it.

Our lawyer from Triple Canopy arrived at around 23:30 but the officers on duty wouldn't allow him to see me. However, at the request of the lawyer, they assembled a committee of people to question me. I was asked about my work in Iraq since 2004; I had to list all the companies that had employed me and the missions I had worked on in Iraq.

I was extensively questioned about my alleged involvement with maritime patrols and was asked if I had ever encountered or interacted with boats that came from Kuwait. 'No,' I replied firmly.

Then I was asked whether we had ever observed any strange boats or activities entering our maritime work area. 'Yes,' I said. 'A boat shot at one of our patrol boats on 7 April, but fled when the TC security team approached them. And during the past week our maritime teams observed unauthorised boats with arms on board entering the maritime work area.'

I also mentioned that Major Sadik had come to see me shortly after the terrorist insurgency in northern Iraq started and asked me to assist them by being on the lookout for any unauthorised movement in our marine area, as the insurgents, he said, might try to infiltrate Iraq from Kuwait in small boats. The Al Faw maritime area was not patrolled by the navy or the Iraqi coastguard.

During the interrogation, an Iraqi man (I learnt later he was an officer from the Ministry of Interior in Al Faw) entered the room and explained to the committee that we treated our guards badly and had refused to re-employ two guards after they had returned from serving in the army. He made further false claims concerning our treatment of the guards. All I could do was reiterate that his facts weren't correct and that we always followed the right procedure.

The interrogation finished after midnight and everybody left. I was taken back to my cell, but from around 01:00 I started vomiting severely. It continued throughout the night, to such an extent that the officers on duty at the cells became worried and called for an Iraqi Army doctor.

I was given tablets that were supposed to stop the vomiting but they didn't help. I was vomiting like I have never vomited in my life. It was so bad that some of the young inmates took pity on me and offered me a pillow, referring to me as '*hadji*', which is their way of showing respect to an older man (normally any man with grey in his beard, which I had aplenty).

The nausea did not relent and by the morning I thought that my bowels were going to come out, as I was vomiting blood by then. The toilet in the cell was a shit-splattered hole in the ground – there aren't enough words to describe what it looked and smelt like. It was slippery, and I fell a few times when I rushed to the hole. In the process I hurt my neck.

At around 07:00, the inmates and guards on duty must have realised something was seriously wrong with me. They called an officer, who took one look at me and ordered two guards to take me to hospital. We had to stop three times on the short trip for me get out of the vehicle and vomit. I was feeling incredibly ill, dizzy and disorientated, and had blinding headaches and vertigo.

When the policemen escorted me into the hospital foyer, the nurses and admin people started murmuring '*daesh, daesh*' – the Arabic slang word for ISIS. They were trying to figure out if I was a foreign Sunni insurgent. It was exactly a month since ISIS had invaded Mosul and started their campaign of terror. Many soldiers from the Shia-dominated southern provinces, and from Basra, had been called up to go and fight in the north. ISIS were killing Iraqi soldiers by the hundreds, and many of the dead and wounded soldiers were from Basra.

The policemen merely shrugged their shoulders, and I received rather hostile glances. I was taken to an examination room where they took my blood pressure and tested my sugar levels. Both were extremely low. I was then taken to a ward where they placed an intravenous line into my arm and ran a bag of saline fluid into my body. None of the nurses or the doctor on duty were even mildly friendly. This took about 30 minutes, and I closed my eyes to take some rest for the first time since the previous morning.

A nurse gave me some tablets for nausea, and about an hour later I was discharged and taken back to the jail facility at the command centre. I vomited on the way back and knew that I must have contracted some kind of bug that would not yield easily.

I was put back in the holding cell until around 16:00, when some policemen came to fetch me and took me into the command centre building. I was asked to wait in a room where I met up with our Basra administrator, Ahmed al-Bahar, who told me that they were going to release me. Apparently, my saviour of many times, Mr Jamal, had got hold of Colonel Oda and Brigadier Walid, who had then contacted the command centre to testify that my work was legitimate, and that I had been working on the project, and in Iraq, from long before the ISIS insurgency.

Their efforts and testimonials, coupled with the speedy deployment of the company lawyer, caught the offenders off guard, as they probably wanted to keep me in jail indefinitely under the Terrorism Act. I was brought before some general, who apologised for the 'inconvenience', and was told that I was free to go. Major Sadik insisted that he would take me back to Al Faw, but I did not want to have anything more to do with any government official, so I asked him to drop me at our villa in Basra.

I stayed there for the night because I was too weak to travel to Al Faw. I drank bottled water and André organised some food, but I could not keep anything down. I took some anti-vomit tablets and tried to get some sleep. Before I could fall asleep, I mulled over the events of the past 48 hours ...

It was never explained to me precisely why I had been arrested or what the charges were (I had to find out through third parties). But the fact that a magistrate had signed a warrant for my arrest indicates that this plot could not have been hatched by some fired guards. There must have been involvement on a higher level for the magistrate to believe that I was a possible threat to the safety and security of Iraq. Most surprisingly, the warrant was obtained without the knowledge of, or consultation with, the General Company for the Ports of Iraq.

Colluding with terrorists can carry the death penalty in Iraq, and it is one of the most serious accusations that can be levelled against a foreigner. If it had not been for my good standing with some high-ranking government officials in Basra, coupled with the speedy deployment of our lawyer, I might have been detained for up to six months without a trial or hearing.

Later on I realised that the men who were with me in the cell could not have been ISIS terrorists because they would surely have attempted to kill me, especially when I was sick and weak. They had probably also been falsely accused of being terrorists. At the time, this was the story to tell the authorities if you wanted to get somebody into serious trouble.

A slow recovery

André and his team took me back to camp the following morning, as I wanted to be in my room and back with my team, although I was too sick to work. The camp medic ran a couple of bags of fluid into my severely dehydrated body and got the doctor in the town to bring some more anti-vomit tablets and to check on me.

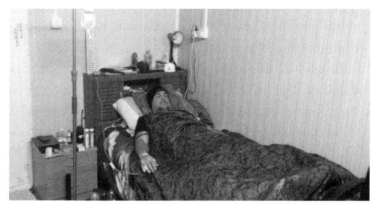

Recovering at the ARCO camp after I fell ill while in Iraqi police custody, July 2014.

After a few days in bed, I had enough energy to fly to Baghdad for a debriefing and to undergo medical tests, as I was still feeling like shit. An X-ray was taken of my aching neck and it turned out to be in bad shape. I also had an MRI scan. The doctors could not make a conclusive diagnosis and it was decided to send me to Dubai for more tests. A neurologist there concluded that my nausea, dizziness and vertigo could be related to my neck injuries, but they wanted to conduct more conclusive tests.

I was in Dubai on a 96-hour visa only, so it was decided to send me back to South Africa for proper medical treatment. After a battery of tests and medical procedures, physicians discovered that I had contracted a viral brain disease while I was in custody. This, coupled with a serious bout of food poisoning and the injury to my neck, had caused a build-up of excessive fluid on my brain. The pressure on my brain caused blurry vision, severe migraines and other symptoms.

I spent August and September in South Africa where a neurosurgeon scheduled surgery to relieve the pressure on my brain for January. I was given a whole host of antiviral drugs, which had serious side effects, but kept me going until the virus had cleared and the pressure on my brain could be relieved.

For various reasons, I decided to go back to Iraq for nearly three months before the surgery in January. Most of all, I wanted to prove to the crooks that they couldn't remove any of our team members. Family members and friends questioned my decision, but I chose to return. I had been in custody for 40 hours and spent only one night in jail, but it had been enough to make me seriously ill.

I was apprehended by the authorities during Ramadan, and around the same time one of the guards on site threatened our guard commander, Willie, with an assault rifle and was ready to shoot him after having been disciplined. Willie managed to defuse the situation. The guard's defence was that his head was messed up because of the heat and fasting. It was almost plausible.

In the meantime, there were some changes to our team. Neil had moved on to another project, and Chris Delport had returned to Iraq from Mozambique and had joined our team. I also brought in two more South Africans, Nicholas Malherbe as a skipper and, a while later, his brother, Russell, who was also a qualified paramedic.

When I got back, I struggled to cope with my workload while

fighting the brain infection. The side effects of the antiviral drugs and the incredibly strong anti-diuretic tablets, which I had to take to keep the brain fluids lower made me feel horrible. I suffered severe headaches, dizziness and vertigo. I felt weak, but I soldiered on. With the help of JoJo and Tuffy, two strong, experienced managers, and the cooperation of a good team, we got our work done.

I obtained information on what had led to my arrest and discovered that it had been a carefully planned set-up. Apparently, a corrupt ARCO employee and some of the local drivers and workers had used their family connections in the police force in Al Faw to get the magistrate to sign a court order for my arrest. A number of other highly placed officers were also involved. According to my informers, it 'only' cost $2 000 to have all these officials sign off and execute the warrant of arrest. It was as if the members of the smuggling gang wanted to show that they could remove any foreigner in a position of power if such a person stood in the way of their activities.

One evening, the colonel from the secret police who had accused me on the night of my incarceration of various wrongdoings walked into my office unannounced. Arrogantly, he told me through an interpreter not to forget that Al Faw was a dangerous place for foreigners and that anything could happen to us. It was of course meant as a warning. This lot still had me in their sights.

Increasing ISIS terror

In 2014, ISIS stepped up their campaign of murder and mayhem. We received reports of kidnappings, torture, beheadings, crucifixions and the persecution of entire groups, such as the Yazidis. Christians in northern Iraq were also executed in droves. This was the insanity of 2006 all over again, but with a new kind of venom and a determined 'marketing strategy' by ISIS.

The Arab Spring uprising, coupled with the persecution of Sunni freedom fighters by the Syrian regime, created the perfect conditions for radical Islamist terror organisations to recruit new members and expand. The situation in Iraq fuelled this problem. A number of Sunni terrorist and insurgent groups, including ISIS, had organised themselves in secret after the withdrawal of the US military. Their priority was to offer resistance to the government of Prime Minister Maliki, as he shunned Sunni Muslims and excluded them from political office.

ISIS started to dominate news headlines and became the most infamous terror organisation in the world. Al-Qaeda remained a threat, but not as much in Iraq as in Yemen, Mali, Algeria, Afghanistan and Pakistan. Many extremists who served with al-Qaeda in Iraq switched to ISIS, attracted by its more radical views. A number of ex-Saddam Baathists also attached themselves to the group.

Over time, the Maliki regime had appointed military and police generals and leaders that were aligned with Shia militia groups. The integration of Shia militias into the Iraqi Army after the capture of Mosul by ISIS in June was seen as the last straw by Sunnis, who felt their arch-enemies had now been given official status.

Other Sunni 'resistance' and insurgent groups that are currently active in Iraq are the General Military Council for Iraqi Revolutionaries, which played a role in expelling the Iraqi security forces from the northern parts of the country, and an older group, Ansar al-Islam, which had a strong resurgence in the northwest.[5] These groups did not always entirely agree with the ISIS mandate, and some came into conflict with the group. Nevertheless, they all shared the same hatred for the Shia-led and Iran-backed governments in Iraq and Syria.

Suicide bomb attacks, rockets and mortars became once again regular occurrences in and around Baghdad. The province of Anbar was controlled by these insurgent and terror groups, and towns such as Fallujah and Ramadi were once again under the full control of the terrorists. Their communication was quite sophisticated thanks to social media, which gave them a large national and international audience, and immediate access to information. Their tentacles even spread to the intelligence services in the Sandbox.

Naseer, my old Iraqi friend, told me the story of how a colleague of his who worked on a construction project in Anbar had been stopped at a checkpoint outside Fallujah by the terrorists. They asked him to produce his identification card. The terrorists had a laptop and access to a database, from which they quickly established that he was working on a construction project in their region, and what the value of the project was. They calculated 10 per cent of the project's value and informed him that he had to pay this sum before he would be released, and that they would kill him if he did not. He made phone calls, and family and friends came up with the ransom money and bought his freedom.

ISIS referred to such extortion schemes as 'taxes', which they raised throughout their self-declared caliphate. They also took over various oilfields in Iraq and Syria and racketeered black-market oil through an extensive network into Turkey. These operations were said to earn them between $1 million and $2 million dollars a day, which they used to pay their fighters, who were now streaming into Syria from all corners of the globe. ISIS marketed themselves very well, luring numerous young recruits with the promise of living in a world free from Western beliefs and one that espoused the ideology of an Islamic caliphate and sharia law.

ISIS tactics, techniques and procedures

The tactics and techniques used by ISIS were nothing new. We had already seen these kinds of barbaric attacks, murders, beheadings, torture and fanaticism in the Sandbox. The grandfather of ISIS, of murder, mayhem and a more radical ideology, Abu Musab al-Zarqawi, had used similar tactics from 2003 until his death in April 2006. The big difference now was that, because of the digital era and social media, these gruesome acts were well publicised and sensationalised by the global media, and herein lay a big problem.

Digital media offered the group an ideal marketing platform. Much of their recruitment, using campaigns cleverly designed by tech boffins, is done through social media and allows them to reach people in all corners of the world. There are even online 'terror manuals' that provide instructions on how to attack, kill and cause anarchy by various grisly and macabre means. These sites are created on the dark web, so they cannot be traced.

The terror group has been especially effective in recruiting young women, many from Western countries, to join their cause, only to be used as sex slaves or suicide bombers. Many ISIS recruits, both male and female, became disillusioned once they spent some time with the terrorists in Syria and Iraq, and tried to leave the group. Some made it out, but many were caught and were either held captive or killed, often by public beheading, as a warning to others.

Their bomb-making skills also stepped up a gear, as there were more electronic gadgets and gizmos available to use as detonation devices than had been the case in the old Iraq. According to an article in the *Sunday Express*, they even had a high-tech laboratory in Raqqa where jihadists researched ways to deliver explosives without the bomber being present – using a remote-controlled vehicle, complete with clothed mannequins so as not to raise suspicion.[6] *The Guardian* reported on an ISIS training academy where jihadists are trained to shoot down passenger airliners with rockets and carry out sophisticated bomb attacks on European cities: 'Footage recorded inside the advanced university of terror reveals how ISIS has achieved a horrifying level of technological competence, developing new weapons which could cause carnage and huge civilian casualties.'[7]

Suicide bombs, delivered by vehicles or people, remain, however, the terror group's most deadly and persistent form of attack. Other tactics, such as ambushes, roadside IEDs, small-arms-fire attacks, rockets, mortars and RPG-7 assaults are common. But they have also developed new forms of terror.

During the Arab Spring uprisings, insurgents and terrorists started using vehicle-mounted anti-aircraft guns.[8] These fire high-explosive warheads (14.5 mm to 23 mm) that are effective up to 2.5 kilometres and remain deadly up to 8 kilometres and beyond. In a military context, these kinds of weapons are mounted on heavy trucks, designed to carry the load and absorb the recoil, but terrorists are able to mount these systems on light vehicles.

These types of weapon systems are not new: the South African SF used the same heavy weapons mounted on light platforms, such as Sabres and Unimogs, back in the 1970s. But the use of these systems on vehicles in the Middle East was new. These weapons are deadly and very mobile, making them perfect for guerrilla-warfare tactics, where hit-and-run operations are effective. Recoilless cannon-type high-explosive projectiles (i.e. 105 mm, 106 mm and 107 mm) are also fitted on mounts on bakkies. These systems, combined with anti-aircraft guns and soldiers on foot delivering RPG-7, machine-gun and mortar fire, are devastating when used to execute a coordinated attack on a target.

These days, people have also become familiar with so-called lone-wolf attacks. This is where an individual commits a terror attack against unsuspecting targets. They use explosives, guns, knives, machetes and vehicles to kill and maim people. (It is a shame that such warped individuals are compared to a beautiful animal like a wolf, but the term has stuck.) Since the latter part of 2014, there have been several such lone-wolf attacks, notably in the US and Western Europe.

Sometime in October 2014, there were rumours that ISIS was closing in on Baghdad International Airport. The media sensationalised this and foreigners in Baghdad updated their evacuation and emergency response plans to find alternative escape routes out of the capital in the event that the insurgents took control of the airport, and possibly parts of Baghdad. Our head office's plan was to move to Basra by road and annex the villa, from where they could run missions. In addition, in the unlikely event of civil war in Basra, they would move south to our location in Al Faw where we would find space for them on the maritime vessels and evacuate to Kuwait.

The theft syndicate and its henchmen kept me under observation. I discovered that four people were the main conspirators behind my arrest. One was a mid-level manager in our client's company. An Iraqi driver was also involved, as well as a police captain and another local official in the town. They bragged about how they had bribed a magistrate to trump up charges against me and had got the Border

Police to carry out the arrest. They warned people that anyone who messed with their business would be taken out in a similar way.

They had worked out their set-up very carefully. On the night that I was arrested, an announcement was made in the mosque in Al Faw that a foreigner working for a US firm had been arrested on suspicion of being a *daesh* terrorist and for abusing the guards.

Time dragged on in the last weeks of the year. I was not feeling good, and I was really looking forward to my rest and recreation in December. I took two months off for the surgery and recovery period. JoJo was seconded to another project and I left the project in the capable hands of Chris, Tuffy and the team.

16

New horizons

I had surgery done to correct the pressure on my brain on 15 January 2015, but there was a complication and they had to open me up again two weeks later. The surgeon booked me off until the middle of March to recover, after which I flew back to Iraq. The project was nearing completion and the client planned to downsize the workforce after June and start demobilising parts of the camp.

At the height of the construction efforts, close to 1 000 personnel worked on the project, half of whom were expats and TCNs. Our security team consisted of 10 expats and 80 local guards. Over the previous two years we had hired and fired a number of locals but the ones who remained had acquired skills in security work after many training sessions and persistent mentoring by the expat team of PMCs.

The fight against ISIS gained momentum in 2015. The US kept increasing the number of special operations forces in Iraq to train, help plan, advise and mentor Iraqi Army units. In the north, the army, with the help of Shia militias – now under the banner of Popular Mobilisation Forces (PMFs) – was planning to take the town of Tikrit back from ISIS. Iranian assistance played a huge part in this first major offensive to retake a city since the June 2014 invasion of Mosul and large parts of northern and western Iraq. It was reported that the elite Iranian Quds Force was involved in the planning and execution of the operation.

The offensive began in the first week of March and lasted until the middle of April. Close to 30 000 Iraqi Army and PMF fighters took part in the battle. The government indicated that between 10 000 and 15 000 ISIS fighters were present in the city. We heard local reports that ISIS eventually killed more than 1 000 Iraqi Army soldiers and PMF fighters in the battle to recapture Tikrit. During the final stages of the battle, about 300 terrorists entrenched themselves in the city centre in government buildings. They rigged the area around them with thousands of IEDs, mines and booby-trapped devices, and offered fierce resistance with no plan to surrender. Eventually, US air strikes were called in. Many influential Iranians voiced their opposition to US assistance (as I've mentioned before, hard-core members of the Iranian authorities refer to Israel as the small Satan, and America as the big Satan).

Meanwhile, ISIS inspired a global network of terrorist organisations to swear allegiance to their cause. More than 20 terror groups, from the Philippines to Nigeria, claimed to be affiliated with ISIS. In northern Nigeria, Boko Haram pledged its support to the new-age caliphate in March 2015. The previous year, they had gone on a murderous spree in local villages and abducted 276 schoolgirls from the village of Chibok. There was an international outcry and the then president of Nigeria, Goodluck Jonathan, decided to act more decisively against the terrorists in the run-up to the presidential elections.

STTEP (Specialised Tasks, Training, Equipment and Protection International), a private military security company chaired by the founder of Executive Outcomes, Eeben Barlow, was contracted to assist in training and mentoring the Nigerian Army to bolster them in their fight against Boko Haram. We received news that many former Executive Outcomes security contractors were doing a good job and that the number of attacks committed by Boko Haram had dropped significantly in March and April 2015.

As I've always said, 'To rid the world of warlords, send in the Lords of War.'

After just a month of combat operations, STTEP had managed to retake and pacify an area larger than Belgium in the northeast of Nigeria. Jonathan wasn't re-elected and his successor decided not to continue employing STTEP. This short but successful deployment of experienced South African PMCs once again showed that even hard-core terrorist organisations can be suppressed and put on the back foot by experienced security contractors.

I believe it is time for the world to accept the need to use ex-soldiers with experience on the international circuit. In operations, they can increase the effectiveness of national armies through training, assistance with planning, logistical support and mentoring.

Returning to Baghdad

The contract to construct the second (western) 14-kilometre break-water pier close to Kuwait was awarded to Korean company Daewoo Engineering. By April their camp was up and running, and they were expanding their operation and construction efforts. This created a new opportunity for the tribal gangs of crooks to worm their way into the logistical supply chain for the Koreans.

The faction that had been supplying most of our goods and diesel also wanted to take control of this project too, but one of the major tribes in Al Faw thought it was theirs for the taking, as they had missed out on the first project. Tensions escalated in the town, culminating in shootings and grenade attacks between these factions, and several people were killed or injured. It was so tense that the central government sent a special squad of police and military personnel from Baghdad to quell the violence.

On 4 April some of the troublemakers managed to use their official police credentials to get into our work area, and a saboteur set fire to the fuel supply boat, which was moored in our area of operations. Our maritime teams saw the smoke from the vessel and reported it to the operations room, but by the time we got to the boat it was blazing out of control. The corrupt police officers in town had managed to use their credentials to enter the port area without being challenged, enabling the arsonist to execute his plan.

The conflict over the diesel supply was now turning into open warfare between the tribes and smugglers in Al Faw. The central government's presence created stability, and apparently the leaders of the tribes met

Martus Visagie and Chris Delport investigating boat sabotage, which was part of tribal conflict in the Al Faw area.

and worked out a way to share the spoils of the logistical supply chain, but it was an uneasy agreement, as there is little honour among thieves.

In May, Jakes informed me about a senior management position that had opened up at the TC management offices in Baghdad and that it was there for me if I wanted it. I didn't hesitate to accept, as I had been on the ARCO project for two years and looked forward to a break from all the headaches generated by Al Faw.

I already knew the set-up at the company offices, as I had been there a number of times. It was a short distance from the Babylon Hotel in Jadriya and was well organised. Jakes and I had a lot to catch up on, and Gert Kruger, the operations officer, and I also knew each other from our SF days. The working hours were shorter and I had Saturdays off if there were no missions. The internet and cellphone services worked well, and we held braais every Friday evening. Life was good.

One thing that had changed in Baghdad in the intervening two years was the number of US military helicopters now flying around the city and the International Zone. It reminded me of the 'good old days' when the US military and the CF were very active in the country. I spotted US Hueys, Black Hawks, Chinooks and Russian Mi-8/17s that belonged to the Iraqi Air Force. From time to time, Apache gunships circled overhead. Just looking into the sky, you could tell that the US had stepped up activity in response to ISIS. I love the sound of choppers flying overhead and it soothed me at night. It was just a shame that the PMC industry was no longer part of the military operations as they had been during the earlier years, which these choppers reminded me of.

During my first few weeks back in Baghdad, a large car bomb went off close to our compound just before midnight on 28 May. Our compound was shaken by the explosion. The blast turned out to have been at the Babylon Hotel, just a few hundred metres away. After the 2003 war, this grand old hotel was a favourite location for PMCs to stay at and meet. It was also the first place I stayed when I first arrived in Iraq. Although the Babylon Hotel had been the target of many an attack in the first few years after the 2003 war, and even had to close down at one stage for repairs, this was the first major attack the hotel had experienced since the US forces withdrew in 2011.

I went to the hotel the next day to look at the damage. The bomb had been detonated by a suicide driver and exploded between the car park and the reception area. Seven people died and around 22 were wounded. The same night, a few minutes later, another car bomb went off at the Sheraton Hotel (now the Ishtar) in central Baghdad. The death toll from both bombings was 15, with another 40-odd people wounded. The midnight bombings came after the government lifted a night-time curfew earlier in the year, which had prevented vehicles from moving freely around the streets of Baghdad.

Rescuing an ex-Recce

In May we received a message through the South African SF network that one of our own was possibly being held against his will by Iraqis in the south of the country. We learnt that JD,[1] an ex-Recce who worked as a PMC, was being held under 'house arrest' somewhere in Basra. Apparently, he had gone there to represent an

Afghan businessman who wanted to start a venture in the Sandbox. He had arranged for one of the local Iraqi security companies to render private security detail services on behalf of his client, but then the Afghan didn't want to pay for the services. The owners of the Iraqi company held JD responsible for the non-payment and decided to confiscate his passport and place him under house arrest at the company's premises until the Afghan paid up.

This charade went on for about seven months, at which point JD realised the problem was not going to be solved. He had a contact at the South African embassy in Jordan, and contacted colleagues and friends to help. His plea reached Jakes, Gert and me. Gert and I asked André Swanepoel to help rescue JD from the house.

Communicating was very tricky, though, because JD had to ask the guards to buy him a SIM card and airtime, which they were reluctant to do. He eventually persuaded one of the Iraqis to help him out with a phone and made contact with some of our South African ex-SF colleagues, who relayed the message to Gert and me. The situation had suddenly turned urgent, as Interpol had released a wire about the South African's kidnapping, which his captors had caught wind of and they were now threatening to take drastic action against him.

Our plan was set for the night of 28 May (the same night as the two hotel bombings). JD would escape through a window, scale a wall and cross a street to an arranged rendezvous point, where André and an Iraqi driver would pick him up and make a getaway run. On the night, there were a few tense moments, but JD managed to get out. We then assisted him with under-the-radar accommodation in the city for a few days.

JD was without his passport, visa or personal belongings. This situation is an absolute no-no for a foreigner working in Iraq, as your passport and visa are your lifeline. At every checkpoint and access control point, foreigners are asked for their passports and visas. To compound matters, the influential owner of the Iraqi security company alerted his contacts in the police and customs to be on the lookout for the escapee.

We therefore faced some serious challenges. JD could not fly out of the country without his passport, and he might also have been flagged as a wanted person on the customs travel list. We could not harbour him for long, as we would then be complicit in a 'crime' in the eyes of the Iraqi authorities. JD had a connection at the embassy in Amman and informed them of his situation. The South African embassy tried to contact the US and UK embassies in Baghdad to request their assistance to get him out of the country, and to inform the authorities that the person in question had not committed any crimes but was the victim of a commercial dispute. While the UK embassy balked, the US embassy supplied paperwork allowing JD into Basra.

In the meantime, another group of British PMC contacts in Baghdad offered to collect JD by means of a special 'envoy', which could pass through checkpoints without questions being asked. We gladly accepted their offer and he was taken to Baghdad where an American housed him until someone could figure out how to get him out of the Sandbox. Once JD was in Baghdad, we visited him at the villa of these Good Samaritans to lend him moral support. It had been a harrowing ordeal for him, and we were all happy that he was safe, even if his problems were far from over, as he was now an illegal alien in a somewhat hostile country.

JD was married to an American woman and they had young children who were US citizens, so his wife asked their state congressman for help. After much toing and froing between embassies and politicians, they could not agree on a concrete solution and the problem was passed from one person to the next.

Several months had now elapsed since JD's capture, and he needed to get home to his family. Eventually, the influential Iraqi who owned the villa where JD stayed used his contacts in the Iraqi government, who agreed to help him get temporary travel documents. Very luckily for him, the Iraqi also provided him with a fixer, who helped him get an exit visa and the necessary paperwork to leave the country. This man clearly had high-level contacts, as he got a judge to sign off on the lost passport. However, he would still have to go to the embassy for the travel documents, which meant entering the heavily guarded International Zone, where they check identity documents rigorously. So the 'right' Iraqi government officials had once again to be found who had the credentials to enter the International Zone, and this was a challenge. In the end, 'contacts' were able to smuggle JD into the International Zone and he was escorted by the British guy to the UK embassy where they started the process of getting him temporary ID and travel documents.

The British embassy in Baghdad has to be credited again with helping another South African PMC who was given a raw deal by Iraqis, even though he wasn't guilty of anything other than being at the wrong place at the wrong time – and of being a foreigner, whom Iraqis see as walking $100 notes. The necessary documents were obtained, a ticket was procured and the very relieved South African PMC could finally fly out of this damned place. In the end, it was the brotherly spirit of the ex-SF boys and other South African PMCs, aided by good-hearted British guys, who hugely helped out a stranded colleague.

Return to the Badra Oilfield

In early 2014, TC had taken over the security for the Chinese workers at the Badra Oilfield, where I'd worked in early 2013. Neil Reynolds was appointed as project manager, and later that year JoJo and Willie were also moved to this project. Teddy Toma joined them as private security detail team leader in 2015.

While I was at TC's country management offices in Baghdad, we needed somebody to fill in for a month on the project while JoJo and Teddy were out of country. I volunteered to go from mid-September to mid-October, as I was curious to see how the project was going since I was there at its inception. I was also looking forward to seeing Jasper, the puppy I'd raised when I was there, which by now must have been a fully grown dog.

The Badra Oilfield had expanded and there was a lot of activity in the area. When I got to the camp, I could not find Jasper, though.

Nobody could look me in the eye and tell me where my dog was. Neil eventually told me that one of the guards had found Jasper's head and skin in a box outside the perimeter the previous December. He had become a Christmas dinner for some of the Chinese. The news hit me like a punch to the gut, but I did not show my emotions. Although I respect other people's cultures and belief systems, I struggled to understand how people could eat a dog, which was also my pet and pal.

When I did some research, I learnt to my disgust that there is a warped belief among some Chinese that torturing a dog before slaughtering it releases adrenaline that makes the animal's meat taste better, and that it also enhances the sexual prowess of the person who eats the meat. What a load of bullshit! Fortunately, a group of US citizens are working with their local Congressmen to raise awareness of this matter, and hopefully it will encourage international condemnation too. It reminds me of the slaughter of rhinos in my own country for their horns, which are exported to the Far East to be used as a sexual enhancer.

It is a good thing I was not in the camp when my dog was killed, as I might have slaughtered a human over this if I had caught them. This episode was another reminder to me of why one should not get attached to animals in the Sandbox.

I did daily private security detail runs with our clients, the Chinese engineers and workers. They were building a new camp in the area of Gharraf, where more pipelines had to be constructed that would lead south to Basra, and eventually to Al Faw. We had to get up 04:00 most mornings and it was almost a two-hour drive to the Gharraf Oilfield complex. The client had to inspect pipelines and pump stations in a remote desert area. This gave me a chance to train the locals in deploying all-round defensive positions when we stopped in these isolated areas, as we used to do in my early days in Iraq. They seemed rather amused by this, as security teams were no longer getting attacked in the new Iraq. Still, I believed that this situation might change and that we had to be prepared for the day when the ambushes and roadside attacks started again.

During one of our trips to the oil pipelines, the engineers had to retrieve the 'pig' – a device placed in an oil pipeline that travels through it to determine the flow rate. We stopped at one of the pump stations where the device had to be retrieved. It was a mission, as it had become stuck and the pipeline had to be opened. A simple job turned into a six-hour one, so one of our team members arranged for someone to bring us food for lunch.

Soon an old rust bucket of a car approached us to deliver the food. I was amazed when they pulled out a rug, laid it in front of our vehicle and placed various pots, dishes, salads and bread on the rug. We took it in turns to eat while the other team members kept an eye on the clients and the area. This was a very special meal and probably the best I have ever been served while on the move.

A five-star desert meal near the Gharraf Oilfield in 2015.

Eventually the engineers retrieved their device, but some of them were now covered in oil and sludge, and I was not prepared to get our vehicle seats stained with oil. I sent the Iraqi team members to fetch plastic bags and cardboard to line the seats of the vehicles before we took them back to Badra.

Mosul Dam – a disaster waiting to happen

During 2015 the state of disrepair of the Mosul Dam became one of the main talking points in Baghdad, and unsurprisingly so. It is the largest dam in Iraq, more than three times the size of the Hoover Dam in the US. It is upstream from the city of Mosul on the Tigris River. It was built in 1981 on top of gypsum, a soft mineral that is water-soluble, making its eventual collapse inevitable. Grouting and strengthening of the dam has been ongoing since its inception, but since the invasion of Mosul by ISIS in June 2014 no maintenance had been done, and this was cause for great concern.

Studies conducted in 2006 by the US Army Corps of Engineers and by the University of Mosul in 2009 determined that if the dam wall broke, an estimated 207 632 cubic metres of water would flood downstream at a rate of 3.5 kilometres per second. The wall of water would be over 25 metres high in the first nine hours of the disaster and half of Mosul city would be flooded.

Such a disaster would affect not only Mosul. According to the studies, the flood wave would displace more than 2 million Iraqis and extend 500 kilometres downstream along both sides of the Tigris at a height of between 3 and 6 metres, reaching as far as Baghdad. It would cause extensive flooding in central Baghdad. Our villa was less than a kilometre from the Tigris, and this posed a possible risk that we had to cater for. After some head-scratching, we came up with an emergency plan for what we dubbed 'Waterworld' – in reference to the 1995 movie of the same name where characters have to survive in a post-apocalyptic world that has been flooded.

The plan included emergency evacuation to southern Iraq if the dam wall failed. This may sound straightforward, but it is quite involved, as sensitive equipment, such as armoured cars, radios, weapons, ammunition, servers, company computers, confidential information, cash in the safes, and so on, has to be either transported or disposed of. In addition, we had to cater for sufficient fuel, water, food and certain other basics to survive on until we reached a safe haven. Another plan had to be worked out in case millions of people fleeing the disaster jammed the roads leading to the south. In such an event, we planned to seal the bottom of the villa with sandbags and other materials, and move to the higher floors or into the roof.

If the dam wall collapsed, residents in Baghdad would have 48 to 72 hours before the water reached the capital. But we anticipated that once such news broke, there would be chaos on the roads, as everybody would try to get out of the city soonest. We filled sandbags and positioned them, and other supplies, such as water and meals ready to eat, in strategic places around the villa.

According to reports, if the dam wall failed, it could be the biggest man-made disaster in recent history, as hundreds of thousands of people might drown, and up to 2 million would be displaced. I couldn't help wondering why the ISIS insurgents who had captured Mosul did not try to blow up the dam wall, but I assume it was because they were based downstream in Mosul and they didn't want to destroy their powerbase. However, now that Mosul has been liberated and reclaimed by the Iraqi government, I still fear ISIS might try to destroy the dam.

Exposed civilians

In October 2015, a top management team from ARCO visited Baghdad to meet with members of the Ministry of Transport regarding their port project in Al Faw. On the day of their departure back to Dubai, we dropped them at the airport in the early evening. About 45 minutes later, just as we were arriving at the villa, we heard several loud explosions coming from the direction of the airport. I counted at least ten blasts and we could tell that these were large explosions.

Our priority was to establish whether all the ARCO executives were safe. Soon they were all accounted for but their flight had been delayed. It turned out the explosions weren't at the airport but at Camp Liberty, which is adjacent to the airport and where Iranian dissident exiles were staying. It was not the first time these poor people had been attacked. As I mentioned before, they had been attacked by the Iraqi Army when they lived in Camp Ashraf, probably at the request of the Iranian regime. These explosions had been caused by thirteen 107 mm Katyusha rockets fired at the camp, killing 23 people, including a woman and a child, and wounding many more.

Rumours started circulating that the explosions were the work of Shia militias closely aligned to Iran. It made perfect sense, as the Iraqi Army and US military contingent based inside the airport area protect the surrounding areas quite well. ISIS and other terrorist groups could not have got close enough to fire the rockets, which have a maximum launch range of 8 000 metres – otherwise they would have done it many times before.

Furthermore, Katyusha rockets are fired from a truck with launch tube platforms. Such a vehicle would never have got through the numerous checkpoints and patrols. However, the militias were now integrated with the Iraqi Army and it was logical to conclude that they were behind the attack. In this part of the world, old scores are settled as a matter of honour in the old-fashioned way – an eye for an eye. It is a disgrace that this kind of score-settling always involves women, children and many other innocent civilians. In Iraq, as in most conflict zones, it was often civilians who ended up in the firing line. I felt equally sorry for the residents of Ramadi after the city was taken over by ISIS in mid-2015.

For some reason, the Iraqi government decided to retake Ramadi, which is further from Baghdad and larger than Fallujah, before they planned to push on to recapture the latter. By the end of February 2016, after more than 800 air assaults by the US and CF air forces, and some fierce fighting on the ground, most of the city was under the control of the Iraqi Army again.

However, it would take months to clear the thousands of IEDs, mines and booby traps left behind by the ISIS fighters. Most main buildings and government offices in Ramadi were also destroyed. I saw haunting images on local television of civilians, including old people and children, fleeing the city in the wake of the fighting. Many travelled to Baghdad to find shelter, but they were halted on the outskirts of the city because the government did not want would-be insurgents hiding among the refugees infiltrating Baghdad and committing further acts of terror.

This led to more animosity towards the Shia government. There was desperation and anger among the refugees, who were mainly Sunnis. In addition, reports of Shia militias committing atrocities against the Sunni population were rife. It does not matter how one looks at this conflict. Over the years, there is one theme that runs right through it: the hatred between the Sunni fighters and the Shia militias.

Karaba mechanic

Since 2003, PMCs had experienced serious problems with the power supply because power grids and infrastructure were destroyed during the war with America. Although the US and the CF spent billions on fixing the infrastructure, including maintenance and building new power plants, the power supplied by the government was unreliable.

If you did not have large generators, you were screwed, especially in summer, when air conditioners are a must. This issue became more of a problem in the new Iraq, as the Iraqi government was busy plundering the Treasury rather than spending money on infrastructure. During the summer months, there would be electricity for around 10 to 12 hours a day in Baghdad, after which you had to generate your own power. Maintaining generators became an expensive and ongoing process.

The Arabic word for power is 'karaba'. At the end of October, nearly 200 millimetres of rain fell over a couple of days, causing severe flooding. There were mass protests against the government of Prime Minister Abadi, who declared a state of emergency, with the protestors accusing the authorities of not having properly maintained the storm-water drains and sewerage systems.

After these floods, we experienced even more disruptions in the supply of city power and had to rely heavily on our generators at the villa. Then one of the generators started giving trouble and our Ugandan logistical manager, Ibrahim (nicknamed '300') Nsereko, had to find someone to fix it. Evidently, the person 300 spoke to on the phone did not understand much English, so he started shouting, 'Karaba

Dodgy electrical connections such as these are a common sight in Baghdad.

mechanic, karaba mechanic, yella, yella!' (literally, power mechanic, power mechanic, let's go, let's go). He meant that he wanted the services of an electrician urgently. But, for once, everyone understood each other. A short while later they were at it, repairing the generator.

On several occasions I would see power nodes and transformers blow up in a ball of sparks. On my travels in Africa, I had come across some dangerously wired electricity cables, but in the Sandbox this was taken to another level. As you drive through Baghdad and other cities, you will see a spider's web of electrical wires rigged between buildings, from the street poles that distribute the power and from areas where communal generators are situated. During wind and rain storms these illegal and amateurish networks of electrical wires often short and blow up, and sometimes cause fires.

In December there were a number of expats and TCNs at the villa who could not take rest-and-recreation breaks. It was also my turn to work, as Jakes and Gert were due for a Christmas break. On Christmas Day the chef made some great food, complete with puddings and cakes. Still, it was the first time in a while that I had not been home for Christmas, and it sucked being in a shithole like Baghdad over the festive season. But this is part of a PMC's life. You begin to lose count of how many family birthdays, anniversaries, Christmases and other important dates you have missed. It is the nature of the business; you just have to accept it and move on.

The team who were on duty over Christmas in 2015.

On New Year's Eve, we experienced the usual senseless volleys of gunfire into the air and the lead rain that followed. On New Year's Day, one of our American team leaders noticed a bullet hole in the roof of his hooch. On closer inspection, he found an AK-47 bullet embedded in the floor of his room — a metre away from his bed. It was his lucky night! Once again, this reminded us in future to rather take cover inside a structure made of bricks and mortar when there is a serious amount of celebratory fire.

17

A history written in blood

After a rest-and-recreation break, I returned to Iraq in March 2016. In May I volunteered to relieve Chris Delport on the ARCO project in Al Faw, which was now drawing to a close. By then I had decided to write this book, and being in Al Faw allowed me the time to focus on writing, as the daily tasks had become fewer and easier by then – unlike during the first two years of the project.

The camp was now a shadow of its former self, as most of it had been pulled down. Just a few hooches remained for key personnel. The gym had been turned into office space and the mess hall was gone. We now dined in a makeshift kitchen. Parts of the camp resembled a scrapyard, with materials and rubbish dumped there. The sniffer-dog area was demolished after most of the security team had been demobilised in July 2015.

Three Greek managers[1] remained on the project, along with a few site supervisors, to oversee the final construction phase. On the security side, there was only one expat manager and about a dozen guards, who kept an eye on the ten or so remaining clients and the few assets left in the camp. The breakwater pier was almost complete. Parts of the structure sank into the mud on a few occasions and then the ARCO team had to rebuild those sections. Close to 8 million tonnes of sand, pebbles and rocks were used to create an engineering marvel 8 kilometres in length, complete with a small naval base and a berthing area.

By then our old security hooches had also been removed. The upside of this was that ARCO now made one of their large expat living units available for the security manager to use. It was the best housing I'd had in my entire time in Iraq. It was not just the usual room and tiny bathroom. It consisted of a large room with plenty of built-in

The eight-kilometre ARCO eastern breakwater pier is a major engineering feat.

cupboard space, a spacious bathroom, and a large section that included a kitchenette and lounge.

The Greeks had not cut corners when it came to comfort or security in the camp. The Greeks say 'bravo' when they have a drink, or if someone has done something good. And I say 'bravo' to them for treating the security team better than any other clients I encountered in my career.

Biblical plagues

Nothing in this forsaken region ever seems to happen in moderation. Towards the end of May and the beginning of June, a swarm of gnats invaded the camp. The creatures were everywhere – they even got into the hooches through the aircon systems. We had to wear long-sleeved shirts, and the guys placed towels over their heads when they went between their rooms and the offices, as these things were onto you in a flash. Their bite produces quite a burning sting for such a small creature.

This was also the moist time of year, when it gets so humid that the ground becomes wet. At night you could see the humidity in the air under the security lights. It got so bad that the paper in our printer would become damp.

When the gnats disappeared, swarms of crickets and flies moved in to take their place. These creatures resembled something like a plague and, having seen them, I can now understand the biblical references to such plagues (and modern-day Iraq forms part of the area of ancient Mesopotamia and Babylonia, which were noteworthy in the scriptures).

I would go for a walk a couple of times a week, working my way to the coast and back. On one of these walks, I encountered a female puppy where the Iraqi subcontractor that supplied building materials had set up a small camp. This good-looking dog reminded me of Jasper.

She followed me, and before I turned off onto the last stretch of road, I gave her some water from my backpack. I knew that I should not get too attached to the puppy, although it was a great feeling to have the company of a friendly animal again.

On my next walk, I took some scraps of meat from the kitchen for the dog, whom I called Queenie. I wasn't sure if the puppy would still be there on my next walk, but when she came bounding towards me as I approached the subcontractor's camp, I knew I had a new pal. I fed her the meat, which she hungrily scoffed down. She followed me on my walk and this would become a pattern. Each time I went for a walk, Queenie would come running up, wagging her tail, and I would feed her some scrap pieces of meat. I always scratched her behind her ears – touching the dog gave me great joy.

Chris got back in the middle of June and I went on a long break. We would now work back to back on the project for ten weeks at a time, giving a ten-week break for the other party. I was looking forward to the break, and I needed a medical check-up because I was still feeling the side effects from my illness and the surgery a year before. I returned in the middle of September.

Queenie, my pal from the desert plains in southern Iraq.

I went for my usual walk as soon as I could to see if Queenie was still there. I did not spot her and felt a bit sad. To make matters worse, I went to Basra a few days later with one of my supervisors and a dog next to the road ran in front of our car and was hit. I quietly hoped that the dog had been killed on impact, but I doubt it. A quick death is a blessing for stray dogs in this country, where they would eventually die a painful death from hunger, disease – or by being eaten by others if they are the weakest in the pack.

On my next walk, Queenie was still not at her usual spot, but after walking for a while I noticed something approaching. To my delight, it was Queenie, only she was now a much larger young dog. She looked thin, though, and I decided that I would bring her some meat more frequently to help her gain some weight. She followed me to our camp but did not enter and went back to her spot at the subcontractor's camp.

I had been back at the ARCO project for six weeks when I received the news that my father had died on the evening of 29 October, which is ironically also my mother's birthday. I was close to my dad and the news hit me incredibly hard, as it was unexpected. I made emergency arrangements for Chris to come back to Iraq, so that I could attend the funeral in South Africa. We agreed that I would take the rest of the year off and that Chris would stay on the project until January 2017.

Third Battle of Fallujah

A major development on a national level in 2016 was the recapture of Ramadi by the Iraqi Army in February, followed by the recapture of Fallujah at the end of June. Fallujah was the first city that had been annexed by ISIS (in January 2014) and was viewed as the group's most important stronghold after Mosul. However, Fallujah had been taken over a fairly long period of time and didn't draw as much attention as the major offensive in Mosul had later that year. Fallujah has traditionally been a terrorism hotbed because insurgents found a safe haven among the majority, and disillusioned, Sunni population. This was the third battle involving Fallujah, as the US military had fought for the city's liberation in March and November of 2004.

Some Shia militias referred to Fallujah as a 'tumour' that had to be destroyed and as 'Fallujah the whore'. They also called it 'a nest of traitors and criminals'. The Shia spiritual leader in Iraq, Ayatollah Sistani, asked the militias to 'respect moral values' when they entered the city.[2] Some militias painted the name Nimr-al-Nimr on the rockets that they fired into Fallujah during the attacks. (Nimr-al-Nimr was a Shia cleric who was executed in Saudi Arabia in January 2016 for terrorism, and this led to a diplomatic spat between Saudi Arabia and Iran, and many Shia Muslims in Iraq were also enraged by his execution.)

There were numerous reports that ISIS kept civilians against their will and used them as human shields when the Iraqi Army and the Shia militias' PMF closed in on the city centre. Some ISIS fighters purportedly escaped the fighting with millions of dollars and a large amount of jewellery, and fled to Mosul. During an intense five-week battle, the Iraqi Army and PMF took control of the city. Hundreds of Iraqi soldiers and militia members lost their lives, and over 2 000 ISIS fighters were killed.

As with Ramadi, much of the city was destroyed and the terrorists left many IEDs and booby traps that had to be cleared and destroyed. Tens of thousands of civilians were displaced and required shelter.

The Battle of Mosul

In October 2016, the Obama administration decided to support the Iraqi Army in its effort to retake Mosul from the terrorists. It was probably no coincidence that this political decision was made around a month before the US presidential elections. (From the end of the previous year, I had followed the primaries in the US with great amazement. I guess it is a sound democratic system, but it still astonishes me how much energy, money and news coverage is wasted on this process.) Was the decision to help the Iraqi Army retake Mosul an attempt to woo voters to support the Democratic Party? Was Obama using a military strategy to bolster the Democrats going into the elections?

We will never know, but everybody in security circles did know that this was not going to be an easy or quick battle, as an estimated 8 000 to 14 000 ISIS fighters had entrenched themselves in Iraq's second city over the previous two years. The Iraqi Army, supported by the Shia militia PMF and some local tribal fighters, amassed a military force of around 100 000, which was augmented by a couple of thousand US troops, to retake the capital of ISIS in Iraq. This large fighting force also had air support from the Iraqi Army, the US and coalition governments, including the UK, Canada, Australia, New Zealand, Spain, Denmark, Norway, the Netherlands and some other NATO countries.

In June 2017, the Iraqi and coalition forces finally won the Battle of Mosul. It had taken nine months.

After the ISIS capture of Mosul, we read reports in which some Sunnis in Mosul and Raqqa (Syria) said it was better living under ISIS than under the Shia regimes in the two countries. Stories emerged of a highly organised system in these ISIS-captured cities, where, allegedly, the residents paid taxes, children went to school, and there were ISIS municipal workers and a police force to ensure their safety. These 'officials', it was claimed, who drove vehicles with caliphate licence plates, provided a state that functioned, unlike the authorities in Baghdad and Damascus. ISIS reportedly provided law and order, so citizens were willing pay taxes, and the municipal councils maintained the electricity and water supply – unlike the Iraqi government, which was seen as taking public money but without providing services in return.

These kinds of sentiments might seem strange to outsiders, but they are an indication of how the Shia regimes in Iraq and Syria have marginalised Sunni Arabs and the Kurdish population outside Kurdistan in places such as Mosul, Kirkuk and Tikrit (more than 95 per cent of Kurds are Sunni Islam believers). This ethnic and religious marginalisation has created ample breeding grounds for ISIS sympathisers, as well as for al-Qaeda and other militant Sunni terror groups, in a country where about a third of the population of almost 39 million are Sunni Arabs, or Kurds who practise Sunni Islam.

Syria experienced the same situation, where, out of a population of around 23 million, almost 75 per cent are Sunni Muslims, about 15 per cent are Shia Muslims, while Christians make up the remaining 10 per cent. Therefore, if one takes both countries collectively, there are some 30 million Sunnis in the region who have been suppressed and given very little in the form of political dispensation or enfranchisement. Terror groups therefore have a vast pool to tap into as a recruitment base. Even if only perhaps 10 per cent of this disenfranchised Sunni community might hold radical views, there is still a huge number – about 3 million – of potential radical Islamist militants willing to be recruited by terror groups.

In my opinion, Iraq and Syria should be split up into three separate independent states: Kurdistan (comprising northern Iraq and northeastern Syria), Iraq (made up of the Baghdad area and the southern and southeastern provinces) and a new Sunni state consisting of part of Syria, Iraq's large western Anbar Province, including Ramadi and Fallujah, and parts of northwestern Iraq.

To illustrate the ethnic tension simmering in the region, Turkish troops entered the northern Kurdish part of Iraq in the latter part of 2015 and moved southwards to just north of Mosul. Initially they were hunting down Kurdish freedom fighters, who are fighting for their independence in southern Turkey. This led to a political spat between the leaders of Iraq and Turkey, with Abadi accusing the Turks of violating the sovereignty of his country. Eventually Turkey joined the fight against ISIS, probably to justify their presence in Iraq, even if it was an uncomfortable arrangement for the government of Iraq.

After the Battle of Mosul, the CF, and in particular the US Special Operations Forces, aided the Kurdish freedom fighters in Syria to retake the de facto capital of ISIS, Raqqa, in the final push to destroy their physical caliphate. The operation was dubbed The Great Battle. The final liberation of Raqqa occurred in October 2017.

Over a period of a year, ISIS had lost vast areas of territory to the Iraqi government forces, aided by the US military's special forces, trainers and advisors. During this time ISIS terror cells detonated several suicide bombs in and around Baghdad in an attempt to distract the Iraqi security forces and to force the government to move some troops back to the capital, easing pressure on the terrorist group in the north.

The Iraqi security forces and their CF partners gained control of Mosul, as they did with Tikrit, Ramadi, Fallujah and other areas previously held by ISIS. The main challenge will be to prevent future invasions and the formation of other insurgent and terrorist groups. Herein lies the challenge.

Without political inclusiveness that empowers the Sunni population in Iraq, and without regime change in Syria and a similar inclusion of the Sunnis there and the Kurds in both countries, it might prove difficult to defeat ISIS and militant Islamic terrorism. It also seems as though the Assad regime in Syria is not going anywhere soon and that Russia, Iran and, to a lesser extent, China, are backing the current political administration there. Moreover, it is very unlikely that Iran and the hardline Shia clerics and politicians in that country will allow much Sunni political participation in Iraq.

These factors will force the Sunni population to turn to insurgency groups to protect them and to fight for their freedom. It will also entice other Sunni countries (i.e. Saudi Arabia, Qatar, Kuwait and the UAE) to sympathise with Sunni freedom fighters, and it might contribute to proxy support for such groups, just as Iran is lending proxy support to the Shia militias and Hezbollah in both Iraq and Syria, and also in the war in Yemen, where Iran is backing the Shiite Houthi rebels, while a coalition of Saudi Arabia, UAE and Bahrain supports the Sunnis in the country.

The wild card in this political struggle will be Turkey. President Recep Tayyip Erdoğan won a referendum for the Turkish public to give him more power in the wake of the failed coup attempt of 15 June 2016. The current regime survived a bold attempt by military factions to take over Turkey in a coup d'état, pointing fingers at a cleric who lives in exile in the US as the person behind the attempt. Turkey is furthermore aggressively hunting and killing Kurdish freedom fighters, whom they label as terrorists.

But, as far as the fight against ISIS goes, the Kurds have been at the forefront, supported by the US and other Western powers. The US, however, has significant military interests in Turkey, so this is the first of a few sticky situations, as they are in bed with both Turkey and the Kurds, who do not see eye to eye.

The next complications are evident in how US military personnel are currently advising and fighting alongside the Iraqi security forces, who, in turn, are heavily augmented by Shia militias, with some direct assistance from Iran. One could therefore argue that the US is cooperating with Iran to fight ISIS. However, if you look a bit further you will see that the US supports certain Sunni freedom-fighter groups in Syria whose goal is to topple the Iranian-backed Assad regime. Meanwhile, hardliners in Iran burn Israeli and American flags, chanting 'death to Israel' and 'death to America'.

The US, furthermore, enjoys good relations with Iraq's current prime minister, Haider al-Abadi, although his cabinet is in a diplomatic row with Turkey and at loggerheads with Kurdistan over their independence and sharing of oil resources. And the previous Iraqi prime minister, Nouri al-Maliki, has his eyes on running the country once again, hoping to promote his more hardline stance against the Sunnis, as he did when the US forces left Iraq in 2011.

Military analysts agree that Barack Obama made a mistake when he withdrew the US forces from Iraq. His second blunder was to underestimate ISIS. After the group's invasion of Mosul, Obama said that not every regional (i.e. Middle Eastern) terrorist organisation would go on to pose a threat to the US. Many in the security industry also shrugged ISIS off as just a band of thugs who got lucky. Today, however, we know that this terrorist organisation poses possibly the biggest security threat to the US, and globally, of all time.

Others in the industry also reckon that Obama had been wrongly advised, that he overestimated the readiness of the Iraqi Army and that Maliki had fooled him. The Iraqi Army at the time of the ISIS invasion in 2014 was mostly useless, and Maliki should have been better controlled by world politicians and should not have been given carte blanche to try to keep insurgent and terrorist organisations suppressed, and on other military matters. But Maliki did not want to maintain a strong army. He knew he could rely on Iran and the Shia militias. They offered their assistance and he could not refuse; in so doing, he made the population believe they needed Iran, even though ordinary Iraqis don't care much for Iran, even in the south. Iran, on the other hand, sees southern Iraq as a province of their Islamic Republic.

This all means that, on some fronts, certain countries are in an alliance, and in other scenarios they are on opposite sides. This highly delicate and complex situation can go wrong at the drop of a hat. The three largest powers in the region, Saudi Arabia, Turkey and Iran, have used Iraq as their punching bag for centuries.

And if Turkey is the wild card, then Israel might be the trump card –

in more ways than one. US President Donald Trump has already shown signs of hostility towards Iran and of a warm friendship with Israel. There have also been rumours of possible cooperation between Israel and Saudi Arabia, as unlikely as that may sound. If and when Iran succeeds in producing nuclear weapons, both these nations might be in Iran's crosshairs, as they are the natural arch-enemies of Iran (alongside the US). The adage of my enemy's enemy being my friend has never rung truer than in this part of the world.

During my career in Iraq, I spoke to a lot of Iraqis from all walks of life, and after the ISIS invasion I heard a number of rumours and conspiracy theories, which I investigated. Recently, local open sources reported that Iran had secretly asked Zarqawi and his terror group, al-Qaeda in Iraq, to kill Shias (their own kind) in the wake of the 2003 war and at the height of the 2006/07 civil war between Sunnis and Shias. Such a move was of course exactly what Zarqawi wanted to fuel anger and hate between the two main branches of Islam.[3] Osama bin Laden didn't support this and eventually distanced himself from Zarqawi, which caused the fanatical Zarqawi to break away and form Islamic State in Iraq, the forerunner to ISIS.

An older, well-informed and educated Iraqi told me that, in the wake of the terrorist group's capture of Mosul, they heard that Iran secretly had some knowledge of an insurgency group that might attack the country from Syria, and that certain elements in Iran convinced the Iraqi security forces in Mosul to abandon their positions after the ISIS invasion. Iran would then, in turn, offer assistance to the Iraqi government to fight this new threat by having the Iraqi government integrate the Shia militias, with backing from Iran, into the Iraqi Army. Iran at the time was already supporting the Assad regime in Syria by fighting the Sunni opposition groups, so this would play well into their narrative.

The fact that over 10 000 members of the Iraqi security forces fled Mosul after only around a thousand ISIS fighters had infiltrated the city might well lend some credence to this story. The Iraqi security forces also had superior weaponry and firepower in the form of tanks, armoured fighting vehicles and weaponry, much of it left behind by the US forces when they left in 2011. All this military hardware was taken over by the ISIS fighters, and after they had pulled off the biggest bank heist in history, they were not only extremely well armed, but also filthy rich. Many observers were dumbstruck by how little resistance the Iraqi security forces offered and this does make one wonder whether the Iran conspiracy was true.

Another theory that makes perfect sense is that Assad allowed ISIS to grow, so that the group would divide his enemies and that he also allowed ISIS to combat the Free Syrian Army rebels, which subsequently happened.

I also heard stories and read reports indicating that ISIS was selling oil and fuel to the Syrian regime. More stories surfaced of Iranian arms smugglers who are selling weapons to the Sunni insurgents. I spoke to one of the American managers who worked with us in Baghdad about this and other rumours regarding possible collusion between Iranian Shia militias, the Shia Assad regime and Sunni insurgent fighters. He was convinced that it could not be true because of the inbred and ancient hatred between Sunni and Shia hardliners. Yet most of it has turned out to be true.

I was told in Basra that Shia militias were looking to kidnap Americans and British people to sell to ISIS after the American James Foley and Briton Alan Henning were beheaded by the terror group's executioner, called Jihadi John. This was a clear indication that people often have no scruples when an opportunity to profit from terrorism, tribalism or crime presents itself, and that arch-enemies will make deals if both sides find value or can profit from such actions.

Towards the end of 2017, the size of the caliphate had shrunk by more than 50 per cent, and by the end of November it had crumbled. But the group's ideology and social-media marketing will persist for a long time to come, and terrorist attacks inspired by this death-marketing mechanism will continue to plague the planet in all shapes and forms.

ISIS will be defeated, but its ideology will not be destroyed. Remnants of the ISIS army will remain and the social-media campaigns in which they spread their ideology will continue. For this reason, the world powers, including Arab states, will have to continue hunting them down. I predict that a virtual caliphate will take over the physical one, and that the only way to destroy a virtual caliphate is to censor and take down social-media publicity and the gore that is spread on various platforms.

This will of course not happen as long as some people in the West, safely cosseted far away from the death and destruction, cry foul over the infringement this would be on human rights. But what about the rights of thousands upon thousands of people who have been killed, tortured, maimed and left broken by terrorists who use the internet as their primary weapon?

When the physical ISIS army is defeated, their remnants will have no support from Sunni countries, and with no funding and resources these jihadist fighters might re-form with al-Qaeda, which has stood the test of time. This would be extremely dangerous. ISIS wants a caliphate and wants to entice the US to come to fight them on their home turf, in their 'holy land'. But al-Qaeda wants to take the fight to America, to the West, by means of monumental attacks like 9/11. They are also not particularly interested in killing Shia Muslims.

America should not succumb by sending in large forces, but should rather keep deploying Special Operations Forces and surgical strikes that provide force multipliers to bolster coalition Arab forces. They should also make use of experienced PMCs as mentors, trainers and planners to help combat this evil. Of course leftists will cry foul when PMCs are used in combat, even if it is to assist the world in the fight against international terrorism. I suspect PMCs will be labelled as mercenaries who are doing it only for the money, and that the UN and other organisations will make it their mission to shut down any private military security company whose PMCs assist in offensive combat operations (i.e. to augment military forces), as opposed to protective tasks.

As my time in Iraq neared its end – I remained in Al Faw until my final month, which I spent in Baghdad before I left the country – two significant events took place that compounded the complexities of the region. On 7 June 2017, ISIS-inspired Iranians launched attacks on the Iranian Parliament and the shrine containing the tomb of the republic's revolutionary founder, Ayatollah Khomeini. There were blasts and gunfire, and some hostages were taken. Close to 20 people were killed and scores injured.

It was the first time since the 2003 war that there had been a Sunni-inspired terrorist attack in Shia Iran. This is significant in many ways. Firstly, it demonstrates that the normally impenetrable Iranian security forces can be penetrated. Secondly, it underscores the fact that ISIS terrorists want to spark an all-out war within Islam between Sunnis and Shia Muslims. Iran immediately blamed Saudi Arabia, their natural arch-enemy, and with whom they are fighting a proxy war in Syria, Yemen and Iraq.

A few days before, another significant event played out in the Middle East. Most of the Sunni-aligned countries in the Persian Gulf (i.e. Saudi Arabia, Bahrain and the UAE) severed ties with Qatar. The reason given was that Qatar supports terrorism in the region. But, soon afterwards, reports indicated that Saudi was angry at Qatar for having paid close to a billion dollars to Iran to free Qatari royals who had been kidnapped by Shia militias while on a hunting trip in southern Iraq the previous year.

Dig deeper and you will see reports that Qatar, one of the largest suppliers of natural gas in the world, had ambitious plans to build a gas pipeline through Jordan, Syria and Turkey to Europe to compete with Russia to supply liquid natural gas to Europe. This move would take billions of dollars out of Russia's economy, as they supply the bulk of liquid natural gas to Europe. With Jordan and Turkey already on board with Qatar, Syria became key to implementing this plan, or preventing it, depending on your agenda.

No wonder Russia is so vehemently supporting the Assad regime – and no wonder it supports Qatar, which 'donated' over $3 billion worth of support to rebel groups. Now rumours have it that Iran is willing to support Qatar with food supplies, as Iran blames Saudi for being behind the boycott against Qatar. This maze of issues in the region makes matters highly complex, and we, as security contractors, must keep our eye on several balls at the same time.

Some time ago, I asked a group of older Iraqis why they thought there hadn't been a revolt against the Iraqi government during the Arab Spring uprisings. Although the situation in Iraq was different for many reasons from that of Tunisia, Libya, Egypt, Yemen and Syria, I was also told that the Iraqis were simply tired of conflict. Civilian Iraqis have become disheartened and tired of all the violence. According to conservative estimates, over a million Iraqis have lost their lives since the 2003 war. These numbers are in addition to another million killed in the Iran–Iraq war (this number reflects deaths on both sides). And many more were wounded or scarred for life.

The current political and sectarian violence in the country and greater region will first have to be resolved if the violence is to stop. It will take nothing short of a miracle to achieve this without a drastic change in the mindset of political and religious leaders, and much more tolerance and cooperation from all parties. Unfortunately, the history of Iraq, and the region, has not seen extended periods without conflict. There always seem to be insurgent or terror groups looking to defend their turf, expand their territories, or forcefully roll out their political or religious agendas.

My views expressed in this book on the eradication of terrorism are based on taking the fight to the enemy and hunting them down before they morph into evil terrorist organisations, such as AQI under Zarqawi and ISIS under al-Baghdadi. People might get the impression that I am a war-monger, but nothing could be further from the truth. I am a peaceful man, I believe in peaceful coexistence, but, unfortunately, the world does not seem to work that way.

War is as old as humanity itself and it is not going to go away. As a combat soldier in the South African military and during my work in the private military security industry, I have seen first-hand in various conflict zones what war does to humanity. There can be no greater evil. If I could wish war away and have to be without a job for the rest of my life, then I would do it. It is heartbreaking to see the effects of war and conflict – people who have been blown up, dead children and innocent people who just wanted to get on with their lives, like you and me.

So-called warriors who brag about how badly they want to go and fight and kill people have in most likelihood never experienced first-hand what war does to a civilian population that gets caught up in the causes pursued by politicians or religious fanatics and very greedy people. In the end, good people will continue to seek protection from tyrants and terrorists, and this will always require the involvement of militaries, and their auxiliaries in the form of private military contractors.

As I finished writing these memoirs of my time in Iraq, many of the political issues there remain unresolved. Who knows what their final outcome will be. But one thing is sure: the bloodshed in the Sandbox and surrounding areas is not over.

Me and two Iraqi drivers from our security team in the ARCO camp outside Al Faw.

After several weeks back home, during which we buried my father and I spent some time with my family, I returned to the ARCO project in the first week of January 2017. By then it was virtually complete and the staff on site were due to remain only a few more months to ensure the breakwater pier had settled. More hooches had been cleared and the camp now felt like a ghost town.

After the project was wrapped up, I spent a few weeks in Baghdad to help out with legal and administrative duties at the TC headquarters. This stint reminded me of how much I hated office work, but also served as a reminder of how any good military, paramilitary or private security company is dependent on the support personnel in the rear echelons, who make it possible for the operators on the ground to succeed in their missions legally, contractually and administratively. In my military days, we sometimes referred to these support structures as the REMFs (rear-echelon mother-fuckers). But in the end these REMFs made it possible for us security personnel on the ground to do our job.

The Baghdad personal security detail team in 2017.

At the end of 2016, I had started contemplating the idea that it was time to close this chapter of my life and go back to South Africa. My health issues had always been a concern to me, and the after-effects of the surgery to balance the fluid pressure in my skull still got to me, particularly when I had to wear tight body armour over my surgical scars and shunt. So, when the ARCO project concluded, a voice in my head told me to call it a day in the Sandbox. It was time to go home and tend to my aches and pains properly.

Although on several occasions my life was threatened in Iraq, in many ways the country has also been very good to me. On a professional level, it gave me the opportunity to do what I like best and to learn much in the process.

When I left the Sandbox in August 2017, it was with mixed emotions. I was leaving behind a career that had become such an integral part of my existence, but I was also incredibly grateful that I'd survived it all – unlike the people listed at the end of this book (see the Roll of Honour), who succumbed to the violent lunacy that the Sandbox seems to dish out so readily.

Epilogue

Although I tremendously enjoyed working in Iraq, it came at a price. I worked myself into a blackout on one occasion and was injured to such an extent that I needed two operations. Many PMCs paid in blood for their work in Iraq. For me, too, the money was earned with blood, even if I felt it was for a good cause.

It takes a special kind of mindset to accept that you might have to give your life to protect strangers in a country that is not your own, and where the culture and beliefs do not conform to yours. During the lectures I gave on working in combat areas to guys who were new to the team, I hammered home this point: if you were not prepared to encounter harm or give your life to protect strangers, then you had to get out of the business, I said. All soldiering and security jobs carry risks, and in the Sandbox the risk was particularly high from 2003 to 2008, especially if you were on convoy-protection missions or stationed at projects in remote areas, at isolated forward operating bases or in remote CF locations.

It is testing to live under conditions where the challenge is to outwit the enemy and stay alive, and where even the slightest mistake or lapse in concentration can cost lives. This, of course, is what true combat soldiers are supposed to do, whether they are in the military or the private sector. Unfortunately, many private contractors who went to Iraq were there only for the money, and once they got ambushed, rocketed, bombed or shot at, they quickly realised that bleeding or dying for another man's cause or war was not for them.

In private-security circles, previously held military rank, position, age and level of appointment mean nothing. And, unlike in the military, any contractor can tell a fellow contractor, even a superior, to shove it where the sun doesn't shine, because there are no court martials or consequences – other than getting fired.

The only way to earn the respect of your fellow PMCs is to prove yourself to them through your own actions – by leading from the front and doing what you would expect from them. Once a company has found the right combination of experienced personnel to work together on missions, it becomes a pleasure to deal with other professionals and you experience a strong sense of camaraderie.

I would like to honour all the US servicemen I met in Iraq. I respected what they did and enjoyed working and interacting with them. I greatly appreciate all their help over the years, especially when I had to set up operations in east Ramadi in 2006. I did not keep the names and contact details of all these men, but if you happen to read this book, then know that I want to thank you again for assisting me and my PMC colleagues.

Many soldiers and servicemen do not like private contractors because they see them as gung-ho, Rambo-like wannabes (they may have a point because many PMCs are indeed like that) who get paid way too much money to perform tasks the military should do. Sadly, there were a number of incidents where PMCs conducted themselves in an unprofessional manner – for instance, by saying that they wanted to 'go out and shoot some Iraqis today' or posing for photos with dead Iraqis.

These kinds of contractors have no place in our business. However, the reality is that between the end of 2004 and 2006, the demand for PMCs outstripped the available number of qualified ex-servicemen with the right training and experience. This meant fortune-seekers and wannabe bodyguards arrived in the Sandbox in droves. Soon the place was flooded with all types of contractors, from former military and police personnel, who had worked in only administrative or logistical roles, to civilian paramedics, firemen, prison warders and even bouncers. These people had little or no experience in guerrilla warfare, counter-terrorist operations or high-threat security.

The demand for PMCs in Iraq and Afghanistan caused tens of thousands of self-styled 'specialists' to enter the market. Many cheated and lied on their CVs, claiming that they were part of the SF or other special-operations groups. I've seen them use information that's available on the internet or plagiarise the experiences of others to draft bogus CVs. Prospective clients scored, as the oversupply of contractors drove down the price for PMC services.

Contractors will often compete fiercely for available positions on the circuit. This created a dog-eat-dog industry in which a bunch of alpha males from military and law-enforcement backgrounds go after the same security contract 'bone'. This led to much rumour-mongering, with certain contractors wanting to promote themselves and discrediting others. When you're working on the circuit, you cannot let your guard down for one moment. The result is a very different environment from the military, where you are all in it together as brothers in arms.

When I returned to Iraq in early 2012, the industry had undergone some changes, in my opinion for the worse. For one, the Iraqi government now had full control over all the permissions, permits, visas and licences required for private military security companies to operate there. Given the ineptitude and corruption prevalent in the Iraqi government, operating there became a huge challenge from an administrative point of view. Instead of focusing on avoiding ambushes and IEDs, we had to concentrate our efforts on outwitting the government – and they were supposed to be on our side.

I also did not particularly like the way certain companies expected us to run security missions. In my opinion, the large 'corporate' private military security companies wanted to deploy a different kind of warrior. These days, it seems like the mark of a good PMC is how well you can prepare endless documents, mainly to protect the company legally, how good you are with spreadsheets that indicate budgets to save money for the company, sometimes affecting your professionalism and screwing the operators out of a decent wage, and how good your English language and communicative skills are on conference calls and in presentations.

Gone are the days when the best leaders and operators were men who were tactically and strategically shrewd, who could closely liaise and cooperate with foreign and local military forces, who could negotiate deals with the local communities and security forces, who knew how to gather human intelligence, instead of relying on reports and the media, and who could outfox the enemy through counter-guerrilla warfare tactics thanks to their insight into high-threat situations. I had to accept Albert Einstein's words that 'the only constant in this universe is that nothing is constant' and therefore I adapted to this new style of running PMC operations.

It is not goodwill, peaceful intent, pacifism and liberalism that protect good people against terrorists, suicide bombers, warlords, militant and fanatical jihadists and criminal syndicates, but soldiers and PMCs. In Iraq my job was to protect good people against bad ones in extremely challenging conditions, regardless of whether the war there was right or wrong.

The handful of South African PMCs who had worked in war and conflict zones before the Afghan and Iraq wars won the respect of other PMCs globally, particularly those who had worked for Executive Outcomes. But, with the advent of these two wars and the boom in the use of PMCs in the new millennium, South African PMCs really came to the fore. From the word go in Iraq, we built a solid and good reputation as hard workers – people who know how to improvise, adapt and fight on their feet. Many of the US and British private military security companies based their standard operating procedures on work done in Iraq by the experienced South African former military and police PMCs.

Over the years, foreign governments and corporations started asking for South African PMCs to be employed on protective tasks, particularly where the challenges were greater than normal. We were always treated as part of the CF expats, in the sense that we were issued with DoD cards, US embassy passes and other access cards – documents that were hard to come by if you were not part of the CF. There are now rumours that the US State Department is considering allowing South African PMCs to work on US diplomatic contracts that were previously only executed by US PMCs with secret clearances. This is another indication that South Africans are trusted and seen as useful by the US government.

I'm also proud to say that mostly the Iraqis took to the South African PMCs. Many of our Iraqi employees learned to speak some Afrikaans and there are even instances where they named their children after us. There are also areas and streets around the country that were unofficially given Afrikaans names or descriptions.[1] I am proud of the accomplishments of the South Africans in the Sandbox, and I often heard complimentary comments from foreign clients and military folks alike.

Looking back on my time in Iraq, three achievements stand out as 'firsts' in PMC circles. Firstly, I managed to get a very complex security plan for Camp Tiger approved, and subsequently to get the convoys into east Ramadi. This was the first commercial project in this highly volatile area, which was a hotbed for insurgent and terrorist activities in 2006. Secondly, I obtained approval for the first non-CF small-aircraft missions into east Ramadi. This was quite a feat due to all the battle spaces that had to be crossed safely, as well as the different entities and authorities involved. Thirdly, I created a new system to allow us to use armed PMCs on maritime patrol boats in Iraqi territorial waters in the Persian Gulf on the ARCO port project. In all of this I was assisted by incredibly competent and experienced South African PMCs. I sincerely thank these men for their loyal and dedicated support over the years.

This book also aims to honour my fellow countrymen who paid the ultimate price in Iraq, and it bears testimony to the reality that PMCs face every day. Over 1 500 private contractors died on duty in Iraq, of whom over 300 worked as security contractors. Of my fellow countrymen, there were 34 who died (plus four presumed dead). I salute these men, and all the other military and private personnel who perished in the Sandbox, as well as those who were maimed and injured. See the Roll of Honour on page 315.

You are all part of history, my brothers. Your names are written in blood. Rest in peace.

Addendum A

The terrorists' arsenal

The combined methods of attack used by terrorists and the weapons they use are referred to in military and PMC terminology as terrorist tactics, techniques and procedures. The following are the most common methods and weapons used by the terrorists in attacks against military forces and PMCs in Iraq.

Shootings

The most common way to attack foreigners in Iraq is to shoot at them. These are known as small-arms-fire attacks (abbreviated in military parlance to SAF). The most common type of firearm used in these kinds of attacks in this part of the world is the Russian-designed AK-47, which has various iterations. The AK-47 is an assault rifle that can fire semi-automatic or fully automatic 7.62 x 39 mm (.308) rounds with a shorter cartridge than a Western .308 calibre (or 7.62 x 51 mm) round. It is a crude but very effective assault rifle that needs less maintenance than Western-manufactured assault rifles, and there were 'gazillions' of them made. Other Russian assault rifles and machine guns in use were the RPK, which was an AK-47 with a heavier barrel and bipod for stability; the RPD, a belt-fed machine gun with heavy barrel and bipod that fires AK-47 rounds, and the PKM, a belt-fed machine gun with a heavy interchangeable barrel and a bipod, which fires a heavier 7.62 x 54 R round to distances of up to 1 000 metres.

Among the initial sniper weapons used in Iraq was the Russian-designed Dragunov semi-automatic, a rifle that fired a 7.62 x 54 R round (like the PKM) from a ten-round box magazine. This rifle, which is effective up to about 500 metres (although it shoots up to

1 000 metres) could be fired with a great amount of training and some luck. Another early favourite was the Tabuk sniper gun, which had a longer, heavier barrel than the AK-47 and fired the same rounds, and was effective up to 300 to 400 metres.

Various pistols were in circulation, including the Russian-designed Makarov 9 x 16 mm and the Tokarev 7.62 x 25 mm. Western pistols, such as the 9 mm Browning Hi Power and the CZ-75, and later Sig and Glock pistols, were also used.

As this unconventional war progressed, all sorts of weapons from all over the world could be found – machine guns, assault rifles, submachine guns, pistols, shotguns, bolt-action rifles. Name it, and there was a chance that it could be found on the black market. But the most common small arms used by the enemy were the ones mentioned above. Typical small-arms fire attacks would be 'spray and pray' operations where attackers would open up fire and try to place maximum fire on their mark before turning and disappearing into crowds, side streets, buildings or the desert. But, as the guerrilla war escalated, insurgents and militias started executing carefully planned ambushes with small arms and machine guns, sometimes complete with explosives, rocket launchers and mortars.

Hand grenades

A hand grenade, or hand bomb, as some Iraqis called it, is a small device that consists of high explosives wrapped in a metal casing that creates shrapnel. The detonator works on a timing device once the safety pin has been pulled out and the fly-off lever has activated the detonation. It takes anywhere between 2.5 and 5 seconds before the grenade explodes. There are too many types of grenades to list here, but the most common ones encountered in Iraq were the Soviet Bloc F1 and RGD-5 defensive grenades (although the insurgents and bad guys used them for anything but defensive purposes). Another favourite was the RKG-3 anti-tank grenade, as depicted in the opening scene of the movie *American Sniper*. This grenade works with a shaped charge, similar to an RPG-7, that can blast through armour. It can be detonated by a direct hit to an armoured vehicle, but was designed to drop down onto the target by means of a small parachute that deploys when the grenade is thrown and charged. The insurgents used various devious techniques to attack their targets with grenades, including placing them, with the safety pins removed, inside dead animals and under the bodies of humans, which would then detonate when the security forces cleared an area. A grenade attack can be survived if spotted quickly enough, and if you execute the anti-grenade drill within seconds after spotting the device.

Indirect fire with rockets and mortars

Not everybody who worked in Iraq had the misfortune of getting shot at, but most contractors in the 'wild era' (2004 to 2008) and occasionally beyond, until December 2011, experienced incoming mortar or rocket fire. Firing rockets or mortars at the enemy is effective, as these weapons can cover large distances (between 1 000 and 8 000 metres), thus obviating the need for direct action with the foe. They carry a payload of high explosives with a metal casing that splinters into fragments and deadly projectiles, which causes psychological panic and fear in the target, as the recipient does not know exactly where these aerial bombs are raining down from. Many terrorist organisations make use of these weapons, which are often seen as the poor man's artillery. In the security world, mortar and rocket fire is referred to as an indirect fire attack.

The smallest mortar rounds were 60 mm, which weigh about 2 kilograms for a high-explosive round. The light delivery system 'pipe', weighing around 10 kilograms, makes this a very mobile attack platform. These mortar rounds have a kill radius of around 25 metres. The next largest mortar round, and the most commonly used, was the 82 mm. This projectile weighs around 4 kilograms and needs a heavier delivery pipe, but it is light enough to be carried on foot. The kill radius is around 40 metres. The big boy of mortar rounds is the 120 mm. A high-explosive round weights roughly 11 to 14 kilograms. The kill radius is around 65 to 75 metres.

The rocket type that was most commonly fired at us was the 105 mm or 107 mm Chinese Katyusha. This is 1.5 metres long and 105 mm or 107 mm wide. The high-explosive payload weighs roughly 5 to 8 kilograms and the body of a rocket is much longer than that of a mortar, as the projectile carries the propellant that drives it, unlike a mortar, which is driven by initial kinetic energy only. The kill radius of the 107 mm rocket is roughly 12 to 20 metres.

Another favourite, but deadlier, rocket is the 122 mm Katyusha projectile (or 'Stalin's organ', as it was known during World War II). These rockets are fired from launch tubes that were designed to be on the back of a truck, normally in 4 x 10 row configurations. This is a large rocket that carries a high-explosive payload, containing over 3 000 fragments, weighing up to 23 kilograms, and with a body tube length of between 1.5 metres and 3 metres. The reach distance of these rockets varies greatly depending on the type of ammunition and launch tubes used; they are effective up to 30 kilometres. The kill radius of the Katyusha rocket is between 30 and 50 metres. The nickname 'Stalin's organ' was coined because the launch pipes resemble a church organ and the sound emitted by the flying rocket sounds frightening at best, much like organ music.

RPG-7

A rocket-propelled grenade is a Russian-designed portable shoulder-fired rocket used to attack light armoured vehicles and personnel. The anti-tank round can penetrate up to 40 mm of armoured steel. The front of the launch tube has a 40-mm opening where the rocket is inserted. There are two types of warheads – the anti-tank high-explosive round and the anti-personnel high-explosive round. The anti-tank round is diamond-shaped and has a shaped charge (explosively formed projectile or EFP) weighing roughly 2 kilograms, which is attached to a 0.5-metre-long container with propellant fuel that drives the rocket for up to 925 metres, after which it self-destructs. RPG-7s have been in use since the Vietnam War, and have been used in numerous guerrilla conflicts in South America, Africa, the Middle East, the Far East, former Russian territories and Baltic State nations. These weapons claimed many lives in the war in Iraq.

Landmines

A landmine is an explosive device concealed under or on the ground, designed to destroy or disable enemy targets. Mine warfare is favoured by insurgents fighting guerrilla wars because mines can be planted under cover of darkness, they can be concealed so that they are impossible to spot with the naked eye, and they engender fear among enemy forces because of the unknown factor. Mines can be divided into two main groups: anti-tank and anti-personnel. Iraq has some of the largest minefields in the world, mostly left over from the Iran–Iraq War. Mine attacks were not as frequent as IED attacks but landmines did claim many lives, especially in the western region of Anbar. The main anti-tank mines in circulation were the Russian-designed TM-46 and TM-57, the Chez PTIII, the Jordanian Type-PRB5 and various others. Types of anti-personnel mines encountered were the PMN, Type-72, various iterations of the Valmara mines, the Russian POM-Z and various types of 'bouncing Betty' or 'jumping Jack' mines. The latter are propelled into the air before detonating and are used against troops on foot.

IEDs

An improvised explosive device is a 'home-made' bomb assembled from destructive and lethal chemicals or explosives, and designed to blend in with normal day-to-day life. This makes it easier for terrorists to hide these powerful, destructive tools without raising suspicion. In Iraq IEDs killed thousands of personnel from the CF and Iraqi security forces, and PMCs and civilians. IEDs are the terrorist's deadliest tools and are regularly used to cause mass casualties in attacks that attract media headlines globally.

Roadside IEDs

In Iraq roadside IEDs caused the highest number of deaths and injuries among the CF, Iraqi security forces, PMCs and civilians. Various high-explosive warheads (e.g. 155 mm shells, 122 mm Katyusha rockets and all kinds of mortars and rocket rounds) were used to rig roadside IEDs. These explosive devices were hidden in ingenious ways to blend in with the surrounding terrain. We received reports in 2004 and 2005 that insurgents had rigged 82 mm mortar rounds in cement blocks, to make them look like building or paving blocks, which were placed close to areas where construction was taking place. Often, devices would be strapped to the metal bars separating highways or buried in the sand next to the road. Devices were detonated by connecting wires to the detonator and hiding it under sand. The terrorists would wait for their target and press the ends of the wires on the positive and negative sides of a battery to set off the explosion. The detonators need as little as 1.5 volts to set off the main explosive charge. Later in the insurgency, the terrorists got smarter and used trip switches, laser-beam cutters and pressure switches to detonate their bombs.

VBIEDs (also known as VeeBids)

A vehicle-borne improvised explosive device – a car bomb in layman's terms – is referred to by the security forces and contractors as a VeeBid. This is a favourite terrorist attack tool, as the delivery vessel, usually an old vehicle, can be packed with a large amount of explosives, it is mobile, and it can be driven close to the target. If the person driving the vehicle detonated the device, it was classified as a suicide VeeBid. Such attacks in Iraq have killed thousands of military personnel, contractors and civilians since the end of the 2003 war. The first female suicide bomber in Iraq was a Belgian convert to Islam, who performed a suicide car-bomb attack on 9 November 2005 against a US military convoy in Iraq. After marrying a Muslim, she moved to Iraq and became radicalised. Since then, a number of female suicide bombers, or sometimes men dressed as females, have been deployed, causing many fatalities and wounding scores of people. Women are more likely to avoid detection and security searches.

Person-carried IEDs

A person-carried IED is a devastating means of attack against groups of people. A suicide bomber will strap explosives around his or her body, often packed with ball bearings, nails or pieces of metal for maximum effect. The device is detonated by the bomber. These kinds of attacks often kill more people than VeeBids and roadside IEDs, as the attacker can infiltrate densely crowded areas before detonating the device. Person-carried IED attacks typically took place at Iraqi Army and police recruitment points, during religious festivals or in crowded markets and restaurants.

Under-vehicle-borne IEDs

Later in the insurgency, terrorists started attaching small IEDs to the underside of vehicles using magnets or glue and duct tape (hence they were called 'sticky bombs' by the locals). Such a device normally kills the occupants of a vehicle, especially if it has a fairly full fuel tank, as the heat from the explosives causes the fuel to catch fire and cause a secondary detonation. This type of IED became very prominent in the new terrorist era from around 2014 after ISIS was formed.

EFPs

An explosively formed projectile, or EFP, was the most devastating and deadly type of IED used by terrorists and militias after the 2003 war. This kind of device was designed to defeat armoured vehicles and requires specialist bomb-making skills to construct. Many US servicemen, CF and Iraqi security forces, and PMC personnel operating in armoured vehicles were killed, maimed or severely injured by EFPs in Iraq.

The device works on a specially shaped charge of high explosives encased in a hard metal casing, usually consisting of steel pipes, with a half-moon-shaped front end that is constructed from a softer and thinner type of material, such as copper (see the illustration of an EFP on page 110). When detonated, the explosive force follows the path of least resistance, which is towards the front where the softer, half-moon-shaped sleeve is seated, and this causes the explosive force to be focused in one dense point that forms a molten copper slug travelling at over 7 000 feet per second. This slices through armoured metal like a knife through butter (see photo on page 110). The copper slug normally breaks into fragments when entering the armoured vehicle and causes havoc by cutting off limbs, and can even penetrate personal protective equipment (body armour).

Some EFPs sliced straight through armoured vehicles – in one side and out the other. Intelligence sources at the time indicated that specialist bomb makers, many of whom had degrees in chemistry or physics, manufactured most of the EFPs in Iran, or they were made by Iraqi bomb makers who went for training in Iran on how to build these devices.

Complex attacks

A complex attack is when terrorists and insurgents use a combination of the above tactics to attack their targets. A complex attack would typically consist of a bomb attack, normally a VeeBid or person-carried IED, at the entrance to an installation, followed by RPG-7 fire, coupled with rockets or mortars fired from a flank, and rounded off by machine-gun fire on the target. This kind of attack is deadly and requires a number of insurgents and coordination.

Chemical attacks

Saddam Hussein had a stockpile of various small- to medium-scale chemical weapons (not to be confused with weapons of mass destruction), including warheads armed with mustard gas, chlorine gas, sarin and other deadly chemicals. The most notorious chemical attack perpetrated by Saddam was in 1988 in the north-eastern village of Halabja, where up to 7 000 people were killed by Iraqi forces. Various systems of chemical weapons were also used against Iranian forces in the Iran–Iraq War from 1980 to 1988. Although the CF found and destroyed most of the chemical weapons in Iraq, some made it into the hands of the insurgents, while other stockpiles were smuggled into north-western Iraq from Syria (the Syrian regime reportedly had stockpiles of hundreds of tonnes of chemical weapons). There were no large-scale or spectacular attacks using chemical weapons, but the few small-scale attacks in the northwestern region were enough to warrant the CF, Iraqi security forces and PMCs procuring chemical-warfare suits and protective clothing, and to participate in chemical-warfare survival training (see the photo on page 51).

Poison

We received several reports of poison being used by insurgents and terrorists to try to disrupt their targets. One famous case in 2005 entailed locals handing poisoned watermelon to Iraqi soldiers at a checkpoint north of Baghdad, which caused them to fall very ill. One soldier died from this attack. Upon investigation, it was revealed that the watermelon was laced with arsenic.

An estimated 400 Iraqis from the minority Muslim Yazidi group were poisoned in northern Iraq in March 2004, apparently from drinking water that had been deliberately contaminated. Cans of Pepsi laced with arsenic were distributed in southern Iraq in June 2006.

Addendum B

Early history of the caliphate (AD 632–750)

The Prophet Muhammad managed to unite most tribes in the Arabian Peninsula after he and his followers fled Mecca when they were persecuted by pagans within their own tribe in the holy city. After his death in AD 632, the Prophet's followers gathered in Medina to choose his successor.[1]

This meeting was interrupted by Abu Bakr al Seddiq, Omar and their supporters, who claimed the title of successor. A group of followers who supported the Prophet in Medina put forward Omar Ibn al-Khattab as caliph. Then, in a surprising move, Omar gave his hand to Abu Bakr and declared him caliph. The Muslim community in Arabia gave their oath of allegiance to Abu Bakr and he became the first of four rightly chosen caliphs. He was caliph from 632 to 634.

Abu Bakr was a modest man and deeply spiritual, but acted decisively against some tribes and clans that rebelled against him. This led to a war in which Abu Bakr emerged victorious. He then decided to expand the kingdom to Persia (modern-day Iran), Byzantium (modern-day Turkey), the Levant and Southern Europe. This launched the Muslim conquests. Abu Bakr instructed his armies not to hurt women and children, not to attack places of worship and to preserve, instead of destroying, conquered territory.

His campaign was successful in Iraq but met with strong resistance from the Byzantines in the Levant (modern-day Syria). In 634 Abu Bakr's Muslim armies gathered to attack the Byzantine armies. The Muslim army was victorious but Abu Bakr died shortly afterwards.

Omar became the next caliph at a gathering by the tribes to choose a successor. He ruled from 632 to 644. He expanded the caliphate and conquered Damascus. Khalid, who was appointed as leader of the Muslim army by Omar, reportedly became rebellious after the victory of Damascus and the caliph had to rein him in.

In 636 Khalid was tasked to lead the army against the Byzantines in the south of the Levant. Khalid defeated their enemy and moved south through modern-day Lebanon and conquered an area all the way to, and including, Jerusalem. Omar was asked to travel to Jerusalem to receive the keys to the city from the Christian leader at the time. He obliged and pledged that his rule would honour and protect the Christian faith. A plaque with this pledge was mounted on a wall at a mosque bearing his name and is still intact today.

By now the Muslim armies controlled the entire Arabian Peninsula, the Levant, the territory from Lebanon to Jerusalem and some terrain in western Persia. However, most of Persia was still intact and was ruled from Ctesiphon, the biggest city in the world at the time. The city was situated on the Tigris River, south of modern Baghdad. To the north of the Levant was the Byzantine empire. These two states had the largest armies globally – both were much bigger than the Muslim armies. Omar wanted to rule both the Persian and Byzantine empires, but in 644 he was assassinated by a Persian slave. Omar was credited for creating military, political, social and judicial structures in the Arabian kingdom.

He was succeeded by Uthman Ibn Affan (known as Osman in the English rendering of his name), who ruled from 644 to 654. Osman deployed his foster brother, Abdullah Ibn Sarh, to lead a 20 000-strong army to the western Sahara Desert to fight the Byzantine armies that ruled North Africa (modern-day Morocco, Tunisia and Libya). Abdullah defeated the North African Byzantine armies and divided the spoils among a group of commanders and confidants. This led to dissatisfaction and mutiny by some of his followers.

In 655 there was an uprising against the caliph's rule, and rebels from southern Iraq in the Basra area marched to Medina to overthrow Osman. In 656 he was assassinated while reading the Koran. This was the second assassination of a caliph, but this time the assassin was a fellow Muslim. Scholars say that after this point there was never again peace in the Muslim world.

The rebels pushed forward Ali Ibn Abi Talib as caliph, as he was a cousin of the Prophet Muhammad. He was reluctant at first because he believed the Muslim community should choose a caliph, but he was pressured by the rebels and finally accepted the position as ruler of the Muslim world, becoming the fourth rightful caliph.

Ali decided to move the capital of the caliphate to Kufa in Iraq. At the time there was a growing threat against him from his wife, Aisha, and some of his close and trusted companions, Talha Ibn Ubayid Allah and Az-Zubair Ibn Al Awam. They wanted Ali to punish the killers of Uthman, but when he didn't comply it led to the Battle of the Camel in southern Iraq where Ali's army defeated those of Talha and Az-Zubair. This battle initiated the first civil war (*fitna*) within the Islamic state, which raged from 656 to 661. Aisha fled and disappeared from public eye.

At the time there were two caliphates, one in what is now Iraq, the other in the Levant. Since 634 Damascus in the Levant had been ruled by Muslims after their armies took the city from the Byzantines. Muawiyah, who stemmed from the same tribe as the murdered Osman – the Umayyad – demanded that Ali find Osman's killers and hand them over to face justice. The ruler wanted to make peace with Muawiyah, but in 661 rebels within his own ranks plotted to kill the caliph, Muawiyah and the governor of Egypt.

In the end, the rebels managed to kill only Ali. This ensured that Muawiyah became caliph, even if he was not a chosen leader. Under Muawiyah's rule, a new way of ruling the caliphate was introduced, which was influenced by both the Persian and Byzantine empires and moved away from the strict guidelines set out in the Koran. For instance, the caliph decided to appoint his son, Yazid, as his successor, instead of being chosen by the people.

In 680 Yazid became caliph after his father's death. Yazid had great ambitions to conquer the world, but strong opposition against his rule was brewing in Medina. Abdullah, the son of Az-Zubair, and Ali, the father of Hussein, resisted the rule of the new caliph. Hussein travelled from Medina to Kufa, his father's previous stronghold. In

October 680 Hussein's forces clashed with Yazid's army at Karbala, in south-central Iraq, and Hussein and most of his family were killed.

However this did not end the resistance to the Umayyad rule. Abdullah Az-Zubair did not succumb to Yazid's rule and travelled to Mecca to take up residence there. In 682 Yazid sent an army to Mecca to confront Az-Zubair, but the caliph died before his forces reached Mecca. Consequently, Abdullah Az-Zubair declared himself caliph.

In Damascus the Umayyads declared Muawiyah II, son of Yazid, the third caliph of the Umayyad kingdom. Muawiyah II died a few weeks after his appointment and he had no sons to take over the kingdom. This created an opportunity for the rival caliph in Mecca, who was bolstered by support from the tribes in Persia, southern Iraq and Palestine, to exploit the situation.

In Jordan, the tribes declared their support to the Umayyads, and in 684 they chose Marwan as their new caliph. Abdul-Malik, the son of Marwan, would eventually reunite the caliphates under one rule of the Umayyads. The Dome of the Rock mosque in Jerusalem was built on Abdul-Malik's orders and he declared it the third holiest site in the Muslim kingdom, after Mecca and Medina, which were under control of the rival caliph, Ibn al-Zubair.

In 691 a ruthless Umayyad general, Al Hajjah Ibn Youssef, was deployed to conquer Medina and Mecca. After an eight-month siege, al-Zubair was killed in the Holy Mosque in Mecca, and Abdul-Malik took control of all areas of the Muslim caliphate, and over the next two decades expanded the kingdom through many conquests. Power was handed down to his son Al-Walid. Then in 708, Al-Walid's armies conquered North and West Africa as far as the Atlantic Ocean and modern-day Morocco. The Muslims had over a period of 50 years conquered all the tribes of North Africa and converted them to the Islamic faith.

In 711, Tariq Ibn Ziyad, a patron from North Africa and converted Muslim, crossed the Mediterranean at the Strait of Gibraltar into what is now Spain and Portugal. He declared the area of Andalusia a province of the caliphate and thereby expanded the caliphate to western Europe.

Further afield, the Muslim armies conquered Iraq, Persia and beyond to Khorasan where modern-day Afghanistan and Pakistan are situated, and all the way to the western Chinese border. The caliphate now spanned an area larger than any empire before it, including the Greek, Roman, Persian and Byzantine empires. Al-Walid was depicted as an emperor, and not a religious leader, and became the most powerful man in the world.

In 732 an Umayyad general, Abdurrahman Al-Ghafiqi, crossed the Pyrenees between Spain and France to conquer the lands of Gaul, or modern-day France. He succeeded in taking control of southern France, and pushed hard in a bid to conquer all of Gaul. However, his fatal mistake was not to make an effort to know the enemy he was about to face (as the quotation from Sun Tzu's *The Art of War* cited at the beginning of this book aptly illustrates). The leader of the Frankish forces was Charles Martel and they clashed in an epic battle in central France in October 732. In this battle, called the Battle of Tours by the French and the Battle of the Place of Martyrs, or Martyrs Yard, by Muslims, the Muslim army was defeated and Abdurrahman was killed. Many historians claim this battle stopped the spread of Islam into Europe.

In 743, around the death of the tenth Umayyad caliph, Hisham Al Malik, the Umayyad Empire was brought into disarray by infighting, after which Marwan II rose to power and was to become the last and 14th Umayyad caliph. The new ruler tried to bring back organised rule, but the chaos persisted and the new ruler was also blind to events unfolding in the east of his empire where a mysterious leader, Abu Moslem, claimed an allegiance to the Prophet's lineage in Medina, with a large following from tribes in Persia (Iran).

Abu Moslem marched to Kufa in 749 to oppose Umayyad rule, and in November that year the tribes in Iraq swore an oath of allegiance, or Baya, to him. His followers declared Abu Al Abbas, who claimed to be a descendant of the Prophet's uncle, the first caliph from the

Abbasid tribe from eastern Iraq/Persia. Around the same time, the Umayyad army fought their final battle against the Abbasids in 750 in Iraq, where they were defeated. Marwan II escaped the battle but was killed shortly thereafter by the Abassids, thus bringing an end to almost a century of Umayyad rule.

Some Muslims in the kingdoms still believed that a caliph should be a direct descendant of and from the same bloodline as the Prophet, and the Umayyads never truly stuck to this principle. This belief, coupled with the violent history of the caliphate since the death of the Prophet in 632, would give rise to the eventual split between Sunni and Shia Muslims.

The history of the caliphate and the fighting for the title of caliph raged on for centuries until the final dissolution of the caliphate in 1924.

Notes

Prelude

1. Beverley Milton-Edwards, Iraq, past, present and future: A thoroughly modern mandate?, *History & Policy*, 8 May 2003, http://www.historyandpolicy.org/policy-papers/papers/iraq-past-present-and-future-a-thoroughly-modern-mandate.
2. The Multi-National Force – Iraq, often referred to as the Coalition Forces, was a military command during the 2003 invasion of Iraq and much of the ensuing Iraq War. The CF were formed to help rebuild Iraq. These forces consisted of some members of the intelligence alliance known as the Five Eyes Countries – the US, Canada, UK, Australia and New Zealand. During the official war, American soldiers had made up the bulk of the CF, followed by those from Britain and some elements from Australia and Poland.

Historical background to the war in Iraq

1. Mujahideen is the name given to Islamic fighters who are engaged in the ongoing religious war, or jihad, usually against non-Muslim forces. Their origins go back to the Soviet–Afghan War of the 1980s.
2. Amy Zalman, The many definitions of terrorism, ThoughtCo, 18 March 2017, https://www.thoughtco.com/definitions-of-terrorism-3209375.
3. Bin Laden backs Zarqawi as al-Qaida head, UPI, 27 December 2004, https://www.upi.com/Bin-Laden-backs-Zarqawi-as-al-Qaida-head-i/51151104180768/.
4. D Jehl and T Shanker, The struggle for Iraq, *The New York Times*, 7 October 2005, http://www.nytimes.com/2005/10/07/world/the-struggle-for-iraq-terrorist-liaisons-al-qaeda-tells-ally-in-iraq.html.
5. Also known as ISIL, IS or Daesh by Iraqis and citizens in Middle Eastern countries.
6. Muqtada al-Sadr, Wikipedia, https://en.wikipedia.org/wiki/Muqtada_al-Sadr.
7. The Peace Companies, frequently mistranslated as Peace Brigades in US media, are an Iraqi armed group linked to Iraq's Shia community. They are a revival of the Mahdi Army created by al-Sadr in June 2003 and disbanded in 2008. See https://en.wikipedia.org/wiki/Peace_Companies.
8. These figures were confirmed by fellow PMC Chris Delport at the US Department of Defense badging office at Camp Victory.

Chapter 1

1. The drills entailed announcing the action (contact front/right/left/rear); turning yourself into the smallest target possible; shooters situated closest or on the side of the contact should return fire; the driver should get of the X mark as quickly as possible; transloading into other vehicles if the vehicle is shot out; applying first aid to the injured, and so on.
2. The world's most dangerous road, *The Sydney Morning Herald*, 8 June 2005, http://www.smh.com.au/news/World/The-worlds-most-dangerous-road/2005/06/07/1118123840061.html.
3. Under the new Iraqi Interim Government, it was changed to the International Zone, although the Green Zone remains the commonly used term.
4. First, I ensured that the barrel was free of obstructions and confirmed that there was a floating bolt with the firing pin in place. Then I did a few tests on the weapon to ensure it cycled, fed rounds from the magazine into the chamber and ejected rounds from the chamber. I also checked that the safety catch was working by removing the mag, ensuring the chamber was empty, cycling the weapon, placing it on safe and pulling the trigger.

5. We wore tactical vests over the plate carriers, which held spare AK-47 magazines and items such as field dressings, a compass and a torch.
6. I thanked the ArmorGroup team leader that day for their assistance and camaraderie, but I didn't take his name or contact details. If you ever read this book, thanks again for helping us out, bro.

Chapter 2

1. 'The circuit' is used to refer to PMC missions globally.
2. Some people in the industry call these specialised security outfits 'private military companies'. I use the term 'private military security companies' to refer to them and 'private military contractors' for the contractors they employ.
3. Initial team members included the likes of Chris Delport (of whom more in this chapter), Craig Kennedy and Greg Garland.
4. MREs were an important part of our lives in Iraq. We relied on them during missions and long protective road trips. They were like the old ratpacks that we survived on during the Border War, but much better.

Chapter 3

1. Soldiers refer to an overseas call of duty as a 'tour', which can be for six or 12 months at a time. PMCs refer to such a deployment as a 'rotation', and the duration varies from company to company, but is typically two to four months, with a three- to four-week break in between.
2. In January 2016, two people were killed and eight wounded at a wedding celebration north of Basra when a partygoer lost control of a PKM machine gun while trying to shoot into the air. He probably lost control of the belt, something we in the industry call a runaway belt. Apparently, the problem of 'lead rain' has now reached such proportions that the Iraqi government wants to prohibit such actions. Good luck to them …
3. The author thanks Virginia al Masoodi for her help in checking these expressions.

Chapter 4

1. I had trained as a medic during my SF days. More on this later.
2. See Al Kasik Military Base, GlobalSecurity.org, https://www.globalsecurity.org/military/world/iraq/al-kasik.htm.
3. Not its real name; I wish to protect the identity of the owner.
4. In a coordinated complex attack, insurgents usually use a mix of tactics, including car bombs or suicide bombers, RPG-7s and machine-gun fire. See Addendum A for more information.

Chapter 5

1. A large, rugged plastic trunk with a suitcase-type handle and on wheels – used by the military and PMCs to transport one's goods and gear.
2. Level B6 armoured vehicles can withstand small to medium blasts and small-arms fire (e.g. from AK-17 and PKM machine guns). They cannot withstand armour-piercing rounds and large IEDs. Level B6 is the industry standard.
3. This manoeuvre, known as the dead-man drill, is practised in the event that the driver is killed. Firstly, the team leader will grab the steering wheel and control the vehicle, while leaning over the centre console with the left leg to control the accelerator. If there are team members in the rear, they will drag the body onto the back seat, so that the team leader can slide over behind the wheel and take control of the vehicle.
4. At this point it was part of the insurgents' propaganda campaign to video beheadings and post them on various fundamentalist websites. Some videos also made their way into the hands of the Western media.
5. The Bronze Star Medal, unofficially the Bronze Star, is a US decoration awarded to members of the US armed forces for heroic achievement, heroic service, meritorious achievement or meritorious service in a combat zone. See https://en.wikipedia.org/wiki/Bronze_Star_Medal.

Chapter 6

1. 'Corpsmen' is the term for US Marine combat medics.
2. During one of the EODT security patrols, they ran into terrorists and survived a shoot-out with the insurgents, during which a South African, Steve Struwig, was wounded in the neck. He was extremely lucky that the bullet had not pierced his carotid artery or spine, and he was fine within a short space of time.
3. The transitional government that ran Iraq after the March 2003 invasion.
4. See Major Jose Garcia, US Department of Defense, Iraqi Army brigade takes lead in Mahmudiyah, http://archive.defense.gov/news/newsarticle.aspx?id=477.
5. Blue Hackle was founded by ex-SAS officer Justin Penfold.

Chapter 7

1. Our heartfelt thanks to Anne Pallotta for her assistance.
2. A store that sells personal protective equipment, tactical vests, magazine pouches, torches, assault-rifle accessories and sight systems, heavy-duty clothing and boots, etc.
3. Katherine Fung, Record number of journalists killed during Iraq War: Committee to Protect Journalists, *Huffington Post,* 19 March 2013, http://www.huffingtonpost.co.za/entry/iraq-war-killed-journalists_n_2907550.
4. See Addendum A for more information on this type of bomb.

Chapter 8

1. An eight-wheeled armoured fighting vehicle.
2. Not his real name.
3. A 'battle space' refers to a unified military strategy to integrate and combine armed forces for the military theatre of operations, including air, information, land and sea, to achieve set military goals.
4. We deployed Renier (PP) Hugo to the road construction project, which was by then nearing completion.
5. Steve Fainaru, Iraq contractors face growing parallel war, *The Washington Post,* 16 June 2007, http://www.washingtonpost.com/wp-dyn/content/article/2007/06/15/AR2007061502602.html.
6. Soon, private military security companies were also contracted to guard key US military installations, which freed up more military personnel to fight the battle against the insurgency.
7. Steve Fainaru, Iraq contractors face growing parallel war, *The Washington Post,* 16 June 2007, http://www.washingtonpost.com/wp-dyn/content/article/2007/06/15/AR2007061502602.html.

Chapter 9

1. Containerised units.
2. A special forces unit of the US Navy; stands for sea, air, land.
3. During the year our expat security team expanded to 14 on duty, with two on rest-and-recreation rotation. I brought four of my old team members from the Al Kasik project days into the fold: Adam Leckrone (USA), James Wheeler, Awie Wessels and Apollo Pallourios (all three South Africans). We had two medics/security members on the team, Manny Louw (South Africa) and Mike Kelly (USA). We also introduced a British member, Andy Johnson, and two South Africans, Craig Spencer and Hein von Berg, to the team.

Chapter 10

1. The late Eric McCann.
2. A slang term meaning 'to be identified as the enemy'.

Chapter 11

1. The X mark is the point of contact, bomb blast or ambush initiation point. If the vehicle is still running, then the drill is to drive the vehicle out of the area.
2. The protocol makes no distinction between defensive and offensive actions, but the US does make such a distinction, in that it does not regard defensive actions by security guards to be combat. See the entry for 'Mercenary' in Wikipedia, https://en.wikipedia.org/wiki/Mercenary.
3. Nicky Woolf, Former Blackwater guards sentenced for massacre of unarmed Iraqi civilians, *The Guardian*, 14 April 2015, https://www.theguardian.com/us-news/2015/apr/13/former-blackwater-guards-sentencing-baghdad-massacre.
4. An extensive survey showed that at least 150 000 people had died in the country in the five years following the 2003 war. The exact numbers are hard to ascertain and some reports suggest that it might have been as many as a quarter of a million people whose lives were cut short because of the violence. See https://en.wikipedia.org/wiki/Iraq_Body_Count_projects.
5. The stoppage had been caused by diesel that was used to clean the belts interacting with the varnish on the rounds in the belt, causing the rounds to get stuck in the belt.
6. PMCs often had to return fire in a contact without knowing where their bullets struck – the main aim was to get out of the contact area as soon as possible, hopefully intact. In this instance, as on other occasions, we didn't know whether the attackers were killed or just wounded. This would only be determined after the US military or CF had assessed the contact.
7. Adriaan Myburgh died in 2010 in the Kurdish city of Sulaymaniyah when the hotel they were staying in caught fire, apparently because of an electrical fault or gas leak. More than 30 people died, many of them expatriates. Three jumped out of the window of their hotel rooms and fell to their death. Adriaan was one of them. RIP, brother.

Chapter 12

1. A hot extraction is the expedient removal of stricken personnel in a war-time crisis, after a coup or natural disaster.
2. A small shop or general store in the Arab world where you can buy anything and everything.
3. As of March 2017, Iraq's oil production was around 4.5 million barrels per day. This figure could have been substantially higher but ISIS and the 2014 insurgency disrupted various oil and gas fields, as well as supply lines in the north and west of the country.
4. Nickname for a member of the South African Special Police Task Force.
5. US dollars.

Chapter 13

1. See Al Faw Grand Port, Archirodon, http://www.archirodon.net/project/584/all.
2. See A time to fast and feast, Muslim Aid, 2017, https://www.muslimaid.org/what-we-do/religious-dues/ramadan/?gclid=Cj0KEQiA_KvEBRCtzNil4-KR-LIBEiQAmgekFzhyPtYqroGYO1eA6E_99D3-unN8ptchCVHUzO0b6kQaAs0n8P8HAQ.
3. B McKernan, Isis tells its followers rewards for bloodshed are heightened during Ramadan, *The Independent*, 5 June 2017, http://www.independent.co.uk/news/world/middle-east/isis-london-bridge-terror-attack-ramadan-greater-reward-terrorism-a7774061.html.
4. Ramadan offensive (2003), https://en.wikipedia.org/wiki/Ramadan_Offensive_(2003).

Chapter 14

1. Mourning of Muharram, https://en.wikipedia.org/wiki/Mourning_of_Muharram.
2. Husayn ibn Ali, https://en.wikipedia.org/wiki/Husayn_ibn_Ali.

Chapter 15

1. Not his real name.
2. A member of the Parachute Battalion of the South African Defence Force.
3. See https://en.wikipedia.org/wiki/Abu_Bakr_al-Baghdadi.
4. Ibid.
5. Other Sunni terrorist groups are the Iraq Baath Party, the Fallujah Military Council, the Council of Revolutionaries of the Tribes of Anbar, the Jordan Conference, Jaysh al-Mujahideen, the 1920 Brigades and the Islamic Army in Iraq.
6. N Gutteridge, Isis now using 15 remote-controlled cars to launch bomb attacks, *Sunday Express*, 25 August 2015, http://www.express.co.uk/news/world/600771/ISIS-Islamic-State-remote-controlled-cars-bomb-attacks-Syria-Iraq-drones-Britain.
7. Martin Chulov, Inside the ISIS terrorism workshops: Video shows Raqqa research centre, *The Guardian*, 6 January 2016, https://www.theguardian.com/world/2016/jan/06/inside-isis-terrorism-workshops-video-shows-raqqa-research-centre.
8. The most common calibres are the Russian 12.7 mm x 108 mm DSKA anti-aircraft gun, and the often twin-barrelled 14.5 mm x 114 mm; 20 mm x 102/110 mm; and 23 mm x 120 mm anti-aircraft guns.

Chapter 16

1. A pseudonym.

Chapter 17

1. Spyridon Tzilalis (site manager), Vasileios Tsitsas (finance manager) and Konstantinos Papageorgiou (geotech manager).
2. See https://en.wikipedia.org/wiki/Battle_of_Fallujah_(2016).
3. Security information director: Iran asked Al-Zarqawi to kill Iraqi Shiites, *Arab News*, 23 February 2017, http://www.arabnews.com/node/1058546/saudi-arabia?ref=yfp.

Epilogue

1. K Greeff, "Briewe uit Baghdad: Die 'monsters' van Irak", Maroela Media, 23 August 2017. See https://maroelamedia.co.za/debat/rubrieke/briewe-uit-bagdad-die-monsters-van-irak/

Addendum B

1. This section is based on the three-part Al Jazeera documentary *The Caliph* (2016). Available at www.youtube.com/watch?v=P3O9d7PsI48&feature=youtu.be, accessed on 4 January 2018. In this addendum, I focus on the power struggles only in the first century or so after the death of the Prophet Muhammad. The period covers the first four caliphs, who were 'rightfully' chosen according to some, and declined by rivals. Throughout the centuries that followed, the history of the caliphate was written in blood.

Roll of Honour

1. The only available lists for PMC deaths in Iraq are on Wikipedia (en.wikipedia.org/wiki/List_of_private_contractor_deaths_in_Iraq) and icasualties.org (icasualties.org/Iraq/Contractors.aspx). They list, respectively, 29 and 20 South Africans killed in Iraq. The list in this book is therefore more complete.

Roll of Honour

For South African security contractors who died in Iraq

The list below was researched as extensively as possible, but unfortunately I could not get hold of family members or people who were eyewitnesses to the deaths of all the men mentioned. I also found that many companies and family members kept the deaths of their loved ones confidential, probably because our government initially had a very draconian reaction to PMCs who deployed in Iraq.[1]

I therefore request family members or colleagues of these men who were privy to operational information that could help complete this list to contact me, or the publisher, so I can update it in any future editions.

	Name	Date of death	Kind of attack	Place of attack
1.	Francois Strydom	Jan 2004	Suicide bomb	Baghdad
2.	Francois de Beer	Apr 2004	Gunshot	Baghdad
3.	Hendrik (Vis) Visagie	Apr 2004	RPG attack	Fallujah
4.	Gray Branfield	Apr 2004	SAF (defending building)	Kut
5.	Klip Nel	Unknown	EFP	Road between Basra and Baghdad
6.	William Richard	May 2004	SAF	Kirkuk
7.	Herman Pretorius	Aug 2004	Convoy ambush	Mosul
8.	Johan Hattingh	Oct 2004	VBIED	Iraq
9.	Johan Botha	Oct 2004	Convoy ambush	South of Baghdad
10.	Louis Campher	Oct 2004	Convoy ambush	South of Baghdad
11.	Johan Terry	Nov 2004	Roadside IED	Basra
12.	Jacques Oosthuize(n)	March 2005	SAF ambush	Road between Tikrit and Mosul
13.	Gavin Holtzhausen	Jan 2005	VBIED	Baghdad
14.	Sean Laver	Jun 2005	Roadside IED	Habbaniyah

315

15.	Willem Johannes Jacobus (Gawie) Venter	Oct 2005	IED	South of Baghdad
16.	Maurice (Assie) van As	Oct 2005	EFP/RPG-7	Baghdad
17.	Naas du Preez	Nov 2005	Suicide bomb	Baghdad
18.	Johannes Potgieter	Nov 2005	Suicide bomb	Baghdad
19.	Miguel (Tabs) Tablai	Nov 2005	Suicide bomb	Baghdad
20.	Jan Strauss	Dec 2005	Roadside IED	Baghdad
21.	Richard Kolver	May 2006	Roadside IED	Baghdad
22.	Edmund Bruwer	Aug 2006	Roadside IED	Iraq
23.	Morne Pieters	Oct 2006	SAF	Basra
24.	Glen Joyce	Feb 2007	Mortar fire	Baghdad
25.	Joe Bresler	Apr 2007	EFP-IED	Iraq
26.	Magrinho Domingos	Aug 2007	EFP-IED	Near Aziziyah
27.	Petrus Kamati	Aug 2007	EFP-IED	Near Aziziyah
28.	Marius Weber	Oct 2007	Convoy ambush	Iraq
29.	Johan (Skip) Scheepers	Mar 2008	IED	Southern Iraq
30.	Frans Brand	Aug 2008	Roadside IED	Iraq
31.	Desmond Milnes	Jun 2008	Roadside IED	Iraq
32.	Andre Botha	Dec 2008	Vehicle accident	Iraq
33.	Adriaan (Eier) Myburgh	Jul 2010	Hotel fire (fell to his death)	Sulaymaniyah
34.	George Tyers	Jun 2012	Construction accident	Basra area
	Missing and assumed dead			
35.	Andre Durant	Dec 2006	Kidnapped	Close to Sadr City
36.	Johan Enslin	Dec 2006	Kidnapped	Close to Sadr City
37.	Callie Scheepers	Dec 2006	Kidnapped	Close to Sadr City
38.	Hardus Greef	Dec 2006	Kidnapped	Close to Sadr City

Many South Africans were injured, wounded or badly maimed in the execution of their duties in the Sandbox. No accurate database was ever kept, but thanks to my knowledge on ground level and some networking, I can estimate that at least 100 of our brothers sustained injuries while deployed here. I salute you, too.

There are a number of South Africans who died during breaks between contracts when they returned to South Africa or went travelling. I did not include their names in this list, but our brotherhood knows who they are and acknowledges their contribution.

Index

Note: page numbers in *italics* indicate a photograph.

About the author

Johan Raath was a private military contractor in Iraq from 2004, where he performed specialised protection tasks for VIPs and sheiks, engineers working on construction projects funded by the US government, oilfield engineers and construction workers.

His tasks, as country security manager for a large consortium of companies, involved setting up missions by liaising with the US military, the Iraqi security forces, tribal leaders and other local stakeholders, and establishing intelligence sources. These multifaceted missions encompassed all components of high-risk security work – personal protection, perimeter security, force protection measures, explosive detection capabilities, convoy security, air operations and maritime patrols.

Raath was a South African Special Forces operator, or Recce, from 1986 to 1992. Then he started a security training and consulting company and went into high-risk security work in Africa. Since the 1990s, he has been involved in security missions in more than 15 countries, including conflict zones such as Libya, southern Sudan, Sierra Leone, Haiti and the Middle East.

Raath also worked as a personal security officer, or bodyguard, for a number of international presidents. His training and protection services have won him accolades from many government organisations, including US government agencies and USAID.

He is also a trained combat paramedic and assisted in various mass casualty scenarios after suicide bomb attacks in Iraq. He is a close-protection and specialised combat instructor, and has trained international security teams in various countries.

From 2015 to 2017, Raath was part of the senior Iraq Country Management team for one of the largest US private security companies in the world, in support of various US diplomatic protective services.